EMPATHY AND DEMOCRACY

EMPATHY AND DEMOCRACY

FEELING, THINKING, AND DELIBERATION

Michael E. Morrell

The Pennsylvania State University Press
University Park, Pennsylvania

LIBRARY OF CONGRESS CATALOGING-IN-PUBLICATION DATA

Morrell, Michael E., 1967–
  Empathy and democracy : feeling, thinking, and
  deliberation / Michael E. Morrell.
      p.   cm.
Includes bibliographical references and index.
Summary: "An interdisciplinary study of democratic
theory, empirical political science, psychology, and
philosophy. Proposes a multidimensional process model
of empathy that incorporates both affective and cognitive
features to demonstrate the importance of empathy in
fulfilling democracy's promise of giving equal
consideration to all citizens in collective decisions"—
Provided by publisher.
ISBN 978-0-271-03659-5 (cloth : alk. paper)
ISBN 978-0-271-03660-1 (pbk : alk. paper)
1. Democracy—Philosophy.
2. Democracy—Psychological aspects.
3. Empathy.
I. Title.

JC423.M724 2010
321.8—dc22
2009032310

The Pennsylvania State University Press is a member of
the Association of American University Presses.

It is the policy of The Pennsylvania State University
Press to use acid-free paper. Publications on uncoated
stock satisfy the minimum requirements of American
National Standard for Information Sciences—
Permanence of Paper for Printed Library Material,
ANSI Z39.48–1992.

CONTENTS

ACKNOWLEDGMENTS

As this work has been long germinating in my mind, there are many people that have contributed to its development, even if they have forgotten they have done so. Among the valued colleagues and students who have helped with my thinking and research on empathy and deliberation, I want to thank Jared Baker, Sarah Barrett, Michael Brooks, William Burress, Erin Cassese, Stephanie Collier, John Gastil, Megan Gieseler, Virginia Hettinger, Richard Hiskes, Alyssa Kelleher, Alisa Kessel, James Kuklinski, Jacob Levy, Jane Mansbridge, Tali Mendelberg, Peter Muhlberger, Diana Mutz, Michael Neblo, Thomas Noggle, Edward Portis, David Redlawsk, Shawn Rosenberg, Jeffrey Smith, William P. Smith, Daniel Tagliarina, Mark Warren, and Elizabeth Wesolowska. Peter Kingstone played an equally important role in helping me along. With my sometimes fleeting memory, I am sure that I have forgotten to mention others who have been helpful, and to them I request that they forgive my oversight. I also wish to thank Robert Bosco, Robert Glover, and Chris Paskewich, who contributed by reading chapters of the book, providing useful comments, and helping in my research. Adam Kanter deserves special recognition for the work we did together that I report in Chapter 5. Cheryl Hall and Sharon Krause provided invaluable comments and suggestions in reviewing the entire book; it is much better for having their input, even if I have still fallen short of their expectations. Sandy Thatcher has been an incredibly responsive, supportive editor and has gone out of his way to help bring this book to fruition. I really cannot thank him enough for what he has done. There are several people who have contributed in less direct, though no less helpful, ways to the writing of this book. I sincerely thank Barry and Tally Satterthwaite, Gary Morton, Mark Guggisberg, Ron Kirkemo, and Skip Rutledge for all that they have done, especially their patience when I thought I knew everything. Jack Crittenden, Rich Dagger, Avital Simhony, Pat Kenney, and Kim Fridkin guided and encouraged me in pursuing the interdisciplinary work of which this book is the culmination; I could never have finished it without them and will be forever grateful that they took me under their wings. Finally, I want to thank my family for their part in getting me to this point in my life. My parents, William and LaDonna Morrell, supported me, sacrificed for me, and taught me many valuable lessons that have led me to be in the position to write the work that follows. Without them, this book would not exist. Most important, I want to thank my wife, Ioana, whose patience, understanding, love, and encouragement was what kept me going even during the difficult times. I could never thank her enough for all that she has brought to my life and done for me, and it is with all my love that I dedicate this book to her.

1

THE DEMOCRATIC PROMISE

There is a promise inherent in democracy: before a society makes decisions that it will use its collective power to enforce, it will give equal consideration to everyone in the community. The development of collective decision-making institutions that take into consideration a wider range of interests did not begin with the rise of modern democracies. Ancient Athens, the ancient republics of India (Thapar 1966, 50–54), the Roman Republic, the Norse *ting*, and the Iroquois Confederation, to name some examples, represent moments in history where the demarcation of those who could have a voice in collective decisions, and thus demand equal consideration, expanded beyond the limits that existed before, and in most cases, after these moments. Yet human history is also replete with examples of societies in which some members of the community counted more than others. A variety of factors—what religion one practices, who one's parents are, what color one's skin is, how one acts, what gender one is, the way one speaks, how effective one's weapons are—have in different times and different places been the criteria by which societies have counted some and discounted others. This perhaps explains the absence of democratic societies through much of history; there have usually been those in human communities who, for various reasons, have been unable to accept the idea that all members of the community deserve equal consideration.

Yet while even many "democratic" societies have built themselves on foundations that excluded the consideration of some, the *idea* of democracy points to the possibility that society can, at the very least, minimize these exclusions. In the last several centuries, there has been a movement toward more equal consideration in democratic societies that has consisted primarily in the extension to ever larger proportions of the population of formal political rights such as the franchise, free speech, and the right to run for political office. While some countries still restrict the political rights of some citizens, the elimination of restrictions based upon race, ethnicity, economic standing, social status, religion, gender, and intelligence has brought about near universal suffrage in many democracies throughout the world. As John Stuart Mill explains, there is an inherent connection between the extension of the franchise and equal consideration:

> Rulers and ruling classes are under a necessity of considering the interests and wishes of those who have the suffrage; but of those who are excluded, it is in their option whether they will do so or not; and however honestly disposed, they are in general too fully occupied with things which they *must* attend to, to have much room in their thoughts for anything which they can with impunity disregard. No arrangement of the suffrage, therefore, can be permanently satisfactory, in which any person or class is peremptorily excluded; in which the electoral privilege is not open to all persons of full age who desire to obtain it. ([1861] 1991, 329–30; emphasis in original)

Despite some of his elitist tendencies (see Mill [1861] 1991, 330–33, 336), Mill recognizes that rulers are unlikely to give equal consideration to all citizens unless there is nearly universal suffrage, and yet equal voting rights are not sufficient. Today's democracies are still struggling to fulfill democracy's promise of equal consideration, and the claim I will defend is that they can do so most fully by giving empathy a central role in democratic decision-making. Without empathy, large modern societies cannot give citizens the kind of equal consideration necessary to make democratic decisions legitimate. To demonstrate why this is the case, I draw upon a unique combination of theoretical positions regarding democracy and empathy and empirical research on the effects of empathy and the role of emotions in politics, including some of my own experimental studies. Before laying out these arguments, I want to place my contention in context by looking at how various theorists of democracy have tried to embody democracy's promise to give equal consideration to all.

Equal Consideration and Collective Decision-Making: Responses in Democratic Theory

One of the recurrent themes in democratic theory has been the attempt to explain how a democracy can give citizens equal consideration while still allowing the community to make collective decisions that it then has the coercive power to enforce, even on those whose considerations the community has chosen to downplay or reject. Democracy promises that all citizens will have the opportunity to voice to their opinions on issues of importance to the community, and yet, in the end, someone or some group must decide what to do regarding each issue. Only on rare occasions will all citizens, or even a large number of them, agree with the final decision. While the democratic process may grant all citizens equal consideration in some form, the final decision will inevitably discount or ignore some members of society. The tension between equal consideration and the need for collective decision-making is certainly not the only lens through which scholars have examined democracy, but I have chosen to focus on it because I believe that this approach will give us a distinctive perspective that will reveal the unique importance of empathy to democracy.

Theories of democracy developed before the late nineteenth century— republicanism, liberalism, and utilitarianism—deal with the tension between equal consideration and collective decision-making by linking individuals and the community in various ways. Republicans eliminate the tension by recasting equal consideration in terms of the common good. They delineate between private interests, the sum of which Jean-Jacques Rousseau calls the "will of all," and the public interest, Rousseau's "general will" ([1762] 1988, 95, 100–101). Each citizen has an equal voice, but if some disagree with the final decision, they have either misperceived the common good or followed their own private interest. As Marsilius of Padua expresses it, while some may disagree "with the common decision through singular malice or ignorance," we should not allow such "unreasonable protest or opposition" to prevent the community from pursuing the common benefit ([1324] 1956). The community can legitimately enforce the decision because it is for the benefit of all, even those who disagree. Liberals eliminate the tension between equal consideration and collective decision-making by positing an original moment of unanimous consent to abide by majority rule in all subsequent decisions, and by circumscribing those decisions to a public sphere defined by law and a private sphere of individual rights. The political community comes into being only when all individuals consent to form it, and at this moment equal consideration and collective decision-making coincide because there is a consensus to give up some individual rights in order to gain the security afforded by joining together (Locke [1764] 1967, 348–49). For subsequent collective decisions, the political community "should move that way whither the greater force carries it, which is the *consent of the majority:* or else it is impossible it should act or continue one Body, *one Community,* which the consent of every individual that united into it, agreed that it should; and so every one is bound by that consent to be concluded by the *majority*" (348–49; emphasis in original). The majority has the power to enforce collective decisions without violating equal consideration because all unanimously agreed that it should have such power at the moment they formed the community. To further buttress equal consideration, liberals (1) guarantee formal political rights so that all citizens have equal avenues to influence the community's decisions, and (2) limit collective decision-making to the public sphere defined by a constitution and the existence of individual natural rights. Utilitarians also circumscribe the proper scope of government action, but instead of basing this upon "natural" individual rights, they rely upon the principle of utility. They build equal consideration into democracy by requiring that all collective decisions follow the principle of utility by maximizing collective happiness defined in terms of all individuals' pleasures and pains equally. Democracy is the form of collective decision-making most likely to result in legislation that will meet the utility principle, at least in the most advanced societies, because, as Mill argues in the passage I have just quoted, rulers will only take into consideration those who can vote. While this might appear to allow the rulers very broad powers as long as everyone is eligible to vote, utilitarians maintain that the principle of utility requires that rulers limit legislation only to those cases that will increase collective happiness. They define the very limits of majority rule by requiring that all decisions equally consider the happiness of all, even those who might be in the minority.

Despite their differences, republicanism, liberalism, and utilitarianism give a warrant for the argument that we ought to extend formal political rights to all citizens within a society. Yet the rise of mass democracies in the late nineteenth and early twentieth centuries, despite the increasing extension of formal political rights to ever larger numbers of citizens, led some thinkers to question previous theories of democracy. As social scientists began to examine the ways in which democratic countries actually functioned, elitist theorists began to argue that democracy could not solve the tension between equal consideration and collective decision-making in the ways put forth by the classical theories of democracy. Though they disagree on several points, writers such as Gaetano Mosca (1939), Robert Michels ([1911] 1962), Vilfredo Pareto ([1916] 1935), and Joseph Schumpeter ([1942] 1976) contend in various ways that societies, even those which are ostensibly democratic, will inevitably tend to serve the interests of the lead-ers or rulers rather than give equal consideration to all. As Mosca summa-rizes, even if citizens have the vote, the inescapable need to make collective decisions will overwhelm equal consideration and allow minorities to dom-inate: "If his vote is to have any efficacy at all, therefore, each voter is forced to limit his choice to a very narrow field, in other words to a choice among the two or three persons who have some chance of succeeding; and only the ones who have any chance of succeeding are those whose candidacies are championed by groups, by committees, by organized minorities" (1939, 154–55). Not only will the need to make collective decisions in large socie-ties predictably lead to the concentration of power in small groups, democ-racies cannot function as previous theorists expected. Schumpeter ([1942] 1976) accuses the supporters of the classical theories of democracy of sev-eral errors: they often place great weight on the common good, which he believes does not really exist; they conceptualize democracy as involving the implementation of the will of the people, which also does not exist; and they arc largely inaccurate in their characterization of democratic citizens, who tend to be ignorant and easily manipulated by political elites. Realisti-cally, we must recognize that the best way to think of democracy is as a free competition among political elites for power by winning citizens' free votes. From an elitist perspective, the democratic promise of equal consid-eration reduces to an equal and free choice of rulers from a limited number of groups of powerful political minorities. Democratic theory since the middle of the twentieth century has consisted largely in attempts to develop an explanation of democracy's ability to allow both equal consideration and legitimate collective decisions that is less minimalist than that found in elitist theorists.

Robert Dahl (1956, 1961, 1989) developed a pluralist model of democ-racy that, while acknowledging that political elites are important to democ-racy, maintains that democracy consists of a constant interplay of various groups of interests all vying for attention from the government. The gov-ernment mediates and adjudicates between the demands of these various groups in the hopes of appeasing enough of them to maintain political power, but this balancing act occurs within a consensus set by certain underlying values that provide the boundaries within which political life functions, resulting in what Dahl calls a "polyarchy." Dahl's conceptualiza-tion of polyarchy has evolved over time, but in his more recent work he spe-cifically addresses the relationship between equal consideration and collec-tive decision-making (1989, 295–308). Political equality and the democratic process are not intrinsically good but are important because they "are the most reliable means for protecting and advancing the good and interests of all the persons subject to collective decisions" (322). Yet the complexity of the modern nation-state precludes a return to a small assembly form of government such as Rousseau advocated. The only practical option is a democratic process that incorporates the institutions of polyarchy: control of government decisions by elected officials, free and fair elections, inclusive suffrage, right to run for office, freedom of expression, availability of alternative information, and associational autonomy (see 221). While Dahl recognizes that these institutions alone will not guarantee equal consideration, he argues that they provide the best foundation from which societies can build toward it. Democracies must still focus on reducing "remediable causes of gross political inequalities" that prevent equal consideration in collective decisions (323). Polyarchy resolves the tension between collective decision-making and equal consideration by relying upon political processes and associational institutions that allow groups of citizens to influence policy decisions made by elected political elites, while always looking for ways to reduce the inequalities that allow some to have a disproportionately greater influence than others.

In contrast to pluralist theories, participatory democrats such as Carol Pateman (1970), C. B. Macpherson (1977), and Benjamin Barber (1984) respond to the elitist challenge by returning to theorists such as Mill and Rousseau in order to argue that mass democracies are simply not democratic enough. Citizens are uninformed and uninterested because they only rarely get the opportunity to participate directly in making the decisions that affect their lives, so the cure for the ills of democracy is to give citizens more effective opportunities for direct participation. Whereas Dahl generally regards a small-assembly democratic model as implausible in a nation-state, participatory democrats envision opening up various avenues of more direct engagement by citizens in democratic processes, either through more localized decision-making or the use of technology. As citizens participate more directly, the political system will give more equal consideration to all and the democratic process will educate citizens in ways that will incline them to take into account interests beyond their own private sphere, increasing the likelihood that collective decisions will serve the public good and thus be more legitimate. The answer to the tension between collective decision-making and equal consideration is to allow citizens to participate directly in decisions in ways that are both quantitatively and qualitatively superior to those found under current democratic institutions. Participatory democrats reinvigorated the idea of a direct, democratic society, but they also faced the difficulties of how to implement the direct democracy they envisioned in large, heterogeneous polities. As the twentieth century came to a close, political theorists searched for a new response to the challenge of how a democratic society can make legitimate collective decisions while simultaneously fulfilling the promise of giving equal consideration to all. They also grappled with the realities of large, heterogeneous societies, and yet aimed at retaining the democratic spirit of the participatory theorists. This new strand of democratic theory arose from what many describe as the deliberative turn.

The Deliberative Turn

There are two related, yet distinct, deliberative "turns" that both occurred at approximately the same time. The first, represented by scholars such as Joseph Bessette and James Fishkin, focuses less on the tension between equal consideration and collective decisions and more on the need for reflective consideration in democratic decisions. Deliberation as reflective consideration implies the need for more equal consideration, and this form of deliberative theory maintains that collective decisions are more democratically legitimate if made after careful reflection. The second variety of deliberative theory, whose main protagonists are John Rawls and Jürgen Habermas, concerns itself more directly with the problems of equal consideration and collective decision-making. Neither Rawls nor Habermas began with fully developed theories of deliberative democracy; Rawls was primarily concerned with justice, and Habermas with capitalist society, political legitimacy, rationality, and moral validity. Yet in developing these other concepts, they not only inspired many of those who theorized deliberative democracy—such as Seyla Benhabib, James Bohman, Simone Chambers, Joshua Cohen, John Dryzek, Amy Gutmann and Dennis Thompson, and Michael James—they created the framework for their own deliberative theories as well. I will discuss both varieties of deliberative theory in more depth in Chapter 2, but for now I want to give a preliminary elucidation of how Rawls and Habermas address equal consideration.

Rawls and Habermas both build equal consideration into the very processes of legitimate collective decision-making. Rawls maintains that when citizens exercise political power in a democracy they must meet what he calls the "criterion of reciprocity" (1996, xlvi). In order to meet this criterion, citizens must be reasonable, which requires that they view "one another as free and equal" and "are prepared to offer one another fair terms of social cooperation" that they are willing to follow as long as others are willing to do the same (1996, xliv). Terms are "fair" if those who propose them "reasonably think that those citizens to whom such terms are offered might also reasonably accept them" under conditions in which all are "free and equal" and not "dominated or manipulated, or under the pressure of an inferior political or social position" (1996, xliv). While there are other important aspects of Rawls's theory that I will discuss more fully later, even at this fundamental level it is clear that citizens can make legitimate collective decisions only if they base them on terms that give equal consideration to other citizens (or at least other "reasonable" citizens).

Habermas also invokes the principle of reciprocity, but his resolution of the tension between equal consideration and collective decision-making in a democracy most clearly begins with his discourse principle. The discourse principle states: "Just those action norms are valid to which all possibly affected persons could agree as participants in rational discourses" (1996a, 107). From this general principle, which regulates a variety of different action norms, Habermas derives the more specific "democratic principle," which applies to legal norms or statutes. "Only those statutes can claim legitimacy that can meet with the assent (*Zustimmung*) of all citizens in a discursive process of legislation that in turn has been legally constituted" (110). There are many complex issues Habermas expresses with these two principles, some of which I will discuss later, but for this brief introduction I want to highlight how he bases the legitimacy of collective decisions in a system that inherently requires giving equal consideration to all citizens in a discursive process of rational opinion- and will-formation.

Though Habermas and Rawls, as well as the theorists they have influenced, disagree on many points, they basically concur that we can resolve the tension between equal consideration and collective decision-making in a democracy through some form of deliberation. They differ from elite theories that question the very possibility of equal consideration or rely solely on the guarantee of equal formal political rights to insure equal consideration and legitimize collective decision-making. They require more of democracy than the pluralist institutions of "polyarchy," and though they share many affinities with participatory democrats, they go much further than participatory democrats in articulating the conditions necessary for democratically legitimate decisions in a large polity.

The Affective Turn

Deliberative theory advances our understanding of how modern mass democracies can make legitimate collective decisions while fulfilling the democratic promise of giving all citizens equal consideration, yet I believe that we can improve deliberative theory by giving a greater place to empathy within deliberation. To begin to understand why, we need to examine a second turn recently taken by scholars that investigates the importance of emotions in a democracy. Although affect has played an important role in many previous studies of politics, in the last several decades, political scientists and political theorists have given greater attention to the importance of affect in politics and its relation to reason. I use the term "affect" to refer to a wide range of concepts including emotions, feelings, moods, and passions. I do so primarily to differentiate these from cognition, though, as I will argue later, I believe that affect and cognition often interact in reasoning and judgment. We can see the affective turn most clearly in empirical political science in the attempts by political psychologists to account for the role of emotions in explaining political attitudes and behavior. In political theory, it has manifested itself most obviously in the increasing interest in the place of passion in politics.

Drawing upon work in neuroscience (for example, Damasio 1994 and 1999) and cognitive science (for example, Zajonc 1980 and 1984) indicating the importance of emotion in human functioning, political psychologists have begun paying special attention to the role of emotion in political reasoning, attitudes, beliefs, opinions, and behaviors (see, for example, Glaser and Salovey 1998, Marcus 2000 and 2003, Neuman et al. 2007, and Redlawsk 2006a and 2006b). Work by George E. Marcus, W. Russell Neuman, Michael MacKuen, and Jennifer Wolak represent one of the major approaches in this area: affective intelligence. Marcus, Neuman, and MacKuen (2000) argue that affective intelligence is crucial to political judgment. Two important systems in the brain execute emotional evaluations—the *disposition system* and the *surveillance system* (see Marcus 2002, 71–75)—and these systems affect how citizens react to political information. The disposition system monitors habitual behaviors and familiar circumstances, generating enthusiasm when we are successful in our habits or confronting familiar friends, and anger or frustration when we are unsuccessful or confront familiar foes (Wolak and Marcus 2007, 172, 177). In contrast, the surveillance system monitors the environment and generates anxiety to alert us when something novel or threatening arises that requires us to shift our focus from the task at hand and pay attention to the intrusion that is occurring. For example, when the surveillance system generates anxiety about the party or candidate a citizen habitually supports, that citizen stops relying on shortcut cues such as partisanship, becomes active, and seeks new information (Marcus 2002, chap. 6). Thus, the model of affective intelligence posits that reactions to political information by preconscious emotional systems are a major determinant of how citizens behave.

In another approach, Milton Lodge and Charles Taber (and their many students and colleagues) propose a dual-process model of motivated reasoning that links emotion and cognition in what they call the "hot cognition" hypothesis (Lodge and Taber 2000, 2005).[1] The model is dual-process because it "distinguishes between automatic and deliberative processing in the formation and expression of beliefs, attitudes, goals, and behavior" (Lodge, Taber, and Weber 2006, 12). While people can certainly engage in reflective processing of political information, their automatic reactions occur before they can engage in conscious consideration of the information, and these automatic responses will always affect the subsequent deliberative processing (15). The underlying source of the automatic response is an "evaluative tally" people create based upon past judgments of "political leaders, groups, issues, symbols, and ideas" that links these objects in long-term memory with either positive or negative affect (Lodge and Taber 2005, 456). Thus, the realization that a news story is about "Jimmy Carter," before any conscious processing of the story, will bring forth an automatic affective response based upon past evaluations linked to "Jimmy Carter" in long-term memory, along with the strongest "Jimmy Carter" cognitive associations. While people may consciously process political information following the automatic response, the automatic affective response will always inform subsequent judgments. As with affective intelligence, therefore, motivated reasoning places affect at the center of political attitudes, beliefs, behaviors, and reasoning.

Although she does not develop a model as fully specified as affective intelligence or motivated reasoning, Rose McDermott also draws on neuroscience when proposing a model of "optimal" decision-making that she calls "emotional rationality," the beginnings of which she bases on "ten cognitive truths" (2004, 700–702). Several of these truths begin with similar

---

1. The use of the label "hot cognition" for this theory is a bit unfortunate, as it tends to reinforce the perception of many that the emotions are frenzied and in need of control by the "cooler" head of reason.

phrasing, so I will summarize them here, noting McDermott's specific enumeration. Emotions (1) arouse individuals to action with regard to an imagined or experienced event, (4) help decision makers focus on important and otherwise inaccessible information, (7) can affect risk perception, (9) may predictably bias decision makers, and (10) can provide the basis of hunches. Mood can affect the selection of (5) memory and (6) historical analogies. Finally, (2) we can understand expected emotional states as part of decision makers' expected utility calculations; and (3) immediate and expected emotion can also increase the perceived discount of future payoffs, increasing decision makers' pessimism about the likely success of their actions. Though McDermott's model needs further development, it differs slightly from both affective intelligence and hot cognition. Those two models focus on explaining people's political beliefs, attitudes, judgments, and behaviors, and while emotional rationality also draws upon evidence about the way people make decisions, it posits that we need to reconceptualize what it means to be a rational human being. Despite these differences, all three models give affect a prime place in the political world.

Political psychologists are not the only scholars who have paid close attention to affect in recent decades; political theorists, too, have taken an "affective turn." The relationship between emotions and reason has a long history in philosophy and political theory (see Kingston and Ferry 2008), but there has been a renewed interest recently in the role of affect in politics (see, for example, Hall 2002 and 2005, Koziak 2000, and Walzer 2002). Several theorists argue that deliberative theory often marginalizes the affective in favor of "rational" argumentation conceived of as unemotional, dispassionate, and disembodied (for example, Young 2000, 39–40, and Sanders 1997). As an alternative, theorists such as Gutmann and Thompson (2004, 50–51), Iris Marion Young (2000, 63–67), and John Dryzek (2000, 52–54, 167–68) open a space for affect by defending the legitimacy of the use of rhetoric, including emotional appeals, in deliberation. James Johnson (1998, 166) and Jane Mansbridge (1999, 225–27) both question the dichotomy between emotions and reason they see in the concept of "public reason"; as Mansbridge writes, "The concept of 'public reason' should be enlarged to encompass a 'considered' mixture of emotion and reason rather than pure rationality" (1999, 213). More recently, a few theorists have developed fuller accounts of how affect might function in a deliberative democracy. Cheryl Hall (2007) argues that we should not simply open up a space for affect within deliberation but must reconceive deliberation by recognizing the important role passion, including its rational and emotional elements, plays in deliberative democracy. Sharon Krause (2008) also addresses the role of passion in deliberative democracy by arguing that it can, if incorporated properly, serve the democratic ideal of impartiality in judgment. Drawing primarily on the work of David Hume, she argues that affect or sentiment plays a vital role in the reciprocity and understanding of others that is vital to deliberation. I believe that Krause is moving in the right direction by arguing that affect is just as important as cognition in a deliberative democracy, and I will return to her arguments in later chapters. It is my contention, however, that the best approach to understanding the role of affect in deliberation is to recognize the importance that empathy holds for helping democracy fulfill its promise to give equal consideration to all citizens. The problem is that most deliberative theorists have not done enough to address either the role of affect or empathy in a deliberative democracy.

Empathy and Democracy

In his book *Reflective Democracy,* Robert Goodin argues for supplementing the face-to-face deliberation advocated by deliberative democrats with a form of internal, reflective deliberation that takes place in the minds of citizens. One of the important facets of this "deliberation within" is that it can activate citizens' empathic imagination (2003, 171). In arguing thus, one of Goodin's goals is to make deliberative democrats' aim of including all those affected by collective decisions in deliberation practical in a large-scale society. Even in face-to-face deliberation, however, it is not enough just for people to have the opportunity to speak; one of deliberative democracy's core differences from other forms of democracy is that it requires participants to actively listen to all those who participate. If citizens simply talk with one another, but fail to take into account the interests, beliefs, and feelings of their fellow interlocutors, we will simply have an aggregative form of democracy with a deliberative face. Empathy is necessary not just for Goodin's "deliberation within," but for any deliberative theory that strives to attain the communication between citizens that is the basis of deliberative democracy. Despite its central importance, neither Goodin nor other scholars fully explore empathy's role in deliberative democracy, either theoretically or empirically; the aim of this book is to engage in this exploration.

As with any exploration, it is necessary first to map the terrain, and in Chapter 2 I begin by charting the different varieties of deliberative theory.

Deliberation has become ubiquitous in discussions of democracy, so it is important to provide some direction for how we can understand the term. I argue that there is one primary division in the literature on deliberative democracy between those who see deliberation primarily as *reflective decision-making* and those who connect it to issues of *justice* and *legitimacy*. Theorists who conceive of deliberation as reflective decision-making, such as Bessette (1994) and Fishkin (1991), focus primarily on deliberation's ability to give decision makers, whether legislators or citizens, an opportunity to gain information and reflect more fully on that information before making a decision. In contrast, Rawls (1996) and Habermas (1996a) maintain that deliberation conducted under specific conditions is necessary to ensure that democratic decisions are legitimate. Most theorists of deliberation, including James Bohman (1996), Joshua Cohen ([1989] 1997, 1996), John Dryzek (1990, 2000), and Amy Gutmann and Dennis Thompson (1996, 2004), follow Habermas and Rawls by focusing on the issue of legitimacy. While these major deliberative theories represent variations on a theme, one theorist who explicitly rejects both the Rawlsian and Habermasian approaches to deliberative legitimacy is Bernard Manin (1987). Although many deliberative theorists cite Manin, I contend that they do not appreciate the challenges he raises for any theory that argues for deliberation as the source of just or legitimate decisions. In order to complete the exploratory map, I conclude Chapter 2 by giving a preliminary description of the role of affect in deliberation. As I alluded to earlier, while some theorists make space for affect within deliberation, the very foundations of their theories—whether reflective decision-making, justice discovered through public reason, or legitimacy grounded in communicative rationality—prevent them from giving affect its proper place in deliberative democracy.

The second step in mapping the terrain is to understand what empathy is. This is the focus of Chapter 3. Empathy is an elusive concept used in a variety of ways both in academia and everyday speech; in order to clarify it, I examine its intellectual history. Empathy began as the German word *Einfühlung*, used in aesthetics to describe how observers come to appreciate a work of art by unconsciously projecting their selves into the object of contemplation. Later theorists expanded the possible target of *Einfühlung* to include human beings, and eventually Sigmund Freud ([1921] 1924) conceptualized it to include the idea that humans could gain an understanding of each other through *Einfühlung*. Before Freud fully conceptualized *Einfühlung* in this way, however, American psychologist Edward B. Titchener

(1909) translated it into English as the word "empathy." From this arose the confusion between empathy as consciously putting oneself in the place of another in order to understand the other's state and empathy as the often unconscious sharing of the emotional state of another. For most of the twentieth century, psychologists influenced by psychotherapy primarily defined empathy as conscious projection and understanding, while social and developmental psychologists mainly defined it as affective congruence. In order to overcome this confusion, Mark H. Davis (1994) proposes a multidimensional model of empathy that incorporates these various understandings. Davis's model moves us in the right direction by demonstrating the connections among various understandings of empathy, pushing us toward greater conceptual clarity and incorporating both affective and cognitive components within the model. Though Davis moves in the right direction, I offer some revisions that strengthen his model. The result is a model of empathy as a process, rather than a state, that not only accounts for the various conceptualizations of empathy and integrates affect and cognition, it also explains the relationship between empathy and sympathy, two concepts theorists often use interchangeably.

Having mapped out both deliberation and empathy, in Chapter 4 I use the process model developed in Chapter 3 to elucidate what deliberative theorists say about empathy. Since theorists who conceive of deliberation as reflective decision-making rely upon conceptualizations of democracy that contrast cool, reflective decisions with passionate, impulsive decisions, it is not surprising that they have little to say about empathy. Theorists who conceive of deliberation as central to legitimate democratic decision-making pay more attention to empathy, though this only becomes clear when we examine their theories in light of the process model. In general, these theorists focus on a process of role taking conceived primarily in cognitive terms, and while cognitive role taking as a mechanism is certainly a part of empathy, it cannot capture the entire empathic process.[2] These theorists also often invoke abstracting mechanisms that have the tendency to impede the process of empathy. By ignoring, downplaying, or rejecting the role of affect in the process of deliberation, these theorists undermine the possibility of achieving the kind of agreements necessary for legitimate democratic decisions that are at the heart of their theories. Deliberative theorists have to acknowledge the role in deliberation of the empathic process as a

2. Throughout the text I employ the terms "role taking" and "perspective taking" as generally synonymous, following the usage of the various authors I am discussing. Any differences between the two are not significant enough to alter my argument.

whole for their theories to be complete, a conclusion supported by empirical evidence.

In Chapter 5 I turn to the empirical evidence on the effects of empathy to demonstrate that deliberative democracy requires empathy if it is to function correctly. Research on group polarization, biases, altruism, helping behavior, reciprocity, and the commitment to continued deliberation indicates that people are highly unlikely to reach the kind of agreement posited by deliberative democrats if they do not engage in the process of empathy. Deliberators are more likely to engage in this process if they have already developed predispositions to empathy that involve both affect and cognition, and if the deliberative process asks them to pay attention to the thoughts and feelings of others. The empirical evidence also indicates that empathy can have positive effects even in a deliberative process that focuses on decision-making in which there are winners and losers, though winning and losing remains a negative influence. The upshot of the empirical evidence is that unless deliberative theory recognizes the importance of the various components involved in the empathic process, it can never achieve the ideals advocated by deliberative theorists. At the conclusion of Chapter 5, I engage in a preliminary discussion of the implications of the empirical evidence for democratic practice.

While Chapter 5 demonstrates that deliberative theorists have to pay more attention to the process of empathy, in Chapter 6 I turn to several theoretical critiques of deliberation to further clarify empathy's importance to deliberative democracy. I begin by explaining the challenge to deliberation raised by political psychologists and political theorists who have questioned the traditional divisions between reason and emotion. I then address a related set of concerns raised by those who criticize deliberative theory for excluding various forms of communication. Theorists such as Iris Marion Young (2000) and Lynn Sanders (1997) maintain that deliberative theory often excludes forms of communication, such as greeting, testimony, and rhetoric, practiced more often by groups that the political system has traditionally excluded from decision-making. Instead of defending affective forms of communication in contrast to reasoned argumentation, I maintain that the process model of empathy demonstrates that forms of communication which open up the possibility for everyone to engage in a broadly conceived process of role taking is necessary for deliberation to function effectively. While Young rejects empathy as central to democratic deliberation because she believes it induces people to project their own beliefs onto the other, I argue that her conceptualization of empathy is incorrect; recent neuroscientific studies demonstrate that maintaining distinctions between self and other are vital to the empathic process. I then examine theorists such as Gary Remer (1999), Bryan Garsten (2006), and Bernard Yack (2006), who defend theories of deliberation that are more open to affect, *pwrive* though they do so from a perspective that focuses on rhetoric. While they have important points to make regarding deliberation, I argue that they do not clarify the place affect should play in deliberation as much as they *conjecture* should. The process model of empathy, I contend, provides us with a heuristic whereby we can judge all forms of communication and their legitimate *theorem* place in a deliberative theory of democracy that takes empathy seriously. Finally, I turn to agonistic democrats, focusing on the work of Chantal Mouffe (1999, 2000, 2005). Agonists posit that by focusing on rational consensus, deliberative democratic theory ignores the importance of contestation in democratic politics. Rather than aim at consensus, democracy must give citizens a place to confront others and contest their differences. Citizens must approach democratic decisions with an agonistic ethos *harm* that leads them to see those with whom they disagree as *mistrust* opponents whom they can respect, not as enemies *distrusted* they must defeat at all costs. Agonistic democrats raise an important point regarding rational consensus, yet they all too often approach the point of fetishizing contestation. *v. evolution as competition - pointless* I contend that deliberative theorists can respond to their concerns by incorporating the process *evolving* model of empathy into the theory of deliberation. Doing so, however, requires a reconceptualization of democratic legitimacy that recognizes the *deductive-only reduce* limits of rational consensus as deliberative theorists understand it.

In Chapter 7 I turn to this alternative conceptualization. I begin by redefining deliberation as a practice in which people contemplate a political object by engaging in an inclusive, attentive communicative exchange that promotes the exchange of information and the process of empathy. *active?* Given this new definition, I maintain that we must reconceptualize the meaning of democratic legitimacy in a deliberative *evolving* society. After rejecting legitimacy as cool, reasoned reflection and justification, I return to Manin's theory of deliberative legitimacy outlined in Chapter 2 and, based upon his observations, argue that deliberative legitimacy constitutes a continuum that I elucidate as follows: a democratic decision is legitimate to the extent that the majority decides only after a process of deliberation that gives all citizens the opportunity to engage in a full exchange of perspectives and induces *which, motivates* them to empathize with one another. Having clarified these new definitions of deliberation and democratic legitimacy, I then answer questions critics raise regarding the feasibility of a deliberative democracy. By giving the process of empathy an important place, my new model of deliberation, I contend, can better answer concerns regarding the problems of economy, domination, and apathy that confront any attempt to implement an actually working theory of deliberative democracy. I end by developing some of the implications for the democratic process of a deliberative theory that takes empathy seriously.

Political theorists have given so much thought and attention to the issue of deliberation that Simone Chambers writes, "Deliberative democratic theory has moved beyond the 'theoretical statement' stage and into the 'working theory' stage" (2003, 307). The argument I make in this book actually addresses both of these stages. As a "working theory," I contend that theorists of deliberative democracy must acknowledge the roles of both affect and cognition in the processes of public deliberation by incorporating empathy more fully into their theories. Beyond this, however, I want to offer a new "theoretical statement" that puts the empathic process at the center of democratic deliberation. Only by doing so can deliberative theory effectively account for the growing body of empirical evidence on empathy, affect, cognition, and reason, as well as answer the theoretical challenges raised by deliberation's critics. Most important, a deliberative theory whose aim is to allow the process of empathy to function is the most likely to fulfill democracy's promise that legitimate collective decisions will give equal consideration to everyone.[3]

3. A note to readers: Since I intend this book to be accessible to a cross-section of readers, I know that there may be times when some find themselves examining material with which they are already familiar. Political theorists and others familiar with the deliberative literature may want to skim the first parts of Chapter 2, focusing on the later sections dealing with Manin and affect. Those familiar with the many aspects of empathy may want to skim the early parts of Chapter 3 and focus on my development of the process model of empathy, though I think that most people will find something novel in my discussion. I think that most readers will benefit from closer readings of the remaining chapters, though I know there will be points here and there when the topics will be well known to them. In those instances, I hope that they will indulge my longer explanations and understand that others might find them helpful.

2

THE DELIBERATIVE TURN IN DEMOCRATIC THEORY

For the past several decades, democratic theory has taken a deliberative turn, and yet, as Samuel Freeman notes, "There is no settled and commonly accepted account of the central features of a deliberative democracy among political scientists and theorists" (2000, 373). In order to recognize why deliberative democracy ought to take affect and empathy more seriously, we need to have a general understanding of how theorists conceptualize deliberation. In spite of various disagreements, I distinguish at the most general level between two major strands of deliberative theory. The first emphasizes deliberation's contribution to more *informed* and *reflective* political decisions, and the second highlights the role of deliberation in the generation of *reasonable* or *rational* democratic decisions. After examining each strand's major theorists, I return to the question of the role of affect in deliberative theory. While some thinkers have begun to address the role of affect in deliberation, I maintain that the best way to do this is through a thorough examination of empathy, something to which I will turn in Chapter 3. I begin, however, with deliberation as reflective decision-making.

Deliberation as Reflective Decision-Making

Several theorists place primary emphasis on deliberation as a process that can lead to informed and reflective decision-making (Ackerman and Fishkin 2002; Bessette 1980, 1994; Fishkin 1991, 1995). This understanding informs the earliest theory of "deliberative democracy" in the recent literature, Bessette's defense of the democratic nature of the U.S. Constitution (1980). In contrast to those who view the Constitution as elitist or aristocratic, Bessette maintains that the framers aimed at insuring that the government's decisions would embody the "deliberative sense of the community" (1980, 106–7). While simple majority rule can result from "spontaneous, uninformed, and unreflective" opinion, the framers wanted to establish the rule of a *deliberative* majority that rests upon sentiments that take "longer to develop" and rely upon "a fuller consideration of information and arguments" (106). Bessette proposes that we can test the democratic nature of these decisions with a hypothetical thought experiment: "If the citizens possessed the same knowledge and experience as their representatives and if they devoted the same amount of time reasoning about the relevant information and arguments presented in the legislative body, would they reach fundamentally similar conclusions on public policy issues as their representatives?" (105–6). If we respond affirmatively to this question, then the decision is basically democratic. On this understanding, deliberation becomes the central component of democracy; simply ascertaining what the majority wants is not enough if that majority has not engaged in a sufficiently deliberative decision-making process.

In a later work, Bessette maintains that deliberation is important because it increases the likelihood that government will formulate good public policy that is in the common interest. He even defines deliberation "most simply as *reasoning on the merits of public policy* . . . in which the participants seriously consider substantive information and arguments and seek to decide individually and to persuade each other as to what constitutes good public policy" (1994, 46; emphasis in original). The focus of this type of reasoning is on how the "public policy can benefit the broader society or some significant portion thereof" (48), though a *public* benefit does not need to be *national* in scope. The public good can be "a locally oriented good (such as a flood control project or a new highway), a good directed toward a broad class of citizens (as with civil rights laws or labor legislation), or even transnational in its reach (such as foreign aid)" (46–47). Thus, a member of Congress working on issues important to wheat farmers may meet "with other lawmakers from similar districts to discuss and evaluate their ideas about how best to promote the interests of wheat farmers," and if the member does so, "whatever the motive, this kind of activity constitutes reasoning on the merits of public policy" (143). Since deliberation requires serious discussion among members about the merits of policies, it will push legislators examining those issues to find some common ground with their fellow members (47–48). Thus, the process of deliberation will increase the likelihood that decisions will reflect what is common rather than just the specific interests of any particular group or individual; by this process deliberation tends toward collective decisions that increase the chances that they will embody a more equal consideration of interests.

While Bessette focuses on deliberation's tendency to result in informed and reflective decisions in U.S. governmental institutions, James Fishkin spotlights the positive effect deliberation can have on ordinary citizens. He argues that political institutions in the United States have sacrificed the deliberative side of democratic politics in order to increase political equality and political participation (1991, 53). While more and more people have become eligible to participate equally in the political life of American democracy, fewer and fewer actually engage in the kind of reflective decision-making characteristic of deliberation. Fishkin advocates the use of institutions such as his deliberative opinion polls to counter the tendency toward relying upon uninformed public opinion. In a deliberative opinion poll, a random sample of a population engages in an extended discussion of a political issue informed by balanced reading materials and a question and answer session with a wide-ranging panel of experts. The primary advantage of the public opinion that results from these polls is that it is more informed than traditional public opinion polling. "The point of a deliberative opinion poll is prescriptive, not predictive. It has a recommending force, telling us that this is what the entire mass public would think about some policy issues or some candidates if it could be given an opportunity for extensive reflection and access to information" (81). Fishkin and his colleagues have conducted deliberative polls throughout the world (Center for Deliberative Democracy 2007), and Bruce Ackerman and Fishkin (2002) have even proposed a "Deliberation Day" before presidential elections in the United States that would allow all citizens to participate. If citizens took advantage of Deliberation Day, they would enter the voting booth with more information, having carefully considered for whom they wanted to vote. These institutions work toward guaranteeing a more equal consideration of interests by including all citizens either directly (Deliberation Day) or virtually through random sampling (deliberative opinion poll). If they also influenced actual political decisions, those decisions would be more reflective and informed, and thus would be more democratically legitimate.

The overriding theme for theorists such as Bessette, Fishkin, and Ackerman is that deliberation will lead to decisions that are more reflective, and this consideration also appears to be one of the prime motivations for many groups promoting deliberation in the public sphere, such as the National Issues Forums, citizens' juries, and the Deliberative Democracy

Consortium. Deliberation may have other important consequences, such as moving decision makers closer to considering common concerns and values, but this only arises within the context of informed reflection.

Legitimacy and Public Reason: John Rawls

In contrast to the foregoing Madisonian vision of deliberation, however, the second major strand of deliberative democracy is more Kantian, focusing on the role of deliberation in allowing democratic decisions that are more reasonable or rational; the most influential theorists to have taken this approach are John Rawls and Jürgen Habermas. While some scholars are reluctant to consider John Rawls a deliberative theorist (see, for example, Chambers 2003, 208), his impact on deliberative democratic theory is undeniable. While influenced by his earlier theory of justice (Rawls 1971), Rawls first elucidated his conceptualization of deliberative democracy in his theory of political liberalism (1996). Political liberalism is his answer to the basic question: "How is it possible for there to exist over time a just and stable society of free and equal citizens, who remain profoundly divided by reasonable religious, philosophical, and moral doctrines" (4). This question highlights his assumption that all citizens are free and equal, but also encompasses what he calls the "fact of reasonable pluralism," the permanent and enduring existence in the public culture of any democracy of important, yet reasonable, religious, philosophical, and moral differences among citizens (36). It is impossible for democratic societies to remain stable and just by basing decisions on some external standard over which their citizens disagree; instead, there must be "fair terms of social cooperation."

Rawls's theory of political liberalism establishes that we can only arrive at decisions about the fair terms of social cooperation under certain conditions. He begins with the idea of the original position, a model in which we conceive of representatives of free and equal citizens deciding on the structure of the background framework for society (1996, 22–28). The most important feature of the original position is the veil of ignorance, which requires that the representatives do not know the "features relating to social position, native endowment, and historical accident" of those they represent, nor their "determinate conceptions of the good" (79). The veil of ignorance assures that the original position treats all citizens fairly by eliminating the asymmetries that result from contingent facts about the real world. What we may call "original position deliberation" consists of our own imaginings about how these representatives, given the limits of the original position, might choose "the appropriate principles of justice for specifying fair terms of social cooperation" (73). Rawls acknowledges, however, that his conception of justice is only one example of a liberal political conception and that the original position itself is just one criterion by which we can generate principles and guidelines for society that are legitimate (226–27). There are many variations of political liberalism that endorse "the underlying ideas of citizens as free and equal persons and of society as a fair system of cooperation over time" (1997, 774). With justice as fairness and the original position no longer primary in his argument, other concepts emerge as central to the role of deliberation in his theory.

As I noted earlier, Rawls maintains that citizens are free and equal, and that there exists the fact of reasonable pluralism. Given these claims, collective decisions backed by the coercive power of the community are only legitimate if they meet the criterion of reciprocity: "Our exercise of political power is proper only when we sincerely believe that the reasons we would offer for our political actions—were we to state them as government officials—are sufficient, and we also reasonably think that other citizens might also reasonably accept those reasons" (1997, 771). That he grounds legitimacy in reciprocity leads Rawls to a deliberative conception of democracy that has three essential elements: "an idea of public reason," "a framework of constitutional democratic institutions that specifies the setting for deliberative legislative bodies," and "the knowledge and desire on the part of citizens generally to follow public reason and to realize its ideal in their political conduct" (772). While deliberative legislative bodies and committed citizens are necessary, public reason comes to the fore as the most important idea in his conception of deliberation because public reason embodies the very idea of reciprocity that gives democratic decisions their legitimacy.

Given the fact of reasonable pluralism, public reason replaces "the ideas of truth or right based on comprehensive doctrines" with a basis of reasoning that all free and equal citizens can share (Rawls 1997, 789). For Rawls, a citizen engages in public reason "when he or she deliberates within a framework of what he or she sincerely regards as the most reasonable conception of justice, a conception that expresses political values that others, as free and equal citizens might also reasonably be expected to endorse" (773). Since there is a "family" of such reasonable liberal conceptions of justice, among which justice as fairness is only one, there will be "many forms of public reason" to which citizens might appeal when deliberating (774). We engage in public reason when we appeal to the standards, ideals, principles, and values of one member of the family of reasonable liberal conceptions in debating fundamental political questions with our fellow citizens (776). We must always remember that these liberalisms represent our best thinking on the values and conceptions of justice that we expect other reasonable citizens can reasonably accept.

Democratic decisions are legitimate only when they are the result of deliberations guided by public reason grounded in conceptions of justice that we believe other reasonable citizens could reasonably accept. Yet there are several ways in which Rawls modifies this general position. He restricts both the scope and the sites of deliberation. One of the reasons some theorists do not classify Rawls as a deliberative democrat is that he limits his theory of deliberation only to "constitutional essentials" and "questions of basic justice" (Rawls 1996, 214, 227–30). While he is open to the possibility that deliberation may apply in other areas—he writes that "it is usually highly desirable to settle political questions by invoking the values of public reason" (215)—constitutional essentials and questions of basic justice help form the framework of the political structure of a constitutional democracy, and he wants to first establish the role of public reason and deliberation in deciding these questions. He is also very specific about the sites at which public reason must guide deliberation. Public reason does not "apply to our personal deliberations and reflections about political questions, or to the reasoning about them by members of associations such as churches and universities" (215), because these are part of the background culture—the area outside the public political sphere—to which the restrictions of public reason do not apply (Rawls 1997, 768). Public reason applies to three discourses of the "public political forum": judicial decisions, especially those made by the Supreme Court; public official discourse, especially that of legislators and the chief executive; and the discourse of candidates and their campaign managers that occurs in public oratory, party platforms, and political statements (768). Outside these three discourses, public reason also relies upon citizens; it can only be effective if citizens think of themselves as "ideal legislators" and "fulfill their duty of civility and support the idea of public reason by doing what they can to hold government officials to it" (769). Thus, public reason applies to the discourses of judges, legislators, executives, and political candidates, but citizens must repudiate any of these whose discourse violates public reason.

Finally, Rawls modifies his position by opening up deliberation in the public political sphere to the introduction of citizens' reasonable comprehensive doctrines. This is permissible only if "in due course proper political reasons—and not reasons given solely by comprehensive doctrines—are presented that are sufficient to support whatever the comprehensive doctrines introduced are said to support" (Rawls 1997, 784). He calls this idea the "proviso," and it helps him distinguish between the "wide view of public political culture" and the "background culture." In the background culture, the use of public reason to justify our stances to our fellow citizens is not necessary, and we can rely upon our own reasonable comprehensive doctrines to make decisions; in the public political culture, though, we must at least eventually be able to justify our positions by recourse to values and arguments we believe other reasonable citizens could accept. As an example, he notes that those in the Civil Rights movement met the proviso because, while their doctrines had religious roots, their positions supported basic constitutional values that were part of a reasonable political conception of justice (785–86). He says that citizens must work out in practice how such a proviso might work, but the central point is that the introduction of comprehensive doctrines in public deliberation is acceptable, and may even be desirable, as long as citizens maintain the commitment to eventually justify their positions by appealing to public reason. This is the only way to fulfill the duties of civility and reciprocity, and thus meet the conditions necessary for legitimate democratic decision-making.

We can see, then, that Rawls insures equal consideration in democratic decision-making by requiring that public deliberation on constitutional essentials and questions of basic justice follow public reason. The duties of reciprocity and civility entail that political decisions are legitimate only when decision makers base them (at least eventually) upon values, guidelines, and principles derived from a political conception of justice that they sincerely believe all reasonable citizens could reasonably accept. A political conception of justice, in turn, must derive from some criterion that treats all citizens as free and equal and respects the fact of reasonable pluralism. Thus, reciprocity, civility, and public reason insure that decision makers consider all (at least reasonable) citizens equally in making decisions. They also provide legitimacy by justifying such decisions. Some reasonable citizens may disagree with a democratic decision, and given the fact of reasonable pluralism Rawls expects nothing less, but as long as those who decide constitutional essentials and questions of basic justice meet the requirements of reciprocity, civility, public reason, and the proviso, the collective force of the community can legitimately enforce the decision, even upon those who disagree.

Legitimacy and Rationality: Jürgen Habermas

Like Rawls, Jürgen Habermas maintains that deliberative democratic decisions are more legitimate than those that result from other forms of rule. Given this, it is unsurprising that there are many similarities between their theories; there are, however, many differences, some of which they have discussed (see Habermas 1995 and Rawls 1995). One similarity that stands out is that both theorists developed their ethical theories—justice as fairness for Rawls and discourse ethics for Habermas—before developing their theories of deliberative democracy. Yet while Rawls is generally clear about the position of justice as fairness in his theory of political liberalism, one of the difficulties with Habermas is that the relationship between his theory of discourse ethics and his theory of deliberative democracy is complex. Since his position on affect and cognition are easier to discern in his discourse ethics, I begin by elucidating his ethical theory before proceeding to his theory of deliberation.

Discourse ethics focuses on validating norms "under conditions of rational discourse" (Habermas 1998, 42) and relies upon Habermas's theory of communicative action. Communicative action delineates how different types of sentences connect to different types of validity claims that people ground through specific forms of argumentation that relate to three different "worlds": the objective, the subjective, and the social (Habermas 1984, 23, 39). Normative sentences raise claims of rightness regarding the intersubjective, social world that regulates our interactions with one another; discourse ethics deals most directly with what happens when people raise objections to validity claims within this intersubjective social world. If someone questions the validity of claims regarding the intersubjective social world, we respond by engaging in discussion (Habermas 1990, 157). In these moments, people's assumptions about the world can no longer guide discussion, and they must take a hypothetical attitude toward what they know that allows them to achieve unanimous, mutual agreement regarding the validity of the specific claim (161). Agreement is necessary because the very nature of communicative rationality "refers to an unclarified systematic interconnection of *universal* validity claims" (Habermas 1984, 18; emphasis added). Discourse ethics specifically describes how to secure universal validity claims through public discourse about moral norms. We rationally confirm the validity of a moral norm through the power to convince interlocutors by the "force of the better argument." "The claim that a norm lies equally in the interest of everyone has the sense of rational acceptability: all those possibly affected should be able to accept the norm on the basis of good reasons. But this can become clear only under the pragmatic conditions of rational discourses in which the only thing that counts is the compelling force of the better argument based upon the relevant information" (Habermas 1996a, 103). If participants assent to the validity of a norm based on forces other than those provided by the better argument, such as deception or coercion, they have not achieved rational, mutual agreement. In contrast with strategic action, in which "participants are primarily interested in bringing about a desired behavioral response" from other participants (Chambers 1995, 237), discourse ethics requires participants to aim at reaching mutual understanding by providing each other good reasons for the validity of moral norms.

Habermas focuses on the force of the better argument because his major goal in discourse ethics is to bring a cognitive content back into moral questions in the face of what he calls our postmetaphysical world. This idea is comparable to, and has similar consequences as, Rawls's fact of reasonable pluralism. While for Rawls citizens must rely upon public reason, for Habermas participants must look to the "intrinsic constitution of the practice of deliberation," from which they can derive a principle that allows them to rationally justify their arguments. He calls this the discourse principle: "Only those norms can claim validity that could meet with the acceptance of all concerned in practical discourse" (Habermas 1998, 41). While the discourse principle provides the foundation for introducing cognitive content into morality, Habermas argues that we still need to specify a rule of argumentation to clarify how we can assess the validity of moral norms in practical discourse. "According to discourse theory, moral norms can appear with a purely cognitive validity claim because the principle of universalization provides a rule of argumentation that makes it possible to decide moral-practical questions rationally" (Habermas 1996a, 155). The universalization principle states: "A norm is valid when the foreseeable consequences and side effects of its general observance for the interests and value-orientations of *each individual* could be *jointly* accepted by *all* concerned without coercion" (Habermas 1998, 42; emphasis in original). The point of deliberation on moral norms is to allow individuals to rationally assess whether they are valid given their understanding of everyone's interests and value-orientations; *each* individual must ascertain whether *all* accept (or could accept) the validity of the moral norm. The cognitive, epistemic goal Habermas pursues requires that, at least in the ideal, there be consensus about the validity of a moral norm. The deliberative process of testing moral norm validity can only reach this goal if it meets certain conditions. These conditions of an "ideal speech situation" include "freedom of access, equal rights to participate, truthfulness on the part of participants, absence of coercion in taking positions, and so forth" (Habermas 1993, 31). Such conditions aim at insuring that the decision-making process really aims at a rational mutual agreement, but when viewed alongside the universalization principle, we can see how Habermas builds equal consideration of all into the very heart of his theory of discourse ethics. Decisions regarding the validity of moral norms that will guide our social interactions must give equal consideration to all and are only legitimate if they do so.

While discourse ethics is clear about how it connects legitimate decision-making and equal consideration of individuals, this relationship is more complex in Habermas's theory of deliberative democracy. In discourse ethics we test the validity of moral norms with reference to the universalization principle, while in deliberative democracy we test the validity of legal norms with reference to what he calls the democratic principle. Though both derive from the discourse principle, they regulate different relationships. "The principle of morality regulates informal and simple face-to-face interactions; the principle of democracy regulates relations among legal persons who understand themselves as bearers of rights" (Habermas 1996a, 233). While legal norms must not violate moral norms (155), they "have different reference groups and regulate different matters" (451). Moral norms look to the interests of all, whereas legal norms focus on particular members of a legal community. To make this distinction clearer, we can think of moral norms as analogous with universal human rights that are valid for all people throughout all human history, whereas legal norms are those rights and laws applicable to those who compose a concrete legal community at a particular point in time.

This change in reference group has important consequences for Habermas's theory. It requires a shift in the way in which the democratic principle, in contrast to the universalization principle, instantiates the discourse principle. The universalization principle admits only moral reasons as legitimate bases for justifying norms, but the democratic principle "expands the spectrum of reason relevant for political will-formation: in addition to moral reasons, we find ethical and pragmatic ones" (Habermas 1996a, 152). The ethical and pragmatic reasons garnered to test the validity of legal norms can only be, by definition, relative to the historically and culturally bounded value orientations, goals, and interest positions of those in the legal community (156). Given the expanded reasons available in legal norm deliberation, the democratic principle does not specify the forms of argumentation and bargaining (460). There is also a shift in what it means to take into account the interests of all those affected. Legal rules require citizens not only to determine what is equally good for all, but also to achieve self-understanding of who they are and decide the best means to achieve the goals for which they strive. These additional questions give rise to "problems of balancing interests that cannot be generalized but call instead for fair compromises" (155).

All of these shifts in emphasis between discourse ethics and deliberative democracy lead Habermas to focus his discussion on what he calls rational opinion- and will-formation. Legitimacy under the democratic principle arises only when legal statutes "can meet with the assent (*Zustimmung*) of all citizens in a discursive process of legislation that in turn has been legally constituted" (Habermas 1996a, 110). The proper constitution of the "discursive process" is what insures that opinion- and will-formation is rational. This changes the focus of his theory "from the level of *individual* or group motivations and decisions to the *social* level of institutionalized processes of deliberation and decision-making" (461–62; emphasis in original). Institutionalizing a legitimate process of deliberative politics requires at least three major components: a system of individual rights; an independent, open, informal public sphere grounded in civil society; and a constitutionally established system of formal political deliberative decision-making.

In order to insure that all citizens are able to participate in the discursive process there must be "a system of rights that secures for each person an equal participation in a process of legislation whose communicative presuppositions are guaranteed to begin with" (Habermas 1996a, 110). These rights form the basis for the autonomy that gives laws their legitimacy by allowing citizens to make the laws to which they are subject, but rights can only be effective if there is a system of opinion- and will-formation that allows citizens to exert influence. Legitimate democratic decisions "must be steered by communication flows that start at the periphery and pass through the sluices of democratic and constitutional procedures situated at the entrance to the parliamentary complex or the courts (and, if necessary, at the exit of the implementing administration as well)" (356). The "periphery" to which Habermas refers is a public sphere of noninstitutionalized communications that allow for "a more or less *spontaneous* processes of opinion-formation" (358). This public sphere, in turn, must "be anchored in the voluntary associations of civil society and embedded in liberal patterns of political culture and socialization" (358). Deliberation in the public sphere, however, is not enough. Communication flows generated there must have influence on the more formalized opinion- and will-formation that occurs in formal democratic political institutions. "To generate political power, [informal public discourses'] influence must have an effect on the democratically regulated deliberations of democratically elected assemblies and assume an authorized form in formal decisions. This also holds, mutatis mutandis, for courts that decide politically relevant cases" (372). While Habermas is not always clear about what "sluices" will allow this flow of power, he does indicate that political parties and general elections intertwine the formal political system with the public sphere and civil society (368).

We can thus see the sociological picture of democratic legitimacy within Habermas's theory of deliberative democracy. A constitutionally established guarantee of rights allows citizens to participate in deliberation within an independent public sphere grounded in civil society. The deliberations that result must then influence opinion- and will-formation within the more formalized political institutions, at least in part through the activities of political parties and general elections. This entire process allows all citizens to be the authors of the laws to which they are subject, thus guaranteeing their autonomy. Yet this entire process itself is not enough. "A legal order *is* legitimate to the extent that it equally secures the co-original private and political autonomy of its citizens; at the same time, however, it *owes* its legitimacy to the forms of communication in which alone this autonomy can express and prove itself" (Habermas 1996a, 409; emphasis in original). Despite his "proceduralism," in the end Habermas argues that deliberative democracy requires a certain political culture to insure legitimacy. Citizens cannot "exclusively use their communicative liberties *like* individual liberties in the pursuit of personal interests," but must use them "with an orientation toward the common good" and "take the perspective of participants who are engaged in the process of reaching understanding about the rules for their life in common" (461; emphasis in original). The array of constitutional guarantees and formal and informal structures for political opinion- and will-formation will only result in legitimate decision-making if the citizens themselves behave in certain ways. The procedures and institutions of Habermas's deliberative democracy move us toward a system that gives equal consideration to all citizens and provides a foundation for legitimate democratic decisions, but citizens must still deliberate such that they fulfill the discourse principle's admonition to take account of the interests of all those affected.

Habermas admits that complex societies could never meet all the conditions of "the model of purely communicative social relations" and that his "model is merely a methodological fiction intended to display the unavoidable inertial features of societal complexity" (1996a, 326). We can use the model as a critical tool to assess the degree to which actually functioning societies meet its various requirements (see, for example, Parkinson 2006). Yet even granting this critical point, it is still important to recognize that the political culture must still meet certain requirements for the system to guarantee equal consideration and legitimate democratic decision-making. While the shift to a sociological viewpoint helps us better understand how a deliberative democracy might function from a broader perspective, equal consideration and democratic legitimacy still depend upon citizens who are willing to deliberate with their fellow citizens with an eye toward providing reasons that are acceptable to others, or at a minimum, to engage in a fair process of bargaining (Habermas 1996a, 165–68). My contention is that empathy is a central psychological trait that will allow this to happen, but Habermas's theoretical positions tend to limit this very possibility.

Bernard Manin's Challenge

Rawls and Habermas have had the greatest influence on deliberative theorists, though much of that influence has derived from their ethical theories of justice as fairness and discourse ethics. This is primarily because the works in which they elucidated their most fully developed theories of deliberative democracy appeared only after many others had published their own ideas about deliberation. Habermas's *Between Facts and Norms* appeared in German in 1992; its English translation came out in 1996. Rawls's *Political Liberalism* came out in 1993, but he explained, expanded, and modified his theory both in the introduction to the 1996 paperback edition and in his 1997 article "The Idea of Public Reason Revisited." Yet before most of the major works in deliberative theory appeared, Bernard Manin (1987) wrote one of the earliest theoretical expositions on the relation between deliberative democracy and legitimacy. Manin's original article appeared in French in 1985, and his 1987 *Political Theory* article was a slightly modified version of this original. Rather than connect legitimacy with ideas such as public reason, rationality, substantive values, or even ongoing cooperation, he bases legitimacy solely on the fact that deliberation occurs before a democratic decision.

Manin's argument begins by criticizing liberal democratic theory, which he believes, because of its foundations in individualism, bases legitimacy on the will of each particular individual. The result is that legitimate power can only exist if all give their unanimous consent (Manin 1987, 340). Democracy does not just concern itself with legitimacy, though; it also addresses efficiency. Since unanimous agreement is very unlikely, democratic practice requires an alternative to consensus as a decision rule: "Thus [democratic theories] must bring into play a more realistic principle of decision-making than that of unanimity, namely the majority principle" (341). There is a tension between these principles of legitimacy through unanimity and decisions by majority rule, and Manin argues that Jean-Jacques Rousseau and John Rawls respond to this conundrum by reducing political decisions to a process whereby citizens apply the appropriate criteria for evaluating what a rational person would decide is best for the common good. In doing so they confer upon the majority will "all the attributes of unanimous will" (342). On this understanding, majority rule becomes a proxy for unanimity, and what the majority decides represents what all *would have* decided, what would have been the unanimous content of all individual wills, if they had all been able to make their decisions rationally. "The process of forming a decision is reduced to calculation . . . the individual is already supposed to know exactly what he wants, or more precisely, he already possesses the criteria for evaluation that will permit him to appraise all possible alternatives" (349).

Manin criticizes this approach because it requires the assumption that individuals "possess an already formed will, already know exactly what they want, and at most only need to apply their criteria of evaluation to the proposed solutions" (1987, 351). He proposes as an alternative that "the source of legitimacy is not the predetermined will of individuals, but rather the process of its formation, that is, deliberation itself" (351–52). It is the process of an open and inclusive search for reasonable and justifiable arguments—the deliberative *process* itself—that gives democratic decisions their legitimacy. The democratic process must meet certain conditions in order to be legitimate, and Manin presents what these would be in a representative democracy. There must be a genuine set of real alternatives, one of the reasons why several organized political parties are important. The process of deliberation must also take place in front of the universal audience of all citizens; this encourages each party to show "that its point of view is *more general* than the others" (358; emphasis in original). The majority must be subject to dismissal by a process of deliberation and vote at regular intervals, and it ought not alter this requirement (362). There are certain actions those with political power may not take, such as excluding anyone from the rights to vote or participate in deliberation, or suppressing fundamental liberties that are the effective exercise of these rights—"freedom of conscience, of opinion, of speech, and of association" (362). The deliberative process itself comes to a close by a vote, and the candidates and points of view that win this vote get to make political decisions.

The fact that a majority of citizens elected these candidates under the required conditions does not, though, grant any special place to their decisions; the will represented by the majority vote gains no special status. "The decision of the majority is only the decision of the greatest number, nothing more" (Manin 1987, 360). The reason their decisions are legitimate is only because they occur "at the close of a deliberative process in which all the citizens (or at least those who wished to do so) have participated. The procedure preceding the decision is a condition for legitimacy, which is just as necessary as the majority principle" (360). Though the minority must now obey decisions that are against its will, the final decision no longer absorbs the minority's will into the general will and forces it to obey laws that it *would* will if it could just decide more rationally or reasonably. The minority maintains its status in opposition to the majority decision, and the majority ought to take into account the opinions of those who disagree with it. For Manin, therefore, there is no conflation of a unanimous will and the majority will; legitimacy still arises from individual wills, but it does so because a process of open and inclusive deliberation leads to political decisions.

While Habermas certainly has his differences with Rawls and Rousseau, all three base legitimacy in an attempt to derive an impartial point of view from which we make practical judgments. Rousseau derives this viewpoint by having citizens engage in internal deliberation about the general will in a society of nearly equally wealth, and self-sufficient citizens who have adequate information and do not form partial associations ([1762] 1988, 101, 116). Rawls develops the impartial stance by requiring that citizens use public reason in justifying decisions, that is, they must base their decisions on a political conception of justice they believe other reasonable citizens could reasonably accept. Habermas's impartial viewpoint derives from the discourse principle, which requires all participants in a rational discourse to assess whether all others could accept the validity of a norm, whether moral or legal. In all three cases there are *rational* or *reasoned* answers to the political questions in a society that we can discover through the general will (Rousseau), a political conception of justice (Rawls), or valid norms (Habermas); and at least in the ideal, if we could all achieve the proper impartial point of view, we could all figure out what those rational or reasoned answers are.

Manin's position may overstate the degree to which Rawls and Habermas expect consensus on answers to political questions, and the two theorists' writings that appeared after Manin's article did alter their positions. Still, there is something at the heart of Manin's critique that is revealing about the later formulations of Rawls and Habermas, but also the deliberative variants proposed by theorists such as Cohen and Gutmann and Thompson. None of these theorists expect deliberation to result in actual consensus or agreement; yet they all still require, on one level or another, those who make decisions to base them on reasons they believe others could (or should?) accept, even if those others patently reject them in actual deliberation. This requirement provides the basis for the *legitimacy* of the decision, and thus lends authority to the decision that it might not otherwise have. As Manin argues, the majority acts, in a sense, as if the minority had actually supported the majority's position. I will grant that deliberative democrats are quick to establish the provisional nature of any majority decision, and the requirements they establish for deliberation do mirror and even expand the requirements Manin himself defends. Yet if, for example, as Gutmann and Thompson claim, "the individual is the only kind of agent who can judge whether a reason should be accepted as a basis for fair cooperation, in accordance with reciprocity" (1996, 151), majorities face a choice in the face of actual disagreement. They must either convince themselves of the minority's misjudgment or, failing this, they must abandon reciprocity.

Manin gets around this problem by not intertwining equal consideration in deliberation with the idea of will or the belief that the reasons one gives others could accept. For Manin, legitimacy simply requires deliberation. Even if the majority chooses to ignore minority opinion at the end of a deliberative process, deliberation insures that the majority's "choice would be a more *deliberate* one than if the majority had believed at the outset that the decision under consideration would meet with no opposition" (1987, 361; emphasis in original).[1] When a majority decision "comes at the close

1. This appears similar to the arguments given by those who connect deliberation with reflective decision-making, though I think Manin's position is even more minimalist than theirs.

of a deliberative process in which everyone was able to take part, choose among several solutions, and remain free to approve or refuse the conclusions developed from the argument, the result carries legitimacy" (359). Political questions do not admit of logical proof, but in deliberation we begin to see that some positions are more persuasively justifiable than others. Manin writes, "Between the *rational* object of universal agreement and the *arbitrary* lies the domain of the *reasonable* and *justifiable,* that is, the domain of propositions that are likely to convince, by means of arguments whose conclusion is not incontestable, the greater part of an audience made up of all the citizens" (363; emphasis in original). For Manin, democratic legitimacy arises simply from the fact that deliberation opens the possibility for a decision-making in which all citizens have the chance to engage in giving voice to their positions under conditions that, at the least, increase the chances that all positions will receive equal consideration. Manin raises a serious challenge that I believe deliberative theorists can answer only by understanding the role empathy must play in deliberation.

Deliberation and Affect

One of the main reasons deliberative democrats miss the importance of empathy is that they have not sufficiently addressed the role of affect in deliberation. I believe this is due, at least in part, to their tendencies to fall back upon conceptualizations of reflection, rationality, and reasoning that give precedence to cognition over affect in human judgment. As I noted in Chapter 1, many political psychologists have begun to challenge the notion that human judgment is independent of affect; our affective responses to things political inherently affect how we reason about them. Most political psychologists concern themselves with the empirical existence of these effects, rather than the normative implications. The normative nature of political theory necessitates that empirical data not drive our theories completely, but when such data indicate a very basic condition about the human experience, political theorists must pay attention. At least one political psychologist has drawn out some of the implications of this new research for the idea of deliberation: George E. Marcus.

Marcus, drawing on his and his colleagues' work that I noted in Chapter 1, argues that deliberative democrats make significant errors in the diagnosis of what is wrong with democracy. Marcus does not wish to claim that deliberation is irrelevant. "It enhances the linkage between the explicit public considerations of government and its appropriate actions and the legitimacy of those actions" (Marcus 2002, 31). Instead, deliberative reforms fail, on Marcus's reading, because they aim at creating citizens who are "more serious, more reasoning, and less passionate" (31). Deliberative democrats both assume that the current level of deliberation is higher than it is and use an incorrect psychological explanation of the use of reason "because emotion is required to invoke reason and to enable reason's conclusions to be enacted" (31). For Marcus, the two emotional systems in the brain—the disposition system and the surveillance system (71–75)—influence the way people evaluate and judge the political world. The disposition system reinforces those habits that have been successful in the past; and in politics, it responds to familiar political objects with either enthusiasm (positive response) or anger (negative response). The surveillance system monitors the environment for unfamiliar or threatening objects, and when it perceives them, triggers an anxiety response. This response in turn leads us to evaluate our environment and situation and contemplate how to respond to the novel or threatening.

Marcus applies this general framework to democratic politics, and the implications are interesting. Citizens react habitually to most political phenomena, relying on the stored knowledge of the disposition system to generate preconscious evaluations of either enthusiasm or anger. Yet these reactions are merely habit; there is no deliberation involved. In contrast, new or threatening objects generate anxiety, and it is anxiety that draws us away from habit and engages us in a formal consideration of the situation. Thus, "when the public feels anxious about something important, it stops relying on habit and it learns about the alternatives, gets better informed about the issues, and when it comes time to make a judgment the public forswears reliance on simple likes and habitual cues for calculated consideration of the most promising alternatives that satisfies its calculated interest" (Marcus 2002, 138). Ironically, therefore, anxiety is what can induce citizens to actually deliberate; absent this anxiety, even in purportedly "deliberative" forums, citizens will rely primarily on their habits in their political judgments. Deliberative theorists who aim at expunging the emotional from politics undermine their very project. Only by being emotional will what Marcus calls sentimental citizens "engage in reason and set aside, if momentarily, their otherwise comfortable reliance on habit" (148). Emotions are also motivating once the deliberation has concluded, "for emotion enables us to put the results of our understandings, new and old alike, into action" (148). For Marcus emotion provides the very opening for the possibility of deliberation, as well as the motivation to follow through on deliberative decisions. At least some deliberative theorists have made some initial moves to address the role of affect in deliberation that may allow them to respond to at least some of Marcus's concerns.

Deliberative theorists, as well as their critics both friendly and adversarial, have primarily addressed affect in discussions of passionate rhetoric. Iris Marion Young, for example, defends the legitimacy of passionate rhetoric in deliberation by arguing that "to the extent that democratic theory and practice privilege . . . a standard of allegedly dispassionate, unsituated, neutral reason, it has exclusionary implications" (2000, 63). Agreeing with Young's underlying position, Gutmann and Thompson argue that "deliberative democrats should recognize that in the political arena passionate rhetoric can be as justifiable as logical demonstration" (2004, 51). Other theorists have made the broader point that deliberation ought to admit affective utterances in a context beyond just passionate rhetoric. Jane Mansbridge, for example, writes, "In both legislative bodies and the rest of the deliberative system, the concept of 'public reason' should be enlarged to encompass a 'considered' mixture of emotion and reason rather than pure rationality" (1999, 213). Here Mansbridge moves even closer to those who recognize that affect and cognition combine in our process of judgments and that we must acknowledge this in deliberation. Few deliberative theorists go as far as James Johnson, who maintains that "there surely are points when 'unreasonable' factors such as anger, frustration, humor, fear, joy, and humiliation quite reasonably and justifiably enter political argument" (1998, 166). Johnson's insight is that political "argument" may not always be "reasonable" in the sense some deliberative democrats require, and yet this is not a difficulty for deliberation if we reconceive it. In Chapter 6, I will return to these arguments in more detail, but for now I want to note that none of these scholars provide a deep account of the role of affect in deliberation; they primarily focus on providing some space for passionate rhetoric or emotions in deliberative democracy.

Recently, though, a few theorists have begun to develop fuller accounts of the role of affect in a deliberative democracy.[2] Cheryl Hall begins by defining passion as a "strong enthusiasm and devotion" for an object one perceives as "deeply valuable" (2007, 87). Since passion involves both a judgment of what one values, as well as an affective link with the object, passion "is inherently rational and emotional" (88). Deliberative democracy

2. See also Thompson and Hoggett 2001.

already involves passion because it motivates citizens to deliberate and helps them discuss with one another what they value. Citizens must "observe and reflect on their passions in order to gain insight into what they really care about, so that they can then weight the advantages and disadvantages" of the subject of deliberation (91–92). Hall argues that we should not simply open up a space for affect within deliberation, we must reconceive deliberation by recognizing the important role passion, including its rational and emotional elements, plays in deliberative democracy. While Hall's discussion of passion is a move in the right direction, I believe that her characterization of passion as a combination of both rationality and emotion still buys into the dichotomy that separates emotion from reason. Rather than talk just of passions, I believe it is necessary for us to understand the role of emotions in the broader sense in how members of a polity engage in political judgment.

Sharon Krause moves closer to this approach to addressing the role of affect in deliberative democracy by arguing that it can, if incorporated properly, serve the democratic ideal of impartiality in judgment. Krause maintains that "there is no such thing as rational justification in the absence of affective modes of consciousness" because "justification always proceeds by appeal to things we care about" (2006, 10). In talking about things we care about, Krause comes close to realizing the arguments of political psychologists like Marcus, and this recognition of the important role affect has in justification requires that we reconceive the idea of reciprocity that is central to deliberative theory. The deliberative process in many of the theories we have examined focus on giving reasons for democratic decisions that are mutually justifiable, or at least persuasive, to all citizens. This reciprocity, if "properly conceived," Krause argues, bears on two deliberative practices: public reason and perspective taking. First, we must recognize that public reason—reason that arises from evaluative standards citizens hold in common—relies upon principles that must have "an affective character if they are to be capable of motivating decisions and actions" and also "themselves rest on, or can be justified in terms of, sentiments" (12). Second, drawing on the work of David Hume, Krause argues that we should understand reciprocity in terms of moral sentiment; doing so reveals how perspective taking relies upon not just cognitively understanding others' arguments but appreciating the affective foundations that guide others' evaluative judgments of the object of deliberation (14–16). Reconceiving reciprocity by acknowledging the importance of affect in both public reason and perspective taking ensures that deliberation involves a recognition of what all citizens care about, and by doing so, helps to ensure that deliberative outcomes are impartial in the sense that they do not privilege the concerns of only some. Thus, Krause does not just make a space for affect in deliberation, she places affect at the very heart of legitimacy in a deliberative democracy. I agree with much of what Krause argues, and I conceive of our two lines of reasoning as complementing rather than contradicting one another. Still, I want to examine areas that she does not and enhance our understanding of the role of affect in deliberation by examining empirical research on empathy. I also want to explore the role of affect in deliberation conceived in ways other than those that focus on reciprocity and the use of public reason. More important, I believe her focus on Hume and his conception of sympathy, while beneficial to our understanding, has its limits. As an alternative, I want to examine the concept of empathy as a way to understand the role of affect in deliberation broadly conceived.

3

THE ELUSIVE CONCEPT OF EMPATHY

As Nancy Eisenberg and Janet Strayer explain, "Because of its wide-ranging application, the notion of empathy is, and always has been, a broad, somewhat slippery concept—one that has provoked considerable speculation, excitement, and confusion" (1987, 3). Jonathan Levy goes even further to state that the "word *empathy* has been troublesome since it entered the language of psychology and psychiatry" (1997, 179; emphasis in original). The slippery and troublesome nature of the term "empathy" becomes apparent if we even briefly peruse some of its uses by scholars and in everyday speech. Depending upon the context of the statement, it can refer to a number of different but related concepts: (1) Some speak of empathy as the ability to feel what someone else is feeling, as when U.S. presidential candidate Bill Clinton, confronted during his first campaign by an AIDS activist, said, "I feel your pain" ("The 1992 Campaign," 1992). (2) A similar but broader notion of empathy indicates having a feeling that is "congruent with the other's emotional state or situation" (Eisenberg and Strayer 1987, 5), even if it is not exactly the same feeling; for example, we may react with frustration or distress when we see someone trapped in a painful situation. (3) Rather than just any related emotion, sometimes "empathy" specifically indicates reacting with positive and supportive feelings in response to others. For example, some researchers measure empathy by asking respondents how they feel about another person using six adjectives: sympathetic, compassionate, softhearted, tender, warm, and moved (see, for example, Batson et al. 2005, 18). (4) Some uses of "empathy" indicate the ability to understand *what* someone is feeling without actually sharing that feeling itself. A parent who has lost a young child may be able to understand the feelings someone else that loses a young child is experiencing, even if she does not relive her own pain and suffering. (5) An alternative notion of empathy as understanding does not focus solely on recognizing *what* someone is feeling but on *why* someone feels a certain way in a given situation. This can occur even when those empathizing are not experiencing, nor might they ever experience, the same feelings in that situation. For example, someone who does not believe that life begins at conception may still recognize that those who do believe this feel frustration or sorrow at the prevalence of abortion in society and understand why they feel this way. (6) Former U.S. defense secretary Robert McNamara has even used the notion of empathy as understanding, of "putting oneself in another's shoes," in a primarily cognitive way. He posits in the film *The Fog of War* that successful foreign policy requires leaders to empathize with their enemies: "That's what I call empathy. We must try to put ourselves inside their skin and look at us through their eyes, just to understand the thoughts that lie behind their decisions and their actions."

These six examples represent only an adumbration of how people use the term "empathy"; and while they certainly have familial connections, they begin to demonstrate the complications that arise in employing the concept. The picture becomes even more complicated when scholars begin to relate empathy with some conceptions of sympathy, such as those by David Hume and Adam Smith (for example, Schertz 2007), or raise questions such as the differing roles affect and cognition play in empathy (for example, Eisenberg and Strayer 1987). One could respond to this seemingly intractable morass simply by stipulating one's own use of the term and then pushing on to other concerns. If we do that, however, we lose insights that can arise from examining how different usages arose, how they are connected, and what contexts have lent themselves to the various conceptualizations of empathy. By examining the historical development of the term, we can begin to understand why people use it in such varied ways and how those different uses relate to one another.[1] Emotion, projection, and understanding have been central to the concept of empathy from its beginnings, and the confusion surrounding the concept arises mainly from the stress users place on particular aspects versus others. By understanding this source of disagreement, we can overcome some of the confusion surrounding empathy by conceiving of it as a *multidimensional process* that

1. I am indebted in my understanding of the history of empathy primarily to Charles Gauss (1973), Arnold Goldstein and Gerald Michaels (1985), George Pigman (1995), and Lauren Wispé (1987), though I have made corrections where I found evidence contrary to their claims.

addresses all of these aspects. This conceptualization reveals that empathy is not a feeling, but rather a process through which others' emotional states or situations affect us. Feelings such as compassion, sympathy, and even anger may result from the process of empathy, but we never "feel" empathy. The process model not only allows us to incorporate the key aspects of the different conceptualizations of empathy, it demonstrates the important roles both thinking and feeling play in the empathic process. The clearer and more complete conceptualization that results from this historical investigation will then allow us to evaluate empathy's importance for deliberation by defining a place for affect in a deliberative democracy.

Einfühlung, Aesthetics, and Wit

The English word "empathy" is just under a hundred years old and is the translation of a German word that only appeared in the second half of the nineteenth century. What becomes "empathy" began as the German word *Einfühlung*, literally feeling-in or feeling-into, and though the idea was around in various forms for many years, Robert Vischer first coined the term in his dissertation, *On the Optical Sense of Form*, written in 1872 and published a year later. In his dissertation, Vischer connects aesthetic appreciation to feelings and emotions, but the problem arises of how inanimate and nonhuman objects can take a form imbued with these emotions. Drawing on Karl Albert Scherner's book *Das Leben des Traums* (The Life of the Dream), Vischer writes: "Particularly valuable in an aesthetic sense is the section on 'Die symbolische Grundformation für die Leibreize' (Symbolic basic formation for bodily stimuli). Here it was shown how the body, in responding to certain stimuli in dreams, objectifies itself in spatial forms. Thus it unconsciously projects its own bodily form—and with this also the soul—into the form of the object. From this I derived the notion that I call 'empathy' [*Einfühlung*]" (Vischer [1873] 1994, 92). The solution to the problem of how inanimate forms can contain emotions is that we bring our own emotions to the objects of contemplation. "If . . . there can be no form without content, then it must be shown that those forms devoid of emotional life . . . are supplied with emotional content that we—the observers—unwittingly transfer to them" (Vischer [1873] 1994, 89). *Einfühlung* describes this process of giving emotional life to objects that do not have it by a projection of the observer's self into the object of beauty: "Thus I project my own life into the lifeless form, just as I quite justifiably do with another living person. Only ostensibly do I keep my own identity although the object remains distinct. I seem merely to adapt and attach myself to it as one hand clasps another, and yet I am mysteriously transplanted and magically transformed into this Other" (104). Vischer maintains that *Einfühlung* allows us to animate a plant, anthropomorphize an animal, and imagine a dead form as a living thing, and though the object's form does have some effect on the process, in each case it is we who are bringing the emotional content to the object.

Though Vischer developed *Einfühlung* to explain aesthetic appreciation, his theory emphasizes three themes that remain important to contemporary understandings of, and disagreements concerning, empathy: *emotion, projection,* and *understanding.* Emotions play a central role in *Einfühlung,* and current uses of "empathy" involve feelings in at least some manner. It is also easy to recognize in many present-day conceptualizations of empathy an influence arising from the presence in *Einfühlung* of a projection of the self into an object. Some contemporary scholars have rejected projection as part of empathy itself, but many current scholarly and everyday uses of empathy maintain this aspect, often by using phrases such as "putting oneself in the other's shoes." Even among researchers who agree that projection is a part of empathy disagree on whether empathy involves an involuntary projection, as in Vischer's theory, or whether this projection can be conscious. Despite these various disagreements, the projection that serves Vischer's aesthetic purposes continues to be important in debates surrounding the concept of empathy. Finally, we can see a more subtle influence in the fact that *Einfühlung* leads to aesthetic appreciation. People generally no longer link *Einfühlung* or empathy with the ability to appreciate beauty, but many of them have adapted Vischer's general idea of understanding something outside the self through projection to explain how we can understand other human beings. As with projection, some scholars maintain that understanding is an outcome of empathy rather than empathy itself, but others place understanding at the heart of empathy. Vischer developed *Einfühlung* to help us understand a phenomenon that is today only tangential to the various applications of the term, but these three key aspects of *Einfühlung* in his theory—emotion, projection, and understanding—influenced much of the later development of the concept.

It is important to note that while Vischer's dissertation focuses primarily on nonhuman objects, he hints that *Einfühlung* could involve interactions between humans. He argues that our emotional life arises from a connection with other human beings, and this connection comes about through something like what he calls *Einfühlung:* "Only by considering our fellow beings do we ascend to a true emotional life. This natural love for my species is the only thing that makes it possible for me to project myself mentally; with it, I feel not only myself but at the same time the feeling of another being" ([1873] 1994, 103). Unlike aesthetic appreciation, in which we bring our own emotions to an object, here he indicates that we can access the feelings of another human. He gives an example of this kind of "feeling of another being" in his discussion of the association of ideas and its relation to *Einfühlung.* "An old, potbellied beer stein, for example, might remind me of some thirsty reveler who once held it. I thus think and feel a person, someone human, in addition to this stein. I can also find myself imagining the reveler in a shape and attitude suggested by this stein. Here [*Einfühlung*] is asserting itself with the association of ideas" (109; emphasis in original). Vischer never fully develops these ideas on feeling oneself into other humans, but those who followed him would take his concept of *Einfühlung* along these lines and open the door to what we now call empathy.

Theodor Lipps took two important steps in this direction by more explicitly conceiving of *Einfühlung* as including reactions to our fellow humans and expanding it beyond the confines of aesthetics. Lipps primarily followed Vischer in applying *Einfühlung* to the problem of aesthetic appreciation: "That I enjoy myself in a sensuous object presupposes that in it I have, or find, or feel myself. Here we encounter the basic idea of present-day aesthetics, the concept of [*Einfühlung*]" ([1905] 1965, 403). For him, this process occurs when observers appreciate and understand an object by projecting themselves into the object, establishing an identification between themselves and the object, and performing an internal imitation of the object (Goldstein and Michaels 1985, 4). In this conceptualization we can again see the aspects of *Einfühlung* Vischer highlighted—the centrality of emotion, projection, and appreciation or understanding—and Lipps's discussion of internal imitation would also influence later understandings of empathy. Lipps's most important contribution is that he extends the concept beyond mere objects to include our responses to humans as well. He delineates several types of *Einfühlung;* and at its highest level, it arises in response to the "gestures, facial expressions, and tone of voice of another" (Gauss 1973, 86). Lipps writes:

The highest evocation of all arises from the sensuous appearance of the human being. We do not know how or why it happens that a glimpse of a laughing face, or a change in that contour of the face,

especially the eyes and mouth, which we associate with the phrase
"laughing face" should stimulate the viewer to feel gay and free and
happy; and to do this in such a way that an inner attitude is assumed,
or that there is a surrender to this inner activity or to the action of the
whole inner being. But it is a fact. ([1905] 1965, 409)

Though this highest level of *Einfühlung* does not quite reach what most
today define as empathy, the idea that one human's emotional state can
affect another's was a central step in the development of *Einfühlung* into
empathy. In addition to expanding *Einfühlung* in this way, he also begins to
go beyond the confines of aesthetic appreciation by arguing that *Einfühlung*
ought be the fundamental concept of psychology and sociology in addition
to aesthetics (Lipps 1907; cited in Pigman 1995, 242). Despite these important moves, Lipps sees inherent limits in the concept: "Whoever speaks of
[*Einfühlung*] and wishes to take part in the controversy about it ought first
of all to know what it means to be giving something aesthetic attention,
to know how to distinguish aesthetic experiencing from the experiencing
of those things that occur in the real world, to know that one must not des-
ignate this experiencing with any term that reminds us of the experience
which practical life and the context of reality force upon us" ([1905] 1965,
412). Thus, while Lipps expands *Einfühlung* to encompass the possibility
of psychological connections among humans, he does so only in a limited
way, and *Einfühlung* remains for him primarily a means of aesthetic appreciation brought about through the inner imitation an object or person
causes in us.

A much clearer application of *Einfühlung* to interpersonal psychological
relationships arises in the work of Sigmund Freud. Freud first uses the
concept in his work on jokes or wit. He discusses how putting ourselves
into the place of others relates to the success of the species of the comic
he calls "the naïve": "Hence we take into consideration the psychic state of
the producing person; we imagine ourselves in this same psychic state and
endeavor to understand it by comparing it to our own. This putting ourselves into the psychic state of the producing person and comparing it with
our own, results in an economy of expenditure which we discharge through
laughter" ([1905] 1938, 766). Without an appreciation of the position of the
naïve person—either the central figure of a joke we hear or someone whose
naïve actions we observe—we would react with indignation. By projecting
ourselves into the other's psychic state, however, we are able to understand
why the other is naïve, and thus find humor in the other's actions or words.

In this passage Freud uses the term *Sichhineinversetzen* and not *Einfühlung*, but it appears that they refer to the same process, and George Pigman (1995, 245) argues that Freud uses the two terms synonymously. Freud specifically uses *Einfühlung* later in the work to explain the comic effect found in the mental and psychic attributes of another person: "As to the comic effect, it is obviously only a question of the difference between the two cathexes [sic] expenditures—the one of [*Einfühlung*], and the other of the ego—and not in whose favor this difference inclines" (Freud [1905] 1938, 773). I concur with Pigman that in this work Freud's uses of "*Einfühlung* refer to understanding others and the examples of 'aesthetic empathy' with inanimate objects occur as examples of 'ideational mimetics'" (1995, 245). Thus Freud was either unaware of the connection between inner imitation and *Einfühlung* so prominent in Lipps's theory, or he consciously chose to distinguish these two concepts, moving *Einfühlung* away from its original use in aesthetics. As Pigman points out, "*Einfühlung* describes for Freud the process of putting oneself into another's position either consciously or unconsciously, and he will continue to use the word in this way for the rest of his life" (246).

Evidence for this comes from Freud's use of *Einfühlung* in his analysis of group psychology. He argues that the mutual ties among group members are due to identifying with one another in an emotional way: "Another suspicion may tell us that we are far from having exhausted the problem of identification, and that we are faced by the process which psychology calls 'empathy [*Einfühlung*]' and which plays the largest part in our understanding of what is inherently foreign to our ego in other people" ([1921] 1924, 66). While he does not develop a full theory of how this process works, he does remark in a footnote that a "path leads from identification by way of imitation to empathy, that is, to the comprehension of the mechanism by means of which we are enabled to take up any attitude at all towards other mental life" (70). While Freud's concept of *Einfühlung* still includes at least two of the central components found in both Vischer and Lipps—projection and understanding—Freud makes several moves that will influence later work in empathy. For Freud empathy is part of a connection between an ego and an other, and while aesthetic *Einfühlung* leads to an appreciation of the art object contemplated, Freud's *Einfühlung* analogously leads to an understanding of another's mental state that goes beyond the level of understanding implied by any of the earlier renderings of the concept. Emotions still play an important part in this understanding, but Freud imbues *Einfühlung* with a much stronger sense of cognition than his predecessors, and perhaps consequently, his conceptualization of *Einfühlung* appears to include the possibility of active projection. While Vischer speaks of feeling ourselves into the object of aesthetic contemplation, he clearly states that we do this "unwittingly" ([1873] 1994, 89). Lipps thought that we have an indescribable part of ourselves that the sensuous appearance of others unconsciously stirs into motion (inner imitation), and from this we experience the affective state related to the expressions we see or hear ([1905] 1965, 409). While Freud is not always clear about how *Einfühlung* works, in at least part of his work he indicates that we can consciously put ourselves into the place of others, and by doing so, gain an understanding of their mental and emotional states. Thus, Freud adds to the principal aspects of *Einfühlung* by more fully developing its interpersonal psychological possibilities, expanding projection to denote conscious as well as unconscious action, including more than just emotions by discussing the psychic state of the target, and moving beyond mere aesthetic appreciation by including the possibility of understanding the mental world of the other. While these additions were vital to the development of "empathy," they would also contribute to the complications we face today in clearly delineating what the concept means.

The Confusion of Empathy

Einfühlung did not migrate to English until the early twentieth century. There is general agreement that Edward B. Titchener first used the word "empathy" as a translation of *Einfühlung* during a series of lectures he gave at the University of Illinois in 1909: "Not only do I see gravity and modesty and pride and courtesy and stateliness, but I feel or act them in the mind's muscles. This is, I suppose, a simple case of empathy, if we may coin that term as a rendering of *Einfühlung;* there is nothing curious or idiosyncratic about it; but it is a fact that must be mentioned" (1909, 21–22).[2] Just as

2. The *Oxford English Dictionary* cites Vernon Lee (a pseudonym used by Violet Paget) as the first to use the term "empathy." In a diary entry from February 20, 1904, she wrote: "But, instead of attributing to this shape merely the act of erecting body and head and spreading out skirts, and then passing on to the aesthetic empathy (*Einfühlung*), or more properly the aesthetic sympathetic feeling of that act of erecting and spreading, the child at once flies to the other acts of which that shape is susceptible actively and passively: dancing, walking, being nursed, dressed, etc., in fact the child thinks of that object *as a doll*" (Lee and Anstruther-Thomson 1912, 337; emphasis in original). Lee herself admits, though, that she did not make the translation: "This phenomenon of aesthetic *Einfühlung*, or, as Professor Titchener has translated it, *Empathy*, is therefore analogous to that of moral sympathy. Just as when we 'put

Lipps argued that the appearance of an object brings forth movements within us, Titchener claimed that empathic experiences involve the feeling or acting of things we perceive in our "mind's muscle." As an example, he admits that he has "practically no gift of musical composition" and that his "skill as a performer is below zero," but he says that his "musical endowment . . . consists in a quick and comprehensive understanding of a composition, a sort of logical or aesthetic *Einfühlung*, an immediate (or very rapid) grasp of the sense and fitness of the musical structure" (205). In this formulation there is no conscious projection, but instead an "immediate" grasp of the music's structure, presumably achieved by movements in the "mind's muscle," though Titchener is not entirely clear about this. His only other example of empathy in these early lectures refers to a time when he was sitting behind a bald man giving a lecture. The speaker used the word "but" very often, and Titchener explains that from that point forward his "feeling" of "but" always included a picture of the bald lecturer. To explain this phenomenon, he writes, "In this particular instance, the picture is combined with an empathic attitude; and all such 'feelings'—feelings of it, and why, and nevertheless, and therefore—normally take the form, in my experience, of motor empathy" (185). Titchener never explains how this type of motor empathy works, but it seems to be one of the "attitudinal feels" he describes earlier (181; see also Wispé 1987, 21–23).

In these early usages, Titchener's "empathy" most closely coincides with an understanding of *Einfühlung* similar to Lipps's. Empathy embodies the main features of *Einfühlung*, such as the centrality of emotions, projection, appreciation, and inner imitation. In later work, though, he seems to move beyond this initial conceptualization. Titchener acknowledges that he translated *Einfühlung* as "empathy" by relying upon the Greek word *empatheia*, literally meaning "in suffering or passion," and formed it on an analogy with "sympathy" (1924, 417).[3] In addition to acknowledging the etymological roots of his translation, he also uses "empathy" in a way that both clarifies

ourselves in the place' or, more vulgarly, 'in the skin' of a fellow-creature, we are, in fact, attributing to him the feelings we should have in similar circumstances" (Lee and Anstruther-Thomson 1912, 20). While Lee wrote her diary entry in 1904, she did not publish the diary until 1912, by which time Titchener had made his translation. It is probable that in editing the diary for publication, she translated the original *Einfühlung* in the entry into "empathy" or "aesthetic empathy." After coming to this conclusion I discovered Pigman's (1995, 243) and Gustav Jahoda's (2005, 161) arguments to this effect, though I had garnered additional evidence. I presume that one of us should inform the OED of this discovery some day.

3. Some have argued that Titchener made an error by not simply translating the term as "sympathy" and that the problems surrounding the concept of empathy derives from this error (see Jahoda 2005). I discuss the problem of disentangling sympathy and empathy later.

and appears to expand the term beyond his initial conceptualization: "We have a natural tendency to feel ourselves into what we perceive or imagine. As we read about the forest, we may, as it were, become the explorer; we feel ourselves the gloom, the silence, the humidity, the oppression, the sense of lurking danger; everything is strange, but it is to us that strange experience has come . . . [t]his tendency to feel oneself *into* a situation is called EMPATHY" (Titchener 1915, 198; emphasis in original). This formulation of empathy still relies upon the centrality of emotion and projection, and there continues to be the implication of some sort of understanding that results from empathy. What is most interesting, though, is that Titchener approaches the line that separates unconscious and conscious projection, but does not cross it. Empathy is still a "natural tendency," implying that we do not consciously engage in the projection, but there is no great distance between a "tendency" to feel ourselves into a situation and to become, "as it were," another person, and a conscious attempt to project ourselves into another's situation that allows us to feel what another feels. As we have already seen, Freud took this step in his conceptualization of *Einfühlung,* and though Titchener does not, the expansion of empathy in these directions would give rise to many of the disagreements surrounding the concept.

Gardner Murphy reflects the problematic state of empathy by the middle of the twentieth century in his compendium of psychological concepts. Murphy literally defines empathy in two distinct ways: "Empathy (E)—(1) Attribution to a natural object or a work of art of the feelings or attitudes aroused in one by the surroundings (actual or depicted) of that object, as when a column seems to plant itself doggedly under a too heavy pressure as a man might do. (2) Direct apprehension of the state of mind of another person, without, as in sympathy, feeling as that other person does. In sympathy, shared attitude is the chief matter" (1947, 985; emphasis in original). The first definition reflects the original, aesthetic understanding of *Einfühlung* as used by Vischer, while the second more closely resembles Freud's usage. That Murphy had to give two very different definitions reveals the ambiguous state of the concept, and while he does include the key aspect of emotion in both definitions, his primary distinction is between the concept's aesthetic and interpersonal applications. His focus is the object of empathy—a natural object or a work of art, or the state of mind of another person—rather than the process by which empathy occurs. Here he says little about projection or inner imitation; and while he implies understanding with the term "apprehension" in his interpersonal definition, he says nothing of appreciation in his aesthetic definition. While his definitions highlight one of the disagreements surrounding empathy (the primary object of the process), it does little to clear up the confusion resulting from other disagreements.

It is interesting, however, that Murphy attempts to distinguish between empathy and sympathy in his second definition, even as he recognizes how difficult this is. In discussing the difference between the two concepts, he deals more directly with projection. "There is no sharp line of cleavage between 'sympathy' and 'empathy'; the latter term is usually applied to *putting oneself in the place* of either a living or non-living thing" (1947, 493–94; emphasis in original). This statement implies that the key difference between empathy and sympathy is projection, but his formal definition explicitly states that sympathy involves shared feeling and empathy does not. In order to differentiate empathy and sympathy more clearly, he gives an example of how empathy can result in a person feeling bitter in response to someone else's success, something that does not occur with sympathy. "When a competitor wins the coveted loving cup, the sight of it becomes an annoyance to the loser; he longingly puts himself in the winner's place, half tastes the sweetness of success, and, in itching perception of the reality, hates him for it" (494). Even in this example, though, the loser's projection into the place of the winner allows a sharing of the "sweetness of success" (even if it is only a half taste). This shared feeling appears more closely aligned with his definition of sympathy, but it results from the loser projecting himself into the winner's place, his definition of empathy. Murphy's attempt to associate sympathy with shared feeling and empathy with projection not only does not allow him to clearly disentangle the two, it also appears to be at odds with many conceptualizations of empathy put forward by researchers both before and after. Distinguishing empathy from sympathy has been a continuing problem, one with which I deal at the end of this chapter, but for now we can see that Murphy acknowledges the role of a conscious projection in empathy in a way that Titchener never does.

Murphy's definitions continued the tradition that emotion, projection, and understanding are key parts of empathy, even though he says little about inner imitation. While retaining these important facets, his definitions also highlight the troubled state of the concept. Eventually, the aesthetic conception of empathy associated with Murphy's first definition lost its importance, but scholars continued to show interest in empathy's use in therapy. Not surprisingly, these researchers defined empathy in ways more closely aligned with Murphy's second definition, and they also tended to move away from those ideas that limited empathy to unconscious projection and inner imitation. They echoed Freud by seeing empathy more as an active process that can result in understanding, but they also faced the problems Murphy had in distinguishing between empathy and sympathy.

Empathy as Cognitive Process: Psychotherapy

We find an example of this move of conceiving empathy primarily as conscious projection in John Dollard and Neal E. Miller's (1950) discussions of learned behavior in children and the role of the therapist. One example of learned behavior in children is the "desire to keep within the culturally defined range of permissible variation" in conformity (Dollard and Miller 1950, 92), and one of the ways society reinforces this is by rewarding or punishing imitative behavior. We learn to copy the behavior of people with prestige, while we learn to be different from other classes of people. This copying of "the other person's feeling or responding with the appropriate signs of emotion is called empathy or sympathy" (93). This conceptualization retains the key importance of emotions, while it implies projection and understanding. It appears, though, to equate empathy with sympathy.

When Dollard and Miller move to a discussion of the role of the therapist, emotion, projection, and understanding remain key, but they again appear to use sympathy and empathy synonymously. "If the therapist has emotional responses attached to the sentences he rehearses, these emotions occur—constituting the basis of sympathy or empathy" (1950, 282). Only toward the end of their work do Dollard and Miller treat empathy and sympathy separately, with sympathy corresponding to Murphy's definition of a shared emotional state. A therapist should sympathize by feeling pity, rage, and fear if a patient describes situations appropriate to these emotions (411). This would at least be a clear definition of sympathy, but shortly after putting forward this claim, they also write that "other kinds of empathy are important, such as a 'sense of humor'" (412). This indicates that sympathy is a type of empathy, with a sense of humor being another type. They go on to claim that the therapist should use empathy to recognize when a patient does not have the appropriate emotional response to a given situation. As they point out, this analysis of empathy "brings the emotional as well as the intellectual dimension into the description of the therapist's work" (412). What empathy is, then, is not clear. It could be copying another person's emotions and emotional responses as a learned behavior, sharing another person's emotional state, understanding another person's psychic-emotional state and recognizing when this is abnormal, or even having a sense of humor. Emotion, projection, and understanding are still important parts of empathy, but Dollard and Miller do not resolve what exactly empathy is and how it differs from sympathy.

Later researchers in therapy more clearly defined empathy, and moved away from sympathy, by focusing on the conscious, cognitive awareness of the psychic state of others. Carl Rogers argues that empathy is one of the most important traits a therapist can possess. He defines empathy and how it functions in a therapist-client relationship: "To sense the client's inner world of private personal meanings as if it were your own, but without ever losing the 'as if' quality, this is empathy, and this seems essential to a growth-promoting relationship. To sense his confusion or his timidity or his anger or his feeling of being treated unfairly as if it were your own, yet without your own uncertainty or fear or anger or suspicion getting bound up in it, this is the condition I am endeavoring to describe" (1967, 93). While emotions, projection, and understanding remain central to this definition, Rogers insists that empathy occurs when the therapist senses the client's feelings without allowing the therapist's own feelings to enter the picture. In his later work, Rogers indicates that he developed this rigorous definition by the mid-1950s (1975, 3), but he calls this his "early definition." His later definition is not as rigorous, and he argues that he believes empathy "to be a process, rather than a state" (3). This process has several components, including, among others, "entering the private perceptual world of the other and becoming thoroughly at home in it," "being sensitive, moment to moment, to the changing felt meanings which flow in this other person," "temporarily living in his/her life, moving about in it delicately without making judgments," and "communicating your sensings of his/her world as you look with fresh and unfrightened eyes at elements of which the individual is fearful" (3). These facets of the empathic process appear at least consistent with his previous definition, though here we see a richer description of empathy as a process rather than simply a state of sensing others' inner conditions as indicated in his earlier definition. The process of empathy involves understanding another's feelings, and sensing as these feelings change, but not judging or actually sharing them. This last point is especially important, since the therapist needs to understand the client's state, but if she also experiences the client's emotions, she may not be in a position to help the client. Rogers himself uses the term "empathic understanding" to describe one of the positive benefits a therapist can gain if she engages in the process of empathy (7). In many ways, and not surprising given its use in therapy, Rogers's definition is an extension of

Freud's usage of *Einfühlung* as the understanding of others' psychic states. While for Rogers empathy clearly involves emotion and projection, the importance of the empathic process is that it allows a therapist to cognitively process the information she senses in others so that she can understand their psychic states and, thereby, help them.

Heinz Kohut, also working in the psychotherapy tradition, conceptualizes empathy in even more explicitly cognitive terms than Rogers. He claims that "empathy is a mode of cognition which is specifically attuned to the perception of complex psychological configurations" (1971, 300). He even goes so far as to call empathy "a tool for gathering psychological data" and cautions against using empathy to explain psychological phenomena (300–301). Though Rogers and Kohut have similar definitions of empathy, there are, at the least, differences in tone in their explications of what empathy can achieve. Rogers believes that empathy on the part of the therapist is a "powerful force for change and growth" (1975, 9). Kohut focuses exclusively on empathy's data-collecting role and argues that if therapists "cannot step beyond empathy, they cannot set up hypotheses and theories, and thus, ultimately, cannot achieve explanations" (1971, 303). Despite this difference, Rogers and Kohut both make clear that the observer must be cognitively aware of the empathic process as it takes place.

Researchers in psychotherapy moved beyond the disagreements that caused confusion regarding empathy by following Freud's lead and defining the concept solely as a conscious, perceptive, cognitive process of understanding the psychic state of another human. Although their definitions retain the central components of emotion, projection, and understanding, they place emphasis on the understanding that results from empathy. This is far removed from the unwitting projection of emotions into an inanimate object originally posited by Vischer and even the unconscious inner imitation in response to objects or humans discussed by Lipps and Titchener. The primarily cognitive understanding of empathy might have held complete sway, in psychology at least, if not for the emergence of empathy in social and developmental psychology.

Empathy as Affective Congruence:
Social and Developmental Psychology

Lauren Wispé maintains that empathy played little role in social and developmental psychology until the 1960s (1987, 32–33). At that time, social psychologists began to examine pro-social behavior, and empathy arose as one of the possible sources for explaining why people acted in positive ways toward others. Though these researchers did not completely ignore projection or understanding, they concerned themselves much more with emotion. Unlike those in the psychotherapy tradition who focus on understanding the psychic state of another, they tend to define empathy as affective congruence between an observer and a target. There are several reasons social psychologists moved in this direction. While therapists are interested in helping others, and empathy can be a tool to do this, social psychologists want to explain human behavior. The social psychologist "understands" the psychic states of others by measuring them, not by empathizing with them. Instead, empathy itself becomes a relationship between two subjects that the researcher must measure, and measurement requires precision. Empathy as a state of affective congruence is much more precise and easier to measure than empathy as understanding the psychic state of another. Additionally, social psychologists are interested in explaining interpersonal behavior and childhood development, and achieving this does not require them to conceptualize empathy in the strongly cognitive terms psychotherapists use. These reasons certainly justify social psychologists' definition of empathy, and while it relates more in some ways to historical antecedents such as Titchener and Lipps, it also both ignores the importance of understanding to empathy and contributes to the problematic nature of the concept.

Though not directly studying pro-social behavior, in his attempt to provide a framework for studying interpersonal behavior Seymour Berger defines empathy specifically as shared emotion: "Personality theorists and social psychologists generally recognize that the emotional responses of one person (performer) may elicit emotional responses from another (observer). When these emotional responses are similar, the relationship between the performer and observer is described as *empathetic*, or one of *identification*" (1962, 450; emphasis in original). Berger does not reference projection or the cognitive understanding of the state of another, but instead, limits empathy to the matching of affect—positive with positive and negative with negative (452). Ezra Stotland gives a similar definition of empathy as "an observer's reacting emotionally because he perceives that another is experiencing or is about to experience an emotion" (1969, 272). Though similar to Berger's, Stotland's conceptualization does not necessarily require affective matching; instead, he refers to an emotional response by an observer that does not match the other as "contrast empathy." Stotland influenced much of the early research in the area of helping behavior (see, for example, Aderman and Berkowitz 1970), and many refer to this conceptualization as "emotional" empathy (for example, Batson et al. 1981). Albert Mehrabian and Norman Epstein summarize the point of the distinction these researchers were trying to make: "There is a critical difference between the cognitive role-taking process and empathic emotional responsiveness. Whereas the former is the recognition of another's feelings, the latter also includes the sharing of those feelings, at least at the gross affect (pleasant-unpleasant) level" (1972, 525). While this distinction may increase precision, it also rejects many important aspects of previous notions of empathy. Emotions are of central importance, as they are in the earliest definitions of *Einfühlung* and empathy, and much more than they are for the definitions advanced by the psychotherapists. The affective congruence definition also opens the door again for inner imitation, though it tends to limit the importance of projection and understanding. Perhaps most important, in making these moves, the primarily affective definition attempts to separate affective reaction from cognitive understanding.

Many contemporary scholars follow the lead of social psychologists that cast empathy in primarily affective terms. Nancy Eisenberg and Janet Strayer maintain that "empathy involves sharing the perceived emotion of another—'feeling with' another" (1987, 5). They define it as "an emotional response that stems from another's emotional state or condition and that is congruent with the other's emotional state or situation" (5). While they acknowledge that empathy involves at least some cognition—differentiation between the self and other—they stress that empathy is an emotional response. Strayer distinguishes between the content of empathy and the process that produces it: "Affect and cognition have been difficult, if not impossible, to dissociate in empirical attempts to measure empathy. Nevertheless, what empathy is (content) and how it occurs (process) are distinguishable issues" (Strayer 1987, 230). Defining empathy in this way, Strayer argues, avoids confusing empathy with other constructs such as role taking, which, while it may be part of the process that produces empathy, is not empathy itself. Becky Omdahl, following Eisenberg, elucidates additional reasons for choosing this type of definition: "Because both historical precedent and practicality strongly indicate that the term empathy should be used to refer to sharing the emotional state of the target, I have adopted that definition for use throughout this book" (1995, 15). For these social and developmental psychologists, empathy requires some form of affective congruence between the emotional states of the observer and the target, whether or not the observer engages in a cognitive process or gains a conscious understanding of the psychic state of the target.

Multidimensional Empathy

The controversy and complexity surrounding empathy has led some scholars to argue that empathy is a multidimensional construct. In his work on moral development, Martin Hoffman defines empathy as *"an affective response more appropriate to another's situation than one's own"* (2000, 4; emphasis in original). While Hoffman follows previous social psychologists in focusing on empathy's affective dimension, he also concerns himself with the "processes underlying empathy's arousal," and his theory "assigns special importance to cognition" (3). Despite discussing the "important contributions of cognition to the arousal and development of empathic distress and generalizing beyond the immediate situation" (93), he continues to maintain that empathy itself is a congruent affective response. Hoffman's extensive discussion of the role of cognition in empathic arousal, however, has influenced the development of a broader, multidimensional model of empathy.

Mark H. Davis writes, "It is a growing belief among empathy theorists and researchers that there are both affective and cognitive components to the empathic response" (1983a, 113). Instead of defining empathy solely as affective responses or cognitive reactions, the multidimensional approach recognizes that affect and cognition are intertwined in empathy. While some theorists stress one aspect over the other, Davis holds that understanding empathy requires an understanding of its many facets. Focusing on one aspect or the other is detrimental to an understanding of empathy and the impact of an empathic disposition on the society and individual.

To address this problem, Davis has developed what he calls an "organizational model" that represents a multidimensional understanding of empathy (see Fig. 1). Davis rises above the confusion surrounding empathy, not by simply putting forward one definition and defending it, but by incorporating the various historical definitions of empathy into one grand model. Drawing on both theoretical and empirical work, Davis divided his model into four major categories: Antecedents, Processes, Intrapersonal Outcomes, and Interpersonal Outcomes. In doing so, he took into account all the key components of *Einfühlung* and empathy: emotion, projection, and understanding.

Antecedents

Antecedents are those personal and situational characteristics that can aid or hinder empathy. Personal characteristics include differences in the capacity to empathize, which individuals may inherit (Davis 1994, 62–70) or exhibit due to environmental factors (70–81). Situational characteristics include how strong the situation is and the similarity between the target of empathy and the observer (14–15, 145–46, 162–63).

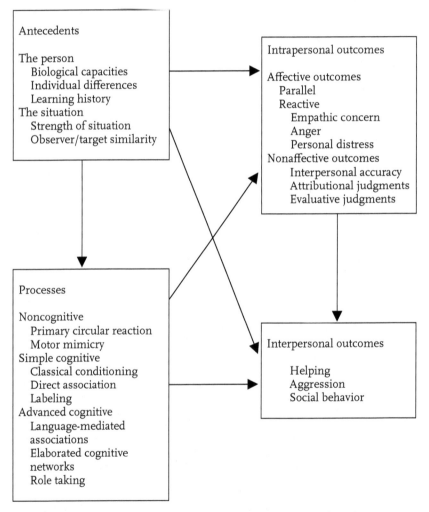

Figure 1. Davis's organizational model of empathy. Modeled on Figure 1.1 (Davis 1994, 13). Davis does not include "evaluative judgments" in the model, but since he mentions them in his discussion of the model, I have added them here.

Processes

Processes are the different ways in which empathy may occur and include noncognitive, simple cognitive, and advanced cognitive processes. The noncognitive methods of empathic arousal are primary circular reaction—such as "the tendency for newborns to cry when they hear another infant crying" (Davis 1994, 37)—and motor mimicry—the emotional state created by "internal kinesthetic cues" when an "observer automatically and for the most part unconsciously imitates the target, both facially and posturally, with small mimicking movements" (39). Both of these refer to the spontaneous affective response of the subject to the unconscious perception of the other's emotional state. Davis's category of motor mimicry incorporates into the model the empathic mechanism of inner imitation that plays the key role in the theories of *Einfühlung* and empathy of Vischer, Lipps, and Titchener. Here Davis has included in his model those processes that represent the unconscious projection that can lead to empathy.

The simple cognitive processes include classical conditioning, direct association, and labeling. Classical conditioning involves "affective reactions to others [that] result from past situations in which the individual perceived affective cues in another person while directly experiencing the same affect" (Davis 1994, 39). Thus, if we have shared an affective moment with another, the cues we have detected in that moment will trigger the same affective response in the future even in the absence of the direct stimulus. Direct association does not require that we have experienced the emotion *simultaneously* with the other, but "only that we have previously experienced an emotion similar to the one we now observe in others" (39). We associate the cues with our own previous affective experiences, and thus experience the affective response from the cues regardless of the stimulus's presence. Labeling occurs when "the observer uses simple cues to infer something about the target's experience . . . regardless of other cues which may be present" (16). If we witness a target involved in a situation that usually produces happiness—for example, a wedding celebration—we will infer from this that the target is happy, regardless of other affective cues. While these processes stand on a middle ground between unconscious and conscious projection, the final category—advanced cognitive processes—embody purely conscious projection.

The more advanced cognitive processes by which empathy can occur are language-mediated association, elaborated cognitive networks, and role taking (or perspective taking). Language-mediated association occurs when "the observer's reaction to the target's plight is produced by activating language-based cognitive networks which trigger associations with the observer's own feelings or experiences" (Davis 1994, 16). The empathic reaction to the target, therefore, results not from inferences drawn from the situation or the target's nonverbal expressions, but explicitly through the language used by the target. This process "does not rely on overt expressive cues by the target, and in fact does not require the presence of the target at all" (40). What must happen is that the observer must "become aware in some verbal fashion of the experiences of the target" (40). A similar process occurs in elaborated cognitive networks, in which target cues cause observers to access their own knowledge and use this to make inferences about the target. The primary difference between these two processes appears to be that elaborated cognitive networks do not focus exclusively on language cues, but both processes involve a deeper cognitive process linking cues to emotional states than the unsophisticated linking that occurs in classical conditioning, direct association, and labeling. The most cognitively advanced process of empathy, though, is role taking or perspective taking. This process "requires a deliberate effort by observers to imagine how they would feel if faced with the circumstances affecting the target" (40). We can characterize it as "the attempts by one individual to understand another by imagining the other's perspective," and it involves "both the suppression of one's own egocentric perspective on events and the active entertaining of someone else's" (17). These more advanced cognitive processes incorporate into the model those mechanisms for empathy described primarily by theorists in the psychotherapy tradition such as Dollard and Miller, Rogers, and Kohut.

Intrapersonal Outcomes

In addition to addressing projection, both conscious and unconscious, Davis's model takes into account the other factors that have historically been central to theorists' interpretations of *Einfühlung* and empathy. It does this by discussing intrapersonal outcomes, which are "the affective and nonaffective responses of the observer that result from the exposure to the target" (Davis 1994, 17). The category of intrapersonal affective responses captures those definitions of empathy that focus primarily on the centrality of emotions, especially those of the social psychologists who utilize empathy in their studies of helping behavior and childhood development. Affective responses can be of two types—parallel and reactive—though the line between the two is not bright. Parallel affective responses are those in which there is "a rough match between the affect of the target and the observer" (124), such as when an observer becomes happy when she observes someone else laughing. Reactive affective outcomes "go beyond a simple matching of affect and consist of the observers' emotional reactions to the target's affect" (105). Thus, when an observer reacts with compassion upon seeing someone who is sad because he has lost a child, we can categorize this as a reactive affective outcome. Davis argues that there are two primary reactive affective outcomes: empathic concern and personal distress (118–22).[4]

Davis does not limit himself, though, to studying only affective intra-personal responses. The nonaffective intrapersonal outcomes he cites are perceptual accuracy, attributions, and evaluative judgments of others. Inter-personal accuracy is the individual's ability to discern the thoughts or emo-tions of the target (Davis 1994, 85–93), and on first glance, it appears to represent the understanding aspect of the earlier definitions of empathy. There are some important differences, though, between accuracy as an outcome and understanding as part of empathy. The studies Davis cites assume that empathy and accuracy are separate constructs and test whether empathy measured as a predisposition or trait has a positive effect on accuracy. Those who define empathy as understanding the psychic state of another do not separate accuracy from empathy, and probably would argue that inaccuracies in perception demonstrate that empathy has not occurred. Another important distinction that such theorists would probably draw is between simply understanding what another feels and why another is feeling the way she does. While empathy may not require the latter, I believe those in the psychotherapy tradition would argue that a full model of empathy would need to take this into account. In addition to perceptual accuracy, Davis lists attributional and evaluative judgments among the non-affective intrapersonal areas that empathy can affect. Attributional judg-ments are "the kind of causal attribution that the observers offer for the target's behavior" (93). Primarily, this refers to whether an actor's behavior is attributed to the personal dispositions of the actor or the situations in which the actor finds herself (93–99). Evaluative judgments of others are those judgments about the likeability, acceptability, or general characteris-tics of others. Davis examines two types of evaluations: liking for individual others and tolerance for out-groups (100–102).

4. While Davis lists anger as one of the reactive affective outcomes in his model, he does not discuss it in the section on reactive outcomes. There are other possible outcomes, such as a feeling of injustice (see Hoffman 2000, 107–8).

Interpersonal Outcomes

The final component of Davis's model examines interpersonal outcomes. These focus on the relationship between empathy and three general areas: altruism and helping behavior, aggression and antisocial behavior, and social relationships and social behavior. Altruism and helping behavior encompass the tendency of an individual to come to the aid of another, whether selfish or unselfish motives induce such aid (Davis 1994, 126–52). Aggression and antisocial behavior are actually "the 'flip side'" of "altruism and helping behavior" (153). In this case, empathy is posited as decreasing the incidences of aggression and antisocial behavior (153–75). Social relationships and social behavior do not actually refer to a type of behavior per se, but encompass "the operation of empathy-related processes and outcomes within the particular domain of social relationships . . . [t]hat is . . . empathy's impact on a variety of behaviors which all occur within the particular context of the formation and maintenance of relationships with other people" (176). Among the behaviors Davis includes under this heading are conflict avoidance/conflict management, good communication, considerate social style, and global evaluation (183–84, 189–99).

Empathy as Process

Davis's model of empathy possesses several strengths, though we need to supplement it to a degree in order for it to be useful in understanding the importance of empathy for deliberative democracy. The model's first strength is that it acknowledges the complex nature of empathy and attempts to embrace it as a complete concept. The scholarly and everyday uses of the term "empathy" often miss different facets of empathy, just as a group of blind people describe an elephant only in terms of the parts they can touch. Davis includes nearly every aspect of previous conceptualizations into a workable model, and even adds to those previous models by bringing in important factors that can affect empathy, such as situational and individual differences, instead of trying to solve the confusion surrounding empathy by rejecting those characteristics of the phenomenon that do not fit a particular conceptualization. The result is a model that allows us to recognize the multiple uses of the concept of empathy and place them in a broader context.

One could argue that Davis's move is not helpful at all, since it only adds to the imprecision of the concept. While this might be the case, there are two reasons why his model still represents an improvement over the current state of things. First, as my historical sketch sought to demonstrate, people already employ the term "empathy" to denote a variety of constructs, and this certainly does little to clear up any confusion. Barring the unlikely development that scholars accept only one conceptualization of empathy, this confusion will only continue. By developing an integrated model we can understand the relationships among the various conceptualizations of empathy, and even if this complicates our understanding, it may lead to a clarity that is currently lacking. The second reason why the model represents an improvement over the current situation follows from this. Including the various conceptualizations within an integrated model requires that we delineate the various components of empathy, which actually forces greater precision in our discussion of the concept. If scholars began to follow Davis's model by discussing the various components of empathy—such as predispositions, processes, and affective and nonaffective outcomes—they would at least be able to clarify points of agreement and disagreement.

For an example of why this is important, we can look to Martha Nussbaum's discussion of emotions (2001). Nussbaum discusses the relationship between empathy and compassion, and while her substantive conclusion is that "empathy is a mental ability highly relevant to compassion, although it is itself both fallible and morally neutral" (2001, 333), the most important point for my purposes is her definition of empathy. She argues that empathy "involves an imaginative reconstruction of the experience of the sufferer" (327). This most closely follows the psychotherapy tradition, which is not surprising, since she often relies upon Kohut in her discussion. She also, though, cites evidence from the experimental work of C. Daniel Batson (1991). In a footnote she notes that Batson's use of empathy is, in fact, equivalent to her use of compassion, and what she defines as empathy, Batson defines as role taking (Nussbaum 2001, 331). While Nussbaum clarifies this distinction, it would be better if we had access to more precise terms to describe what we are studying. Batson and his colleagues have taken a step in this direction by describing what they study as "empathic emotion" (see, for example, Batson et al. 2003, 1192), not simply empathy. Davis's model opens up the possibility that we can develop a more precise lexicon to describe the various facets of empathy, and as I will show, the use of empathy by deliberative democratic theorists demonstrates how not doing so can lead to confusion that can interfere with theoretical development.

The model's other strength is its integration of both cognitive and affective components. Though often discussed within the context of emotion or affect, empathy is not, in and of itself, an emotion. Though we often speak of "feeling" empathy, what we feel instead is, to name some examples, sympathy or empathic concern, shared embarrassment, anger at injustice, distress for those in need, or the pain of others. Even Batson and his colleagues equate empathic emotions with "feelings of sympathy, compassion and the like" (Batson et al. 2003, 1192). Thus, there is no "empathy" that we feel; instead, empathy is a process through which others' emotional states or situations have an affect upon us. Davis's model recognizes this by separating out the processes of "feeling" with others or putting ourselves in their place from the outcomes that result from these processes. We can empathize with someone else, which may result in feelings of compassion or sympathy, for example, but we never feel empathy. In addition to clarifying affect, the model does not ignore cognition. We may empathize through various mechanisms, and these range from noncognitive to higher-level cognitive processes; in pointing out these different paths to empathy, Davis's model incorporates various levels of conscious and unconscious projection highlighted in prior conceptualizations of *Einfühlung* and empathy. It also recognizes that the empathic process may have nonaffective outcomes that have cognitive implications. For example, that empathizing may affect our evaluative judgments demonstrates that the process does not necessarily result only in affective outcomes. Thus, the organizational model provides a framework that allows us to discuss both the affective and cognitive aspects of empathy.

While these strengths recommend Davis's model in general, I suggest four improvements. The first change is somewhat minor, though still important. Davis names his framework the "organizational model," leaving the term "process" to describe one component of the model. Davis's intent in providing the organizational model was to make "clear the similarities and differences between the various constructs that fall within empathy's roughly defined domain" (1994, 11). I believe we should follow Rogers instead and model empathy as a process, not a state; I will therefore refer to this as the process model of empathy. This will clarify that empathy is not, in and of itself, a feeling and will focus our attention on those factors that influence the process, the mechanisms by which it occurs, and the various outcomes that can result from empathizing. Instead of calling the means by which empathy occurs processes, I will refer to them as mechanisms.

The second improvement I want to suggest for Davis's model is to incorporate more directly the understanding component of empathy as defined by those in the psychotherapy tradition. As I noted, while interpersonal accuracy gets at this to some degree, it does not fully capture what these theorists have in mind when they discuss understanding the psychic state of another. Therefore, under the nonaffective intrapersonal outcomes, I have added an additional component that I call empathic understanding. The third adjustment simplifies the model by removing several of the causal connections between the antecedents and the outcomes. While the antecedents can affect the outcomes, they will only do so by working through the mechanisms. An empirical test that finds direct effects from the antecedents to the outcomes will do so only because it has not adequately measured which mechanisms are functioning in the empathic process. Removing the connecting paths highlights the fact that the process of empathy must always work through some mechanism and has the added advantage of simplifying the model's causal pathways. The final improvement relates to empathic understanding, but not to it alone. In Davis's model, the antecedents can affect the mechanisms; the mechanisms can affect both the intrapersonal and interpersonal outcomes; and the intrapersonal outcomes can affect the interpersonal outcomes. What Davis's model does not take into account is the degree to which there may be an interaction between the affective and nonaffective outcomes of the empathic process. I may have an initial affective response that then affects my nonaffective judgments or understanding; for example, a nineteenth-century reader of *Uncle Tom's Cabin* may have found herself feeling pity for the slaves in the novel and, as a result, reevaluated her judgment about the humanity of the slaves. It is also possible that the judgments and understandings I reach through empathy may result in further or altered affective responses; a secular humanist who gains an understanding of why an evangelical Christian feels so strongly about her religion may feel more compassion toward her. To indicate the possibility of this feedback loop between affective and nonaffective outcomes, which also more accurately captures the possible interactive nature between affect and cognition, I divide the affective and nonaffective outcomes into separate components of the model and include a feedback loop between the two. I present the resulting model in figure 2. As I will show, this model will best allow us to recognize an important role of emotions in deliberative democracy by demonstrating how both cognition and affect function in the empathic process.

Empathy and Sympathy

As we have already seen, disentangling sympathy from empathy has been difficult for many theorists. Murphy (1947) was not very successful in his attempt to separate the two concepts; Dollard and Miller (1950) tend to equate them; and many others simply do not address the distinction. Gustav Jahoda (2005) suggests that Lipps considered *Einfühlung* and sympathy as indicating the same phenomenon. For Eisenberg and Strayer, sympathy "is 'feeling for' someone, and refers to feelings of sorrow, or feeling sorry, for another" (1987, 6). For them, sympathy may result from empathizing, though they say it may also result from cognitive perspective taking, which they do not consider to be empathy. They acknowledge, however, that others do not agree with their definition, especially clinicians (6–7). The problem with defining sympathy in this way is that it ignores its etymological roots and historical uses.

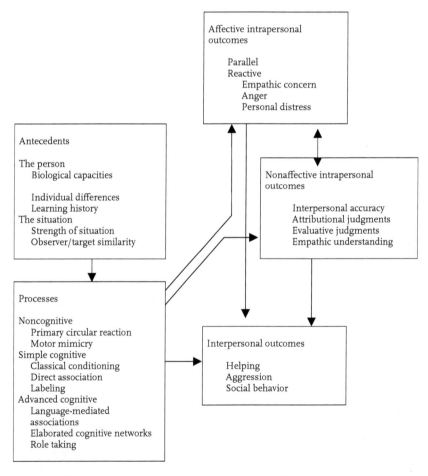

Figure 2. The process model of empathy. Modeled on Figure 1.1 (Davis 1994, 13).

As derived from its Greek roots, sympathy actually comes much closer to the definition of empathy given by Eisenberg and Strayer. It literally means affected by like feelings, and included among the definitions the *American Heritage Dictionary* gives of sympathy are "a relationship or an affinity between people or things in which whatever affects one correspondingly affects the other" and "the act or power of sharing the feelings of another." Sympathy also has a conceptual history in moral philosophy in which it parallels what many today call empathy. Adam Smith explains moral judgment by writing, "We either approve or disapprove of the conduct of another man according as we feel that, when we bring his case home to ourselves, we either can or cannot entirely sympathize with the sentiments and motives which directed it" ([1790] 2005, 99). Smith is not referring to whether we feel pity or compassion for the sentiments of the other person, but whether we can feel the same as that person if confronted with her situation. We engage in the same process when judging our own actions: "We either approve or disapprove of our own conduct, according as we feel that, when we place ourselves in the situation of another man, and view it, as it were, with his eyes and from his station, we either can or cannot entirely enter into and sympathize with the sentiments and motives which influenced it" (99). Here again sympathy indicates parallel affect, though Smith also points to placing ourselves in the situation of another, a clear parallel to the projection aspect of empathy, and from this projection we gain something like an understanding. Yet Smith's description delineates between the projective process and the sympathizing that has to occur as a result of this process in order for us to judge our actions as morally correct. David Hume also discusses sympathy in relation to moral judgment, though he discusses it in other contexts as well. He writes, "No quality of human nature is more remarkable, both in itself and in its consequences, than that propensity we have to sympathize with others, and to receive by communication their inclinations and sentiments, however different from, or even contrary to our own" ([1739–40] 2003, 225). Though not quite as clear as Smith, Hume uses sympathy in a similar manner to represent the sharing of affect, or sentiments, between humans.

Because of the influence of Hume and Smith especially, philosophers tend to use sympathy to describe something at least similar to what many psychologists call empathy. What Eisenberg and Strayer call "sympathy" may result from what Hume and Smith call "sympathy," but this will not always be the case. Yet Eisenberg and Strayer's definition of sympathy matches many common usages of sympathy, connecting it to feelings of pity or compassion. The fourth definition the *American Heritage Dictionary* gives demonstrates this: "a feeling or an expression of pity or sorrow for the distress of another; compassion or commiseration." The answer to this difficulty is to again return to the process model of empathy. By representing empathy in more complete terms, the model can incorporate the various conceptualizations of empathy and sympathy and represent the possible relationships among them. It includes parallel affective reactions to another's state or condition, what many social psychologists call "empathy" and Hume and Smith call "sympathy," as one of the outcomes of empathizing. It also recognizes that such parallel affect may result from a variety of empathic mechanisms, some more cognitive than others. The model also acknowledges the possibility of reactive affective outcomes, including concern or pity, which Eisenberg and Strayer call "sympathy" and others have called sympathetic or empathic concern. Instead of using the intractably confused concepts of empathy and sympathy in only one of the traditional ways, the process model focuses on engaging in empathy or empathizing and allows us to speak more precisely about the antecedents, mechanisms, and outcomes of empathizing and to recognize more clearly the role theorists give empathy in deliberative democracy.

4

EMPATHY IN DELIBERATIVE THEORY

Most deliberative theorists pay scant specific attention to empathy, and while using the process model of empathy reveals that this silence is not as pervasive as it may seem on the surface, their theories still miss some of empathy's important contributions. In order for theories of deliberative democracy to address the tension between equal consideration and legitimacy, we must supplement them by developing a fuller account of the role of empathy by addressing the role of affect in deliberation. To establish the warrant for my position, I want to return to the various theories of deliberative democracy and clarify the ways in which they incorporate, or fail to incorporate, empathy into their reasoning. Put most simply, deliberative democrats employ ideas that relate to certain components of the process of empathy, but in doing so, they tend to focus primarily on cognitive role taking.

Ignoring Empathy: Deliberation as Reflective Decision-Making

It is not very surprising that theorists who conceive of deliberation principally as reflective consideration, such as Bessette and Fishkin, have little directly to say about empathy. One of the primary reasons for this is the way in which they and others often conceptualize reflective consideration as an alternative to impulsive reaction. On this understanding, deliberation represents a "cool" activity based in "reason" that can mitigate the dangers inherent in acting upon passionate impulses. This is precisely the understanding of deliberation advanced by the American founders James Madison and Alexander Hamilton, who influenced especially Bessette, but also Fishkin.

Bessette argues that for Madison and Hamilton, one of the primary reasons for many of the institutions established in the U.S. Constitution was to allow for deliberation. Hamilton points out that allowing the deliberate sense of the community to guide public affairs "does not require an unqualified complaisance to every sudden breeze of passion, or to every transient impulse which the people may receive from the arts of men, who flatter their prejudices to betray their interests" (Hamilton, Madison, and Jay [1788] 1961, 432). While Hamilton's point is that the government should not give in to every public demand, he associates public errors with sudden breezes of passion or transient impulses. On such occasions, "It is the duty of the persons whom [the people] have appointed to be the guardians of [their] interests, to withstand the temporary delusion, in order to give them time and opportunity for more cool and sedate reflection" (432). Madison echoes Hamilton when he argues that institutions such as the Senate "may be sometimes necessary as a defense to the people against their own temporary errors and delusions" (384). While the "cool and deliberate sense of the community" ought always to "prevail over the views of its rulers," there are times "when the people, stimulated by some irregular passion, or illicit advantage, or misled by the artful misrepresentations of interested men" desire something that is disadvantageous to their interests (384). The Senate can act as a "temperate and respectable body of citizens" that will "suspend the blow mediated by the people against themselves until reason, justice, and truth can regain their authority over the public mind" (384). While Hamilton and Madison never condemn passion or impulses wholesale, they connect the deliberative institutions within the Constitution to cool, sedate, reasoned decision-making.

Despite moving to mitigate the influence of passions, Madison does discuss the importance of sympathy in his defense of the House of Representatives. Since "it is essential to liberty that the government in general should have a common interest with the people," it is necessary for the House to "have an immediate dependence on, and an intimate sympathy with, the people" (Hamilton, Madison, and Jay [1788] 1961, 327). The most efficient guarantee for this is frequent elections, but making sure that all laws the House passes apply equally to everyone, including the representatives and their friends, will also create a "sympathy of sentiments" between the rulers and the people that prevents the House from passing oppressive laws on the people (352). Ultimately, the House must be only as large as necessary *for the purposes of safety, of local information, and of diffusive sympathy with the whole society*" (360; emphasis in original). Alexander Hamilton also explores the subject of sympathy in his discussion of the House's power of taxation. Hamilton seeks to respond to the objection that the House of Representatives is not large enough "to combine the interests and feelings of every part of the community, and to produce a due sympathy between the representative body and its constituents" (214). While having such representation may sound good, he argues that it is both impractical and unnecessary. In reality, any legislative body chosen by the free votes of people will nearly always be composed of landholders, merchants, and members of the learned professions (215) because members of some classes will normally choose representatives from other classes who share the same interests and are better able to defend those interests in the legislature. This is not a problem because these three groups can understand and attend to "the interests and feelings of the different classes of citizens" (215). While this is partly because of the nature of the three groups—landholders will protect landed property, merchants commerce and industry, and the learned will act as impartial arbiter between the two with the general interest in view—Hamilton parallels Madison by citing the dependence of representatives on the votes of the people and the fact that laws apply to the representatives and their posterity as reasons why there will be "strong chords of sympathy between the representative and the constituent" (216). For Hamilton, therefore, diffusive sympathy indicates a "knowledge of the interests and feelings of the people" demonstrated by an acquaintance with "the general genius, habits, and modes of thinking of the people at large, and with the resources of the country" (217).

For Hamilton and Madison sympathy indicates a regard for, or more correctly, a confluence with the interests and feelings of others. Mapped onto the process model, their use of sympathy most closely matches parallel affect, though it also hints at empathic concern. There is some tension, however, in their account of the object of sympathy. At points, it is most important for representatives to sympathize with their particular constituents, and their reference to frequent elections as a guarantee of sympathy leads in this direction. In other places, they focus on the need for a diffusive sympathy whose object is the entire citizenry, but they appear to posit that the House as a whole, with each member sympathizing with his or her own constituents, will embody this diffusive sympathy. There is little need for representatives to sympathize with citizens from other constituencies, or citizens to sympathize with one another, with the possible exception that those from the learned professions will serve as impartial arbiters by taking account the general interests (and feelings?) of the entire society. Some components of the process model of empathy, therefore, are present in the writings of Madison and Hamilton. Yet even setting aside the issue of whether the House of Representatives is large enough to bring the interests and feelings of society into deliberation, and the implications this debate has for equal consideration and democratic legitimacy, the sympathy they invoke is limited. In Madison's discussion of keeping the House from becoming too large, the limits he wants to place on the influence of passions in deliberation again come to the fore: "The more numerous any assembly may be, of whatever characters composed, the greater is known to be the ascendancy of passion over reason" (Hamilton, Madison, and Jay [1788] 1961, 360). Deliberation requires representatives to sympathize with the interests and feelings of constituents, but deliberation must insure that those feelings do not overwhelm reason.

Since Bessette's definition of deliberation aligns so closely with Madison's, it is hardly surprising that he does not expound upon empathy or affect beyond the need for sympathy between constituents and representatives. Fishkin says even less about empathy and affect. Although Fishkin analyzes the need for deliberation by ordinary citizens, and Bessette focuses on Congress, their definitions of deliberation lead them both to ignore the importance of empathy and affect in deliberation. Yet why would cool, sedate reflection on an issue lead to a better decision than acting on passion? First, a passionate impulse may cause those making a collective decision to act in a way that they will come to regret because they will ignore other objects of desire, and if they take the time to talk with one another, they will realize their error. This does not indicate that the object of the original passion is unimportant, just that it is less important than other objects the action may affect negatively. Second, a passionate impulse may lead decision makers to misread the correct means to achieve the object of the passion, and again deliberation can clarify their mistake. In this case, the object of passion is not the issue, but rather the misperception about how to achieve that object. And finally, a passionate impulse may itself cause misperceptions about the objects of desire themselves. This is similar to the first example, but in this case deliberation may reveal that people do not (or should not) really desire the object of the passion regardless of its effects on other objects. If they deliberate with one another, they can discover in a kind of therapeutic sense that they are mistaken about their passion. In the first two cases, the conflict between passion and reflection is complex. In the first, passion for one object simply overwhelms passion for other objects that are more important. In the second, passion still aims at its object, but has mistaken the means for achieving it. In both, there remains a passion or desire for a particular object. It is only in the third case that passion is completely mistaken, and yet if there are no other objects of desire that come into conflict, it is hard to see how this case will be the norm or even likely. It is also possible that cool, sedate, reasoned reflection might lead decision makers to ignore a passion in ways that they will come later to regret, lamenting a missed opportunity. What these examples demonstrate is that deliberation will rarely mean ignoring or eliminating passion, and when it does, it may lead to regrettable decisions.

Bessette and Fishkin tend to focus more on the information participants may gain through deliberation than on passion. Setting aside critiques of this possibility, it is important to ask what type of information deliberation may reveal. Deliberation is most likely to reveal factual or probabilistic information on nonsalient, technical, or rapidly changing issues; in these cases, reflective consideration may indeed lead to better decisions. On issues that are salient or more easily understood, it is hard to see how deliberation will add to the store of this knowledge. Another possibility is that deliberation may reveal affective information about an issue. Citizens and legislators may be able to gain technical or factual information on an issue without deliberating, but it is much less likely that they will understand how others feel without talking with one another. Deliberation opens up the possibility for the empathic process to occur, resulting in the gain of both affective and cognitive information about others' perspectives. Yet if we conceive of deliberation as cool, sedate reflection, this may mitigate against the very processes that empathy requires, including language-mediated association and role taking. To be fair, Bessette and Fishkin are not overtly hostile to this possibility, and their theories may be able to take it into account, but their general silence on affect and empathy leave their theories, to my mind, inadequately developed.

Impeding Empathy: Rawls, the Original Position, and Public Reason

John Rawls says very little about emotions in his theories of justice or political liberalism, and after close scrutiny, I found no mention in them of empathy. Despite this, several theorists have proposed that his theory of justice implicitly relies upon both affect and empathy, especially in the original position. We saw in Chapter 2 that Rawls considers justice as fairness, even when formulated as a freestanding political conception, as only one possible avenue in determining the values appropriate for public reason. Since most theorists have focused on his theory of justice, relying especially on the original position, to elucidate Rawls's position on affect and empathy, it is necessary to begin there. While several theorists indicate that Rawls's arguments, at least implicitly, require giving empathy a central role in "justice as fairness," I believe that they overstate both Rawls's position and the compatibility between the two. While his theory would require something like perspective taking, he falls short of incorporating a full conceptualization of empathy such as that represented by the process model.

Susan Moller Okin maintains that empathy and other feelings are central to Rawls's theory of justice, even if he does not explicitly acknowledge this. Her reading of his theory of justice "suggests that Rawls is far from being a moral rationalist and that feelings such as empathy and benevolence are at the very foundation of his principles of justice" (1989, 238). In the original position, since the parties behind the veil of ignorance do not know whom they represent or what the probability is that they represent any specific type of person, they must take on the perspectives of all in order to determine which principles they might want to accept. Okin gives the example that those in the original position would have to imagine what it would be like to be both a religious and a nonreligious person, which would require both "strong empathy and a preparedness to listen carefully to the very different points of view of others" (245). Since the original position requires us to give equal consideration to everyone, it inherently requires us to be able to empathize. "If we, who *do* know who we are, are to think *as if* we were in the original position, we must develop considerable capacities for empathy and powers of communicating with others about what different human lives are like" (246; emphasis in original). Yet empathy alone is not enough, according to Okin. She argues that we also "need as well a great commitment to benevolence; to *caring* about each and every other as much as about ourselves" (246; emphasis in original). Given the structure and purpose of the original position, it requires both empathy and benevolence to function. Okin argues that this reading of Rawls requires jettisoning some of his Kantian and rational choice leanings, but it does not undermine the basic structure of the theory.

Several theorists follow Okin's reading in attributing to Rawls a position on affect and empathy that is not always apparent in his text. Sharon Krause (2005) argues that even beyond the motivational problem that affective ties among citizens might correct, Rawls's original position requires empathy. Participants in the original position "need empathy to inhabit hypothetically the standpoints of all the people they could turn out to be, to feel the rational desires of persons differently placed, and so to reason their way to the most advantageous arrangements for social cooperation. . . . Reasoning about justice is an affective and not only a cognitive activity" (368). She points out that at the end of *A Theory of Justice* Rawls refers to the original position as "a certain form of thought *and feeling* that rational persons can adopt within the world" (Rawls 1999, 514; emphasis added). Michael Frazer posits that for Rawls the "demand for empathy on the part of actors in the original position captures an important element in our intuitive understanding of the value of respect" (2007, 765). In support of this, he quotes Rawls: "Mutual respect is shown . . . in our willingness to see the situation of others from their point of view, from the perspective of their conception of their good. . . . Thus to respect another as a moral person is to try to understand his aims and interests from his standpoint" (1999, 297). He even makes a connection between Rawls and the concept of "sympathy" found in the theories of Adam Smith and David Hume. He argues that actors in the original position "cannot rely on instrumental reason alone for purposes of the relevant deliberations, but also must possess the emotional and imaginative capacity of well-developed empathy, something akin to what the English-language sentimentalists of the eighteenth century called 'sympathy'" (2007, 764).

Certainly Rawls incorporates perspective taking of some sort into the original position, but it is hard to see how he can overcome the tension between this requirement and the Kantian strains in his theory. In the passage cited by Frazer, for example, Rawls argues that mutual respect requires that we give reasons "in good faith, in the belief that they are sound reasons as defined by a mutually acceptable conception of justice which takes the good of everyone into account" (1999, 297). Yet we cannot have reasons defined by a mutually acceptable conception of justice until *after* we engage in the thought experiment of the original position behind the veil of ignorance, which cuts parties off from knowing about those whom they represent. This leads Michael Sandel, for example, to critique Rawls for positing decision-making by an "unencumbered self" detached from particular circumstances, a person "wholly without character, without moral depth" (1984, 90). Richard Dagger argues that Sandel's criticism fails to distinguish between abstract and concrete selves: "A conception of the self is abstract and general when it tries to capture the features common to all selves; it is concrete and particular when it refers to features that vary from one self to another. The self—the self in the abstract, general sense—is always a part, but never the whole, of the particular self that I or you or anyone else has" (1999a, 189).[1] Yet even if Sandel mischaracterizes the unencumbered self, there is something in his argument that rings true from the perspective of empathy, at least for Rawls's original position.

Parties behind the veil of ignorance do not know any particular information about those they represent, the society in which they live, or to which generation they belong (Rawls 1999, 118). They do not even "know the social positions or the particular comprehensive doctrines of the persons they represent" (Rawls 2001, 15). The reason this is important is that "the parties must not know the contingencies that set them in opposition" (Rawls 1999, 119). On the interpretation presented by Okin, Frazer, and Krause, since the parties do not know anything about the particular persons they represent, they must decide on the principles of justice from every possible perspective, including future generations. Yet Rawls is unclear whether this is what he means to happen behind the veil of ignorance. He argues that "since the differences among the parties are unknown to them, and everyone is equally rational and similarly situated, each is convinced by the same arguments" (1999, 120). Given this, we could select at random one of the parties in the original position and she would choose the same principles that all others would choose. Without "restrictions on particular information," however, it would be impossible to have "a unanimous choice of a particular conception of justice" (121). Specific, contingent information should not provide some people with advantages and cannot be the basis for reasons supporting a particular conception of justice; it must not come into play in the original position. Yet if the parties only know general facts about human society, political affairs, economics, and human psychology—if they only know general, abstract information—it is hard to see how they can empathize with *particular* selves. As Diana Meyers argues, arguments such as Okin's show "how completely the introduction of empathy into moral reflection eclipses impartial reason" (1993, 29).

As we move from his theory of justice to political liberalism, the tension between Rawls's abstract, rational Kantianism and empathy remains. Even though Rawls lists the original position as only one way to derive a freestanding political conception of justice, his description of it remains consistent with that in "justice as fairness." He argues that in the original position we must "leave aside how people's comprehensive doctrines connect with the content of the political conception of justice . . . by putting people's comprehensive doctrines behind the veil of ignorance" (1996, 25n). Rawls maintains that the veil of ignorance has no metaphysical implications and that in thinking from the original position we are merely engaging in role-playing such as an actor taking on a part in *Macbeth* (25). Rawls does not want us to think of the parties in the original position as mirroring the psychology of actual persons or citizens in a well-ordered society. If the original position is supposed to allow us, at least preliminarily, to construct principles of justice that treat all citizens equally, yet we have to put behind the veil of ignorance all the particulars about people in the real world, then it is hard to see how empathy can enter into our reflections.

If we examine the role of public reason in political liberalism, we begin to see the same restrictions on empathy in Rawls's theory. It is important to remember that public reason, by definition, appeals to values or standards arising from what people see as the most reasonable political conception of justice, which people derive from procedures such as the original position. Yet the central component of public reason is reciprocity, which requires that we give reasons for our political actions that we think other citizens would reasonably accept (Rawls 1997, 771). This seems to imply that we would have to engage in something like empathy in order to discover what reasons other citizens would accept, but in the end, we do not have to do so fully. We only have to take account of reasons other reasonable citizens *would* agree with, and since reasonable citizens by definition realize that they cannot rely upon their own comprehensive conceptions of the good to determine the political conception of justice, we can ignore the reasons (and I would argue the feelings implicit in the reasons) other citizens derive from their comprehensive conceptions. As with the original position, we do not have to empathize with *particular* others, but only with abstract, reasonable citizens. Giving others equal consideration becomes a practice of ignoring differences among citizens and only paying attention to the areas of agreement exemplified by an overlapping consensus.

In the end, therefore, neither justice as fairness nor political liberalism can incorporate the process model of empathy. As Manin charges, Rawlsian deliberation reduces to the discovery and application of abstract principles that set aside the particular differences among individuals. Though Rawls hints at a perspective taking that might correspond to parts of the process model, his attempt to ground political legitimacy on public reasons that all would accept derived from a reasonable conception of political justice discovered in the original position behind a veil of ignorance forces him to basically ignore the importance of empathy for deliberation.

Inhibiting Empathy: Habermas and the Generalized Other

As noted in Chapter 2, one of the difficulties in analyzing Jürgen Haber-mas's theory of deliberative democracy arises from trying to parse out the connections and distinctions between discourse ethics and deliberative democracy. Writing about discourse ethics, Thomas McCarthy maintains that "Habermas's discourse model, by requiring that perspective-taking be general and reciprocal, builds the moment of empathy *into* the procedure of coming to a reasoned agreement: each must put himself or herself into the place of everyone else in discussing whether a proposed norm is fair to all" (1990, viii–ix; emphasis added).[2] McCarthy's argument is based on Habermas's requirement that participants in discourse engage in ideal role taking (see Habermas 1990, 121). In general, though, Habermas limits the role of affective appeals in the validation of moral norms, indicating that for him role taking is primarily a cognitive activity. He does maintain that "empathy," which for him is primarily affective, plays an important role in discourse ethics by supporting role taking and providing the basis for solidarity. Yet even while assigning empathy this high place, Habermas gives the affective a subordinate role to the cognitive in his discourse ethics because it is usually not universalizable. Habermas certainly incorporates the cognitive side of empathy in his theories of discourse ethics and delib-erative democracy, but the affective side of empathy has only a limited place in both. There are only a few *direct* references to "empathy" in Habermas's work, all of which occur in his discussions of discourse ethics, primarily when he examines moral feelings. It is also in his work on communica-tive rationality and discourse ethics that Habermas most fully and directly addresses affectivity in general.

In his discourse ethics, Habermas describes empathy as primarily an affective ability, attitude, or predisposition that serves two primary func-tions. The first role empathy plays is to serve the cognitively directed ideal role taking necessary in discourses of justification. Given that participants must test the validity of moral norms by guaranteeing that they can meet with the free consent of all, they must take on the perspectives of all; this is where empathy can aid participants. "At the very least, empathy—the ability to project oneself across cultural distances into alien and at first sight

2. McCarthy's claim is a perfect example of why we need a fully specified model of empa-thy such as the process model. What he describes here as empathy corresponds most closely to the cognitive process of role taking, but there is little indication that "empathy" on this model involves affective role taking.

incomprehensible conditions of life, behavioral predispositions, and in-terpretive perspectives—is an emotional prerequisite for ideal role-taking, which requires everyone to take the perspective of all others" (Habermas 1993, 174). Habermas argues that the cognitive operations of ideal role taking "are internally linked with motives and emotional dispositions and attitudes like empathy" (1990, 182). Here he seems to consider empathy an emotional disposition or attitude, not specifically an ability, but again the point of empathy is to help participants engage in the demanding cognitive operations that perspective taking requires. The primary reason empathy is important is that it allows the cognitive function of ideal role taking, with-out which participants could never guarantee that the moral norm under discussion is acceptable to all.

In these passages, Habermas uses the term "empathy" to describe an ability, attitude, or disposition. Mapping this on the process model indi-cates that empathy for Habermas indicates an antecedent to the empathic process embodied in an individual's ability or predisposition to feel *with* others, which is not the same as feeling *for* them. This affective ability or predisposition is linked with the cognitive process of ideal role taking, because people must be able to understand how others feel about a norm to determine whether or not that norm can meet with the consent of all. There is also an antecedent predisposition or ability to engage in perspec-tive taking that is more cognitively oriented; this leads people to under-stand what others are thinking rather than feeling. Thus, while Habermas uses the term "empathy" only to describe the affective side of the process, by linking empathy with perspective taking, he incorporates both affect and cognition into the practice of moral norm validation. Yet while Habermas appears to link affect and cognition, a closer look at *ideal* role taking reveals the limitations of his model.

Ideal role taking is an abstracting process that allows for social control rather than simply opening people up to the experiences and interests of others. G. H. Mead writes that "the exercise of what is often called 'social intelligence,' depend[s] upon the given individual's ability to take the rôles of, or 'put himself in the place of,' the other individuals implicated with him in given social situation, and upon his consequent sensitivity to their attitudes toward himself and toward one another" (1934, 141). The process of role taking requires a conscious act on the part of the observer; it cannot simply be an unconscious reaction to the emotional state of others. "The common term for this is 'putting yourself in his place.' It is presumably an exclusively human type of conduct, marked by this involution of stimulating one's self to an action by responding as the other responds" (366). Yet Mead's theory of ideal role taking, focused on what he calls the generalized other, cannot embody the broader conceptualization of empathy represented in the process model.

Mead argues that role taking is essential for us to be in "possession of selves" because "we can and do take the attitudes of others toward ourselves and respond to those attitudes" (1925, 272; see also Mead 1913). An individual does not, however, "assume the attitudes of the numberless others who are in one way or another implicated in his social conduct, except in *so far as the attitudes of others are uniform under like circumstances*. One assumes, as I have said, the attitudes of generalized others" (275; emphasis added). By taking up the generalized attitudes of others, we "attain to the levels of abstract thinking, and that impersonality, that so-called objectivity that we cherish" (272), and we are able to respond to our own selves with approval or condemnation based upon these attitudes. Our responses to our own behavior guided by the generalized perspective lead to social control. "Social control, then, will depend upon the degree to which the individual does assume the attitudes of those in the group who are involved with him in his social activities" (274). The basis of this social control is a common object of the group that can be the focus of cooperation: "If we can bring people together so that they can enter into each other's lives, they will inevitably have a common object, which will control their common conduct" (276). Social control, therefore, arises when humans take on the attitudes of the generalized other and thereby discover a social object that can be the basis of cooperation.

Yet Mead indicates that generalized attitudes only arise when all (or presumably almost all) people react uniformly under like circumstances. The process of ideal role taking does not help us understand the attitudes of others per se, but only to recognize when the social group has a generalized attitude about something. "Generalization is not simply a quantification of individual situations. There is an organized common attitude. Certain gesture-response action sequences have socially agreed meanings, such as those to do with rights, social order and geo-politics (e.g. the League of Nations)" (Dodds, Lawrence, and Valsiner 1997, 497–98). If we contravene the generalized attitude, then we judge ourselves negatively and will change our behavior. Thus, ideal role taking results in social control through individual self-discipline in reaction to socially shared attitudes. Mead is hopeful that as people gain exposure to a wider circle of others, the generalized attitudes will push them in positive directions. He gives examples of the

World Court and the League of Nations as possible social objects around which all humans might cooperate if they could overcome their "national selves" (1925, 277). Yet such objects can only serve as loci of cooperation under circumstances in which all, or nearly all, people in the social group react to the same object in the same way; there must be an already existing generalized attitude.

Habermas follows Mead in focusing on *ideal* role taking, not just any form of role taking. Empathy serves ideal role taking by allowing us to understand how others feel about a moral norm, and yet the goal is not simply to understand what others feel, but to be able to recognize when there is a *generalized* attitude about the validity of a norm. This move toward generalized perspective taking can lead to two very different outcomes. On the one hand, it might indicate that people, after taking the perspective of all, only declare as valid those norms to which they believe everyone would give their assent. This would appear to give everyone a veto on the validity of moral norms, and there are moments when it appears that Habermas means to conceptualize ideal role taking in this way. Yet ideal role taking can also lead to what Mead calls abstract thinking, impersonality, and objectivity, all of which imply that while we try to understand how all individuals feel about a particular norm, we do not determine moral validity solely from their perspective. Instead, we can weed out those perspectives that are clearly not general. We then declare moral norms valid that would meet with the assent of all from this generalized perspective. Mead seems to take this approach because ideal role taking would never lead to social control if each person could simply veto the attitudes of others; individuals must internalize the most general attitudes of the social group. This is clear when he argues that if some people could overcome their "nationalized selves," selves that are generalized relative to their own nation but not humanity in general, then institutions such as the World Court or League of Nations might be able to prevent the world from once again engaging in war. Habermas's use of ideal role taking comports most closely with this reading of what it means to test the validity of moral norms by looking at them from a generalized perspective. This becomes clearest when we examine Habermas's theory of communicative rationality, the very basis of his theories of discourse ethics and deliberative democracy.

In his original theory of communicative rationality Habermas discusses five types of statements: descriptive, normative, expressive, evaluative, and explicative. Expressive speech acts are "constitutive for . . . dramaturgical action" (1984, 327) in which "participants form a visible public for each other and perform for one another" (90) by bringing forth their subjectivity for public display. If the public finds such performances sincere, they will attribute to the performers those desires and feelings they express (90–91). The validity claim in public performance is different from others in that people can only show it, not truly ground it. While "cognitions, beliefs, and intentions also belong to the subjective world . . . they stand in internal relation to the objective world" (91) and thus have a ground for their validity. Feelings and desires, in contrast, "can *only* be expressed as something subjective" (92; emphasis in original).[3] Individuals have privileged access to feelings and desires, and the public can only judge whether actors are being sincere in their self-expressions. Habermas argues that inclinations and desires represent the volitional side of needs—that which aims at need satisfaction—while feelings represent the intuitive side of needs—that which perceives the relationships between our needs and the situations in which we find ourselves. As they are both aspects of *subjectively* defined needs, feelings and desires are *subjective* experiences; to communicate subjective experiences actors express them in language through evaluative statements that can "serve to make predilection understandable" (92).

The expression of needs in language allows actors to go beyond subjective experience by creating a "bridge between the subjectivity of experience and that intersubjective transparency that experience gains in being truthfully expressed, and on this basis, attributed to an actor by onlookers" (Habermas 1984, 92). Feelings and desires can achieve "intersubjective transparency," but they cannot reach the same level of intersubjective recognition of validity as descriptive or normative expressions. The link between subjective expressions of feelings and desires and intersubjectivity arises with evaluation expressions: "Evaluative expressions or standards of value have justificatory force when they characterize a need in such a way that addressees can, in the framework of a common cultural heritage, recognize in these interpretations their own needs" (92). People can justify or make plausible the predilections expressed through statements of desire or feeling, what we might call affective statements, through evaluative expressions that are generalizable. Recognizing one's own needs in another's interpretation of needs implies that the public has achieved some level of intersubjective understanding that goes beyond the performer's purely subjective inner world. Yet Habermas equates evaluative expressions with claims regarding the "appropriateness or adequacy of value standards (or the 'good')"

---

3. Jürgen Habermas does say that certain feelings (e.g., obligation, shame, and guilt) can stand in relation to the social world.

(39). Since values relate to cultural definitions of the "good," they cannot rise to the level of universal validity claims; instead, they are "located within the horizon of the lifeworld of a specific group or culture" (42). Claims made through expressive and evaluative statements are culturally specific, and thus they are distinct from claims made through descriptive and normative statements, which are universalizable. Yet the concept of communicative rationality "refers to an unclarified systematic interconnection of *universal* validity claims" (18; emphasis added). Habermas claims that any actor who engages in communicative action, and is thus oriented to reaching an understanding with her interlocutors, must make three validity claims: "truth for statements or existential presuppositions, rightness for legitimately regulated actions and their normative context, and truthfulness or sincerity for the manifestations of subjective experiences" (99).[4] Expressive statements and dramaturgical action clearly connect with the third type of claim, but it is the only claim that cannot achieve universal validity; subjective experience can only become intersubjective through evaluative statements that are always dependent upon culturally specific statements of value. Participants can directly redeem the validity of descriptive and normative statements through argumentation in deliberation, but for expressive statements they can only do so if there are need interpretations that can transcend culturally specific values.

   If I am correct, then, that most affective statements are encompassed in Habermas's conceptions of expressive statements and dramaturgical action, it seems that they must play only a secondary role in his theory of communicative action, and concomitantly in his theory of discourse ethics. As Krause similarly argues, because Habermas retains a commitment to the opposition between reason and affectivity, his "theory cannot fully embrace the fusion of these elements, although its success depends on doing so" (2005, 379). Yet Habermas appears to be inconsistent. It is unclear whether expressive statements can achieve some sort of intersubjective recognition outside culturally specific values that give validity to evaluative expressions. Perhaps there are need interpretations that are universal, and if so, they may provide the basis for universal evaluative statements that could be the foundation of moral norm validity. Even if this is so, however, the role of empathy in ideal role taking would follow Mead by allowing us to eliminate the affective expressions others make regarding a moral norm that are not generalizable. We test a moral norm's validity by the force of the better

---

4. Habermas no longer makes this claim in regard to all forms of communicative action, but this does not affect the argument I present here (see Cooke 2001, 4).

argument, and since affective expressions will rarely, if ever, embody need interpretations that are generalizable in the same way as nonaffective normative claims or even descriptive statements, affectivity cannot help but play a limited role in discourse ethics. Thus, the affective side of the empathic process in discourse ethics primarily serves at the behest of a cognitive, abstract, generalized role taking.

The inclusion of moral feelings and empathy as necessary dispositions in moral discourse, I believe, results from Habermas's recognition that excluding feelings from moral discourse is untenable and unrealistic. In the end, though, his project requires that he downplay the role of affect in discourse ethics. The reason this tension reveals itself in his theory has to do with his overall project. He is attempting to construct a moral theory that is deontological, cognitivist, formalist, and universalist; in doing so, he must defend his theory against neo-Aristotelian, emotivist, and skeptical moral theories. His original downplaying of emotions results from a need to ground a universal and cognitive theory, the assumption being that emotions are primarily subjective and cannot achieve the same level of universal recognition as cognitive normative arguments.

While allowing participants to engage in ideal role taking is the primary position Habermas specifically grants empathy, there is a second, related responsibility that empathy carries. There are two principles that must guide any discourse ethics: justice and solidarity. Justice emphasizes "the inviolability of the individual by postulating equal respect for the dignity of each individual" (Habermas 1990, 200). Solidarity aims at protecting "the web of intersubjective relations of mutual recognition by which these individuals survive as members of a community" (200). For Habermas, these two principles are inseparable. If "justice is what is equally good for all," then "universal justice also requires that one person should take responsibility for a stranger. . . . From this perspective, solidarity is simply the reverse side of justice" (Habermas 1998, 29). These principles, therefore, are like two sides of a coin, and at least in part, empathy is a vital metal in forging this coin. "These two complementary aspects correspond to the principles of justice and solidarity respectively. The first postulates equal respect and equal rights for the individual, whereas the second postulates empathy and a concern for the well-being of one's neighbor" (Habermas 1990, 200). On first glance, it appears that here Habermas is more open to the affective side of empathy, encouraging the development of a solidarity based upon a concern for the well-being of one's neighbor, what he calls elsewhere a generalized compassion. This appears to link his use of the term "empathy" with the antecedent predisposition to empathic concern highlighted in the process model. This generalized compassion, though, still links with the even more important cognitive processes: "It is unlikely that one would be able to perform this demanding cognitive feat [of ideal role taking] without the generalized compassion, sublimated into the capacity to empathize with others that points beyond affective ties to immediate reference persons and opens our eyes to 'difference,' to the uniqueness and inalienable otherness of the other" (Habermas 1993, 174–75). Thus, even though he recognizes the importance of the integration of cognition and affect in what he calls "the mature capacity for moral judgment" (Habermas 1990, 182), it remains for affect to serve the cognitive process of role taking.

In Habermas's theory of deliberative democracy affect is rarely discussed directly, and empathy does not seem to be present at all. In deliberative democracy we are concerned with a wider range of questions (pragmatic, ethical-political, and moral) than occur in the arguments concerning moral norms found in discourse ethics. In this context, we are also concerned with legal norms, and he seems to allow affect only a slightly more important role in the legal than the moral sphere. In discussing the general public sphere, that open sphere in which political opinion- and will-formation can occur, he writes, "Here new problem situations can be perceived more sensitively, discourses aimed at achieving self-understanding can be conducted more widely and expressively, collective identities and need interpretations can be articulated with fewer compulsions than is the case in procedurally regulated public spheres" (Habermas 1996a, 308). We can infer from this that expressive modes of communication may be legitimate in the general public sphere, although they still seem to be less appropriate in procedurally regulated public spheres such as parliamentary bodies. Habermas's openness to expressive utterances in the general public sphere can be explained because legal norms must "regulate the life context of the citizens of a concrete legal community" (153). The culturally specific nature of statements of value, upon which expressive utterances depend, no longer threatens the rationality of the discursive process. In fact, "as soon as rational collective will-formation aims at concrete legal programs, it must cross the boundaries of justice discourses and include problems of value (that depend on the clarification of collective identity) and the balancing of interests" (154).

Despite the somewhat greater role allowed affect in deliberative politics, there is still an undercurrent in Habermas's theory that is dismissive of expressions of feelings. In discussing deliberative politics, he acknowledges that in any complex society there will be deviations from the model of purely communicative social relations. In addition to systematic constraints, there will be individual differences in abilities and resources; evidence of this includes what he describes as "the opportunistic attitudes, affects, prejudices, and so on, that detract from rational will-formation" (Habermas 1996a, 326). While this does not condemn affect in general, only affect that detracts from rational will-formation, here we can recognize the theme we have seen throughout the rest of Habermas's work: affect is, at best, a supporting player in communicative rationality.

We can thus conclude that Habermas's use of the term "empathy" matches the antecedent individual dispositions to affective role taking and empathic concern of the process model. This affective side of empathy plays a role, though a very limited one, in deliberative democracy; desires and feelings are primarily subjective and can only reach intersubjective recognition if all citizens share values or need interpretations that can serve as the basis for intersubjective evaluations. Empathy primarily serves to allow for ideal role taking, which, given the influence of Mead, represents for Habermas a primarily cognitive process. While ideal role taking would appear to match with the role taking process in the model, because it only focuses on generalized attitudes, it is actually a limited version of what it means to empathize. Certainly we must begin by looking from all perspectives, but we do so only to discover an abstract, generalized perspective. This must inevitably involve the elimination or weeding out of perspectives that are not generalizable, a process that can lead to distortions and biases. Habermas also mistakes the relation between cognition and affect in political judgment, a theme at which I have already hinted and will return to in the future. For now, though, I want to simply claim that Habermas's theory does not persuasively incorporate the entire process of empathy.

Incremental Inclusion of Empathy: Deliberative Variations

Deliberative theorists who follow Rawls and Habermas closely also focus almost exclusively on the cognitive or role-taking dimension of empathy and unsurprisingly pay little attention to its affective side. Whenever they discuss or begin to hint at something like empathy, they concentrate primarily on the cognitive process of role taking. John Dryzek's early work is a good example. Because of his emphasis on rationality, he does not discuss empathy explicitly or directly address the affective side of human beings. Instead, when he comes close to discussing ideas related to empathy, they involve something like perspective taking. He notes that "*phronesis* assumes and requires a background of shared norms and socialization experiences on the part of participating individuals. People from different cultural backgrounds are unlikely to come to agreement" (Dryzek 1990, 42). The answer to this difficulty is for participants to work to understand each other's perspectives. "If [a substantial shared background on community norms] is absent . . . participants can still reach consensus based on reasoned *dis*agreement, by striving to understand the cultural tradition and/or conceptual framework of the other participants" (42). Such an understanding of each other's perspectives, one could infer, is vital in any heterogeneous group engaged in deliberation, which presumably would include most groups in any large society. It would also be safe to infer that such an understanding would be nigh impossible without the empathic process described by the process model of empathy. Simone Chambers echoes Dryzek in her adaptation of Habermas, and is even more explicit about the need for perspective taking. She writes, "Impartiality is achieved by putting oneself in the position of the other and trying to see the situation from her perspective" (1996, 100). Without seeing "how the world looks to other people," we can neither achieve mutual understanding nor even get to the point of a "rational disagreement" (100–101). Though both Dryzek and Chambers clearly refer to concepts that are part of the cognitive component of the process model of empathy, neither explores these issues in depth, and neither has much to say about the role of affect in deliberation.

James Bohman: Uptake in Deliberation

James Bohman is explicit about the need for perspective taking, but he too provides little discussion of the affective side of empathy. We can distinguish his theory from other deliberative democrats primarily from a distinction he makes between discourse and dialogue. In contrast to discourse, "dialogue is the mere give and take of reasons. It does not necessarily aim to produce well-justified claims; rather, it aims to produce claims that are wide enough in scope and sufficiently justified to be accountable to an indefinite public of fellow citizens" (Bohman 1996, 57). Public deliberation is a dialogical process in which citizens exchange reasons in order to resolve problems, rather than a justificatory process; the best defense for deliberation "is that it is more likely to improve the epistemic quality of the justifications of political decisions" and be based in reasons that will "reflect the broader input of all the deliberators who are affected" (27). The distinction between discourse and dialogue is important because "it is only in dialogue with others—in speaking to them, answering them, and *taking up their views*—that the many diverse capacities for deliberation are exercised jointly" (24; emphasis added).

With this different understanding of deliberation, Bohman reconceptualizes the role of public reason in deliberative democracy. Rather than a single public reason drawn from an overlapping consensus as in Rawls's theory—or even based on the force of the better argument—he contends that the reason of the public must be plural (Bohman 1995). We should not construe reason giving in public deliberation "narrowly as formal argumentation" (Bohman 1998, 410). Instead, plural public reason admits a variety of reasons, perspectives, and even styles of communication as citizens exchange reasons in dialogue. At least one of the justifications for an open public deliberation is the democratic promise of equal consideration. "If equal standing contributes to the value of a procedure and the willingness to accept its outcome, then deliberators should not be quick to exclude a reason as nonpublic" (410).[5] Not only is plural public reason open to a variety of reasons and communication styles, since it does not presuppose "a single norm of reasonableness" in deliberation, "agents can come to an agreement with one another for *different* publicly accessible reasons" (Bohman 1996, 83; emphasis in original). Instead of envisioning deliberation as aiming at a consensus on values and principles that can then provide the basis for democratic decisions, Bohman argues for seeing "deliberation as an ongoing cooperative enterprise that does not require that citizens be always fully convinced by the public reasons offered by others in deliberation" (1998, 407). On this understanding, the reasons given in deliberation are legitimate "when they are convincing enough to motivate each citizen, even a dissenter, to continue to cooperate in deliberation even after the decision has been made" (Bohman 1996, 35). Thus, the criterion for determining deliberation's success is not whether citizens reach consensus based upon the same reasons, but whether they agree to *continue deliberation* even when they are on the losing end of a decision.

Instantiating this general idea of democratic legitimacy within the legal system leads Bohman to formulate the conditions for legitimate laws: "Laws are legitimate on the following conditions: (1) if they result from a fair and open participatory process in which all publicly available reasons have been

5. Other than equal consideration, James Bohman also cites the democratic ideal of liberty as a justification for a pluralist accommodation of views (see Bohman 2005, 719–20).

respected, (2) if the outcome is such that citizens may continue to cooperate in deliberation rather than merely comply, and (3) if this process makes the public deliberation of the majority the source of sovereign power" (1996, 187). Here democratic legitimacy arises not just from ongoing cooperation, but also from a system that allows full participation and consideration of all publicly available reasons, as well as the connection between such deliberation and sovereign power. In order for this sovereign power to function, "democracy requires new structural connections between deliberation and institutions that reflect the practices of inquiry in a multiperspectival polity" (Bohman 2004, 39). Yet while institutional structures connecting public sphere deliberation and decision-making is necessary for democratic legitimacy, in order for public deliberation to meet the requirement of openness that will allow ongoing cooperation, the background culture in which deliberation occurs becomes key.

In a survey of deliberative theory, Bohman maintains that "rather than simply limiting themselves to an ideal of public reason, most accounts of justification in deliberative democracy recognize the role of background understanding and social conditions in deliberative practices" (1998, 412–13). Without the appropriate background conditions, deliberation will never be able to insure equal consideration and democratic legitimacy; one such condition is that citizens demonstrate tolerance of a specific type. Bohman argues that evidence of intolerance includes "the inability of citizens to raise vital and significant concerns in deliberation," "the exclusion of relevant reasons," and "the illicit and unspoken generalization of the dominant or majority perspective" (2003, 775). Deliberative toleration is not simply allowing others to think and speak as they wish, guaranteed by a system of rights and immunities; there must be a genuine openness to the perspectives of others without any preconceived reservation of what perspectives are reasonable or rational. "If we regard the persons whom we tolerate as citizens, then we must as such also regard them as entitled to put forth reasons that are valuable from their perspective" (758). Yet dialogue requires citizens to go beyond just allowing others to give whatever reasons they believe are important; they must be open to the possibility that others' contributions will affect their own perspectives. This process of different perspectives affecting one another through open dialogue is what Bohman calls, following J. L. Austin, "securing uptake" (1996, 58–66). The ability of dialogue to secure uptake of various positions is vital to democratic legitimacy. If the minority remains unconvinced that deliberation could lead to the incorporation of its perspectives, either presently or in the future, the system of deliberation cannot serve as the basis of ongoing cooperation in the face of political disagreement. At the heart of Bohman's theory of deliberation, and what undergirds both equal consideration and democratic legitimacy, is a genuine openness on the part of citizens to the influence of others' reasons. He builds equal consideration into the very heart of his deliberative theory, and the mechanism by which equal consideration can occur is uptake.

Dialogue can secure uptake through various mechanisms, and here Bohman specifically follows Habermas in advocating role taking as of prime importance for deliberative democracy, but he even more explicitly limits this to a cognitive exercise.

> Some dialogical mechanisms employ the capacities for perspective taking and role-taking implicit in communication—capacities for *thinking* from the standpoint of everyone else. The mechanism here is that of shifting and exchanging perspectives in the course of dialogue—shifting between speaking and listening. In order to convince you I may have to take your perspective and vice versa. Even if I do not adopt your views, a change in perspective may cause me to modify my own reasons, particularly if they do not convince those who disagree with me. Such mechanisms build upon the sorts of *cognition* involved in resolving face-to-face conflicts. (Bohman 1996, 63; emphasis added)

Bohman even links this kind of perspective taking to Mead's theory of taking the perspective of the generalized other, further demonstrating how he limits perspective taking to a cognitive exercise. "Perspective taking of this sort aids deliberation by making reasons more convincing relative to the whole body of deliberators. The generalized perspective enables deliberators to see the cogency and intelligibility of reasons in new reflective ways, along with the multiple perspectives and views of others" (65). The one time Bohman makes a link between perspective taking and empathy he downplays empathy's importance. In his discussion of dialogical mechanisms, he highlights several that are not dependent upon shared values and commitments; one of these is discussion of differences in personal and collective historical experiences. Bohman claims that this mechanism is "more than simply hearing someone's confessional discourse or listening to someone's self-expression" (61). The problem with simply listening to confessions or self-expressions is that listeners' uptake in such cases "is minimal

and dependent upon the listener's own capacities for empathy or identification" (61). For Bohman, therefore, as for Habermas, empathy has its limits and cannot be "a means of solving problems" (61). Instead, a primarily
cognitive-focused exchange is necessary if deliberation is to be successful.

William Rehg: Reason and Emotion

One theorist influenced by Habermas who more specifically addresses
empathy and the role of affect, though like Habermas he does so in a discussion of discourse ethics, is William Rehg. In the introduction to his
book *Insight and Solidarity*, Rehg examines three possible functions emotions and feelings might play in argumentation situated within a theory of
discourse ethics. In doing so he highlights the complex nature of empathy:

> Attempts to incorporate empathy into the moral point of view suggest
> that "feeling" (in some sense) could actually improve one's under-
> standing for the other's position, and thus allow for a fairer moral
> judgment. To be sure, definitions of empathy vary, and a purely cog-
> nitive concept of empathy would not support this claim. Nonethe-
> less, even if one defined empathy as a cognitive grasp of the other's
> predicament, one might draw on some of the arguments sketched
> above and propose that feelings of care and concern could guide and
> enhance such empathetic understanding. In either case, the attempt
> to grasp the other's position and arguments in a process of moral
> argumentation might be considerably aided by certain emotions.
> (Rehg 1994, 13–14)

Rehg acknowledges that a purely cognitive understanding of empathy might
not allow empathy to play a role in reaching the mutual understanding
necessary for fair moral judgments; at the same time, he begins to point
toward a complex understanding of empathy as being more appropriate for
discourse theory by suggesting that at least some feelings should guide our
understanding. He goes even further by suggesting that "one might argue
that emotions can actually amount to something like arguments or coun-
terarguments" (14). Thus, the cognitive and the affective, under this understanding, interact to allow the kind of mutual understanding necessary to
truly test the validity of moral norms.

   While he recognizes the need for a multidimensional understanding of
the role of empathy in discourse ethics, Rehg only hints at how we ought

to conceptualize this. He acknowledges, "An adequate treatment of these issues ultimately exceeds the scope of this book. Nonetheless, a plausible account of discourse ethics must at least set out the systematic basis for developing the above connections between reason and feeling" (1994, 14). In the rest of his work there are scattered references to the part that empathy might play in discourse ethics, several of which focus on how empathy helps mitigate problems associated with impartialist or generalist moral theories. He argues that moral discourse "must include an empathetic sensitivity to the concrete other, as well as an attention to the particularities of the concrete situation. This allows a conception of morality that overcomes an excessive orientation to general rules" (17). Further, he writes, "The impartiality defining the moral point of view is likewise double-sided. The participants must be able to present their needs and interests in the language of others, a task that requires at once a degree of imaginative abstractive capability with respect to one's own need interpretations *and*, just as much, the ability to understand the other's position—something like empathy, only in a cognitive sense. This demanding empathic presupposition is often overlooked by criticisms of impartialist moral theories" (77). Rehg also argues that empathy can be helpful when we must engage in what Habermas calls discourses of application as we apply moral norms to specific situations: "To this extent, the notion that application requires perception or an intuitive weighing still retains some validity. Moreover, insofar as discourse ethics can allow for such particularistic assessments, notions such as care and empathy have a role in moral reasoning" (205). He elaborates further on this in his discussion of how the ethics of care can inform discourse ethics; he writes that "the importance of care and interpersonal responsiveness for moral reasoning in such situations would substantially fill out a discourse-ethical theory of practical reasoning. If affectively charged attributes such as care, compassion and empathy play a significant role in the assessment of concrete cases, then the proponents of discourse ethics cannot ignore the relation between reason and emotion" (206–7).

Thus, even though he does not fully develop his theoretical position, Rehg acknowledges the vital role that empathy must play in discourse ethics. If we predicate this sort of ethics on the ability to reach mutual agreement through understanding each other's positions and convincing each other of a moral norm's validity, empathy must be a central theoretical concern. "Precisely the effort to convince others of the justice of a normative expectation demands that I *attend empathetically* to its effects on others' welfare. Both the community whose cooperative structures are at stake in moral deliberation as well as the concrete others involved in such cooperation enter into the very constitution of justice under the aegis of a rational solidarity" (Rehg 1994, 245; emphasis added). Rehg has taken a first step by highlighting the role of empathy in discourse ethics, as well as the need to understand the relationships among affect, cognition, reason, and emotion; we still, though, need to more clearly theorize what this role is and how these relationships work.

Seyla Benhabib: The Generalized Other and the Concrete Other

Seyla Benhabib (1992) briefly examines the role of empathy in discourse ethics, though her conclusion differs slightly from Rehg's. We have already seen how Habermas's reliance upon Mead's ideal role taking leads him to focus on generalized attitudes that inhibit the role of empathy in deliberation. Benhabib criticizes Habermas's discourse ethics, as well as Rawls's original position, for their lack of sensitivity to these differences between a "generalized" other and the "concrete" other present during deliberation. And although she discusses Okin's argument for the role of empathy in Rawls's original position, unlike Okin she downplays the importance of empathy. "I therefore trust much less than Okin (and even Gilligan) the sentiments of empathy and benevolence" (1992, 168). Instead of relying upon empathy, Benhabib turns to Hannah Arendt's conception of an enlarged mentality: "As Arendt also has noted, the capacity for exercising an 'enlarged mentality,' the ability to take the standpoint of the other into account is not empathy although it is related to it" (168). Yet Arendt rejects empathy altogether in favor of a sort of projection that dismisses how the other feels. She argues that we form political opinions by "considering a given issue from different viewpoints, by making present to [our minds] the standpoints of those who are absent" (1968, 241). This type of representation "does not blindly adopt the actual views of those who stand somewhere else, and hence look upon the world from a different perspective; this is a question neither of empathy, as though I tried to be or feel like somebody else, nor of counting noses and joining a majority but of being and thinking *in my own identity* where actually I am not" (241; emphasis in original). An enlarged mentality allows individuals to examine how they would think and feel if they were in the place of another, and Arendt follows Kant in positing that this is what allows us to judge something. Arendt's notion of an enlarged mentality appears to be something like role taking, but it really is more of a cognitive projection of the self into the place of another without worrying about what the other thinks or feels. Benhabib understands empathy as "the capacity to 'feel with, to feel together'" (1992, 168), and people who feel with others, she claims, may lack an enlarged mentality in the Arendtian sense. She claims this is so because empathic people are unable to distinguish between the self and other and are thus unable to see the standpoint of the "concrete" other. Instead, she agrees with Rawls that because the objects of empathy or benevolence often oppose one another, we need "principles, institutions and procedures to enable articulation of the voice of 'others'" (168).

I will return to Benhabib in Chapter 6, but here I want to note that her definition of empathy as the capacity to feel for or feel with others is more limited than the process model definition. That empathy is a capacity indicates that she sees it as an antecedent individual ability to either feel for (empathic concern) or feel with (affective role taking) others. Yet her reference to an "enlarged mentality" more closely aligns with what the process model calls role taking, even though Arendt's conception of role taking is limited. Benhabib does improve upon Habermas's and Rawls's versions of role taking by arguing that we must examine the concept from a concrete rather than a generalized perspective. Her mistake, I believe, is to separate the cognitive and affective sides of empathy. As the process model indicates, both an "enlarged mentality" in the broad sense and "feeling for" or "feeling with" others work together in the empathic process. Further, a growing body of evidence from neuropsychological studies indicates that humans have neurological mechanisms that tend to prevent a conflation of the self and other during empathy (see Decety and Grèzes 2006, Decety and Jackson 2004 and 2006, Decety and Lamm 2006, Decety and Moriguchi 2007, Decety and Sommerville 2003, and Ruby and Decety 2004). People who empathize experience what others are feeling while still maintaining a distinction between the self and other. Evidence from studies in social psychology also indicates that while empathy can lead to bias if one limits those with whom one empathizes, empathy and predispositions to empathy can actually increase tolerance of, decrease biased behavioral attributions toward, and increase cooperation with both concrete and generalized others (see Chapter 5). While some people may be unable to maintain the distinction between self and other, research indicates that this is not as strong a threat as Benhabib believes it is. I believe that Benhabib and Arendt are wrong in rejecting empathy as an important component of an enlarged mentality. The process model is an advance by incorporating both affect and cognition in the process whereby we come to understand others' situations and experiences, but a persuasive theory concerning the relationship between empathy and deliberation must take into account the concerns Benhabib raises about the differences between the concrete other and the generalized other.

Amy Gutmann and Dennis Thompson: Reciprocity and Mutual Respect

While theorists influenced by Habermas tend to engage in only limited discussions of empathy, those for whom Rawls is a stronger influence do so even less. Amy Gutmann and Dennis Thompson go even further than most deliberative democrats in putting forward requirements for legitimate democratic decisions. As with Rawls, one of the central concepts in their theory of deliberation is reciprocity, the giving of reasons that others can accept. "When citizens make moral claims in a deliberative democracy, they appeal to reasons or principles that can be shared by fellow citizens who are similarly motivated" (Gutmann and Thompson 1996, 55). Reciprocity requires citizens to "publicly appeal to reasons that are shared or could be shared, by their fellow citizens, and if they take into account these same kinds of reasons presented by similarly motivated citizens, then they are engaged in a process that by its nature aims at a justifiable resolution of disagreement" (25). If citizens can reach agreement in this deliberative process, they achieve mutual justification: "Insofar as moral reasoning in politics succeeds in finding [mutually recognized] principles, the conclusions of deliberation become mutually justifiable" (56). Under these circumstances everyone agrees with the decision, seemingly based upon the same principles, so there is no question of whether it is justified or not. Moral disagreement may exist, but it can be of two types. Nondeliberative disagreement occurs when "one side does not have reciprocal reasons for rejecting the other, and thereby signifies that it is not motivated to find fair terms of cooperation (at least with respect to the policy at issue)" (78). In cases of nondeliberative disagreement, "citizens do not have any obligations of mutual respect toward their opponents" (3). Even citizens who are motivated to find fair terms of social cooperation and follow the principle of reciprocity, however, may disagree about moral principles and their interpretation. The result is deliberative disagreement, and this requires that citizens follow the principle of moral accommodation.

Moral accommodation requires that democratic decision-making embody the value of mutual respect. Citizens can uphold this value by following the principles of civic integrity—integrity in speech, action, and principle—

and civic magnanimity—acknowledgment of the moral status of opposing views (Gutmann and Thompson 1996, 79–91). Deliberation that proceeds along these lines will lead to the recognition of "the idea that the only mutually justifiable route to gaining collective acceptance of individual moral beliefs is through mutually respectful deliberation" (93). Mutually respectful deliberation represents a mutually justifiable "view on how citizens should publicly deliberate when they fundamentally disagree" (93). While citizens may not accept the decision itself as correct, they can accept that deliberation—if it embodies reciprocity, mutual respect, civic integrity, and civic magnanimity—is a mutually justifiable way of reaching decisions in the face of moral disagreement; it is the only way that citizens who are committed to fair terms of social cooperation can resolve their disagreements. Yet the procedural limits implied by the principles of moral accommodation are not the only requirements reciprocity and mutual respect entail. In criticizing purely procedural theories of democracy, Gutmann and Thompson also highlight substantive limits on majority rule, and in so doing, link justifiability and legitimacy.

Gutmann and Thompson claim that "no one has yet proposed a decision-making procedure that is *generally* more justified than majority rule (and its variations)" (1996, 31), and yet the "procedural defense of majority rule as the manifestation of popular will does not satisfy even the most minimal understanding of reciprocity" (30). The reason for this is that reciprocity not only requires moral accommodation, it also implies that democratic decisions must respect the substantive principles of basic liberty and opportunity (30, chap. 6). The claims people make based upon the principles of liberty and opportunity "have their limits, but all the reasonable limits entail rejecting the proceduralist claim that majority rule is legitimate, whatever its outcome" (31). Thus, legitimate democratic decisions not only face the procedural restraints of moral accommodation, they also must protect basic liberty and opportunity, both of which arise from the principle of reciprocity. Deliberative democracy has a place for majority rule, but majority decisions are legitimate only if they do not violate the principles or values of reciprocity, mutual respect, moral accommodation, civic integrity, civic magnanimity, basic liberty, and basic opportunity. Gutmann and Thompson acknowledge that their arguments concerning these principles and their interpretations of them are always subject to further deliberative scrutiny (51), but it seems impossible to abandon the general idea that certain procedural and substantive principles restrain legitimate majority decisions without undermining their theory.

Gutmann and Thompson go a step further, though, and explain that deliberations that meet their requirements are likely to have a psychological effect on the perceptions of citizens such that they will recognize the process as fair, and thus legitimate, even if they lose out in the deliberations. Citizens will recognize their form of deliberation as the only mutually justifiable way, and thus the only fair way, to make democratic decisions. It is fair because deliberation characterized by reciprocity and mutual respect eliminates irrelevant considerations from the process; by doing so, it embodies equal consideration. "Deliberation contributes to the legitimacy of decisions made under conditions of scarcity. . . . The hard choices that democratic governments make in these circumstances should be more acceptable even to those who receive less than they deserve if everyone's claims have been considered on their merits rather than on the basis of wealth, status, or power" (41). Citizens will take a much different attitude to these decisions than they would if power politics taints the process: "Even with regard to decisions with which many disagree, most of us take one attitude toward those that are adopted after careful consideration of the relevant conflicting moral claims, and quite a different attitude toward those that are adopted merely by virtue of the relative strength of competing political interests" (Gutmann and Thompson 2004, 10). For Gutmann and Thompson, equal consideration provides the very foundation for the democratic legitimacy of collective decisions, yet they are never clear on the specific psychological mechanisms that will contribute to this legitimacy and have very little to say about empathy.

Gutmann and Thompson never explicitly discuss empathy, though their discussions of reciprocity and mutual respect touch on something akin to the cognitive process of role taking. Reciprocity "asks us to appeal to reasons that are shared or could come to be shared by our fellow citizens" (1996, 14). It is difficult to imagine that this could occur without at least some perspective taking, especially since reciprocity can only occur if there is mutual respect among interlocutors. Mutual respect "requires a favorable attitude toward, and constructive interaction with, the persons with whom one disagrees" (79), and it encourages "citizens and public officials to appreciate the moral character of the positions of people with whom they disagree" (90). One could infer that this constructive interaction and appreciation could only occur if some form of role taking also occurs, but this is appears to be the closest that they get to discussing the role of empathy in their theory of deliberative democracy. They give some space for a cognitively oriented role taking, but fail to account for the affective side of the empathic process.

One way in which Gutmann and Thompson advance deliberative theory, however, is to respond to critics who have argued that passionate rhetoric should be part of deliberation. I will return to this more fully in Chapter 6, but for now, I want to note that they point out that deliberative democrats should not accept the given of "a dichotomy between passion and reason" (2004, 50). This will lead deliberative theory to "recognize that in the political arena passionate rhetoric can be as justifiable as logical demonstration" (51). While the move toward recognizing the importance of both passion and reason in deliberation is encouraging, I have a few criticisms of their approach. The dichotomy between passion and reason, or passionate rhetoric and logical demonstration, does not necessarily map onto the distinction between affect and cognition. Affect involves more than just being passionate, and reasoning, as we have seen, involves both affect and cognition. More important, though, it is hard to determine what they mean when they say that passion is justifiable. On the one hand, they argue that theorists and politicians since Aristotle "have recognized the legitimacy of modes of persuasion in politics that combine reason and passion" (51). This seems to indicate that speech infused with emotion can be the legitimate basis for decision-making, though they place reason in opposition to passion, and since they base their whole theory on giving reasons others could accept, it is not clear whether affect can be a reason within deliberation. This becomes less clear when they then argue that "rhetoric may properly have to tip toward passion in some circumstances" (51). Unless some citizens are willing to act with passion, "making statements and declarations rather than developing arguments and responses," some issues may not even make it onto the public's agenda (51). In such cases, deliberative theory suspends its deliberative requirements to allow for more deliberation than might otherwise occur or if it leads "to future occasions for deliberative criticism of injustice" (51). Despite their rejection of a passion/reason dichotomy, and though they are open to allowing passionate rhetoric in deliberation, Gutmann and Thompson retain a bias toward rational argumentation as the source of democratic legitimacy in deliberation; most important for my purposes, this prevents them from developing a full theory of empathy for deliberation.

Jane Mansbridge: Beyond Adversary Democracy

Though most deliberative democrats spend little or no time discussing empathy, one of the earliest expositions on the role of empathy in deliberation

occurred well before the publication of the more fully developed deliberative theories. Jane Mansbridge (1983) references empathy fairly extensively
in her study of a New England town meeting and a crisis hotline. As early
as her preface, Mansbridge writes:

> Readers should be warned in advance that when I use the term "inter-
> ests" I do not mean self-interest narrowly conceived. My "interest"
> includes concern for others and concern for a principle. If my friends
> and I want to help starving people in Biafra, but a rival group in
> our organization with different priorities schedules the crucial meet-
> ing while I and my friends are out of town, we would say that our
> interests have not been represented at the meeting, even though we
> had come to our decision in favor of the Biafrans through *empathy*
> or through commitment to a principle like justice. (1983, xii; empha-
> sis added)

Mansbridge demonstrates what will become the most important role empathy plays in her theory: the creation of a common interest. She argues,
"All three distinguishing features of a unitary democracy—equal respect,
consensus, and face-to-face meetings of the whole—encourage members
to identify with one another and with the group as a whole. This process of
identification in turn helps develop common interests" (1983, 5). The development of common interests within a unitary democracy not only relies on
empathy, it seems to be part of what empathy is: "Empathy can lead individuals to make another's good their own. Individual interests do not then
overlap; instead, the separate individuals fuse, in a sense, into one" (27).
Mansbridge also clearly recognizes the centrality of affect in role taking: "A
third reason for adopting a consensual procedure is that empathy among
members of a group has proceeded so far that the line between mine and
thine has become indistinct, and each member feels the grief or joy of others in the body almost as if it were his or her own" (256). Here empathy
results in what the process model terms a parallel affective response; it
leads deliberators to feel what others are feeling, and through this affective
identification, creates common interests similar to the way that Habermas
talks of solidarity. Yet Mansbridge takes empathy further than Habermas.

Mansbridge argues that the contact created by direct participation is
the source that evokes empathy. On its face, this process appears to be like
Mead's role taking: "Selby's citizens also create common interest when they
adopt as their own the interests of fellow citizens. They do not call Harvey

or Mildred on the carpet for not having the figures right in the town report because they are likely to think: 'What if I were in their shoes?' . . . This empathetic protection is a general predisposition in a town meeting" (1983, 73). Yet despite talking about being in the others' shoes, Mansbridge's use of empathy does not approximate the generalized ideal role taking of Mead. For her, the focus is much more on the concrete other in a face-to-face setting. "Experience teaches us, however, that in practice, face-to-face contact increases the perception of likeness, encourages decision-making by consensus, and perhaps even enhances equality of status. . . . On the positive side, [face-to-face contact] seems to increase the actual congruence of interests by encouraging the empathy by which individual members make one another's interests their own" (33). Mansbridge recognizes, as specified in the process model, that the closeness with a target can affect the possibility of empathy. Face-to-face contact creates a closeness that increases the chances for empathy to occur. Later, however, she appears a bit more vague: "The rule of consensus seems not only to reflect empathy but to create it" (256). Here empathy results from the fact that consensus is the decision rule, not that deliberators adopt consensus because they already empathize with one another.

Thus Mansbridge incorporates more components of the process model of empathy into her discussion of deliberation than any of the theorists discussed to this point. She recognizes the importance of role taking, though it is not just a cognitively oriented practice focused on generalized others. She highlights the parallel affective outcomes of empathy, and even hints at the reactive affective outcome of empathic concern. She acknowledges the importance of similarity between target and observer, and points out that face-to-face discussion can increase this possibility. In the end, though, I think Mansbridge misses some key points for deliberation. She recognizes that the possibility of empathy is limited, having occurred much more easily in the Vermont town of "Selby" than at the crisis hotline center. There is no guarantee that face-to-face decision-making will result in greater identification among deliberators, as anyone who has been to a public hearing or town meeting can attest. She also does not fully discuss several of the components of the process model—the critical omissions being individual predispositions to empathy and nonaffective outcomes. Finally, in focusing on face-to-face interaction, Mansbridge runs up against one of the criticisms aimed at participatory and deliberative democratic theories that Dryzek (2001) calls the problem of economy and legitimacy. Even at the level of the New England town meeting, it is usually impossible for all citizens to deliberate together, thus undermining the very basis of democratic legitimacy in deliberative theories. If empathy depends upon face-to-face interaction, and deliberation requires empathy, then this only further complicates the legitimacy issue. Mansbridge has done much to make the role of empathy clearer in deliberative theory, but there still remains more to do.

Robert Goodin: Internal-Reflective Deliberation

What this review so far makes clear is that we need a better theoretical explication of the role of empathy in deliberative democracy. Robert Goodin (2003) has begun to make this connection more explicit, though even in his theory of reflective democracy he spends little time exploring the complexities of this connection. Goodin argues that we need to *supplement* our more traditional understanding of face-to-face deliberations with what he calls "internal-reflective" deliberation. These are the deliberations that take place inside each citizen's mind, rather than those occurring in interpersonal communication. One of the ways this can happen, he argues, is through empathy. Goodin writes that correctly "crafted deliberative processes can produce preferences which are more reflective," and one of the ways in which this is so is that the preferences are "more *empathetic* with the plight of others" (7; emphasis in original). Once we acknowledge that there are problems with making everyone present in large-scale deliberations, Goodin argues it is a small step "to suggesting that empathetic imagining can be an important supplement to, and at the margins can occasionally substitute for, interpersonal conversation in the sorts of deliberations which democrats desire across mass societies" (171).

Like other theorists, Goodin does not spend much time explaining exactly what he means by empathetic imagining. It appears, at points, to be a kind of perspective taking. "Whatever more particular story we tell, the general idea is invariably that we make sense of others, their utterances, and their actions, by mentally 'putting ourselves in the other's place' in some sense or another" (Goodin 2003, 179). He even goes on to cite Habermas's reliance on Mead's version of ideal role taking in achieving intersubjective understanding. Yet there also appears to be an affective component to his theory. One of the ways he argues that we can induce internal-reflective deliberation is through fiction and film. In explaining this argument, he writes, "The larger point is that those lessons come packed with more emotional punch and engage our imagination in more effective ways than do historical narratives or reflective essays of a less stylized sort" (181). From the limited evidence in his exposition, it is clear that Goodin comes closer to understanding empathy as multidimensional and provides a provisional answer to the problem of scale. Both he and Mansbridge incrementally improve our understanding of the importance of empathy to deliberation, but neither can fully account for the various aspects of the process model of empathy and how these can contribute to deliberative democracy.

We have seen that most deliberative theorists focus primarily on the cognitive practice of perspective taking, and they often argue for this in generalized or abstract terms. Some pay attention to the affective components of the process model of empathy, or the connections that might be important between affect and cognition in the practice of citizens' empathizing with their fellow deliberators, and yet even those who recognize the affective side spend little time teasing out the importance of affect for deliberation. Only by doing so can we gain a full understanding of how and when empathy might occur in deliberation, why we would want it to occur, and what the positive benefits might be if it were to do so.

5

EMPATHY'S IMPORTANCE—
THE EMPIRICAL EVIDENCE

We now have a model of the empathic process that allows us to discuss the various aspects of empathy in a more complete way, but I have yet to make the case that such an account is vital to our understanding of deliberative democracy. There are both empirical and theoretical reasons why I believe that the process model of empathy I have defended is necessary for establishing a persuasive case for deliberative democracy. My first argument is that empirical research indicates that a clear conception of empathy is absolutely necessary for a theory of deliberative democracy to address the issues of equal consideration and legitimacy. Empirical evidence in several key areas—group polarization, individual biases, out-group perceptions, altruism and helping behavior, and reciprocity—points to the importance of the empathic process for deliberation. Further empirical results also indicate that there are important links between cognition and affect in both the process of empathy and moral judgment. These linkages highlight the need for a full conception of the role of emotions and thinking in deliberation; the process model of empathy gives us insight into how to achieve this.

Group Polarization

One critique leveled against deliberation is what Cass Sunstein calls the "Law of Group Polarization" (2002; see also Schkade, Sunstein, and Hastie 2007). Sunstein defines polarization as occurring when *members of a deliberating group predictably move toward a more extreme point in the direction indicated by the members' predeliberative tendencies*" (2002, 176; emphasis in

original). Sunstein gives many empirical examples of the tendency of deliberating groups to polarize, and what factors tend to increase the likelihood of polarization. Polarization can obviously be harmful for deliberative
democracy, but Sunstein recognizes that it is not inevitable. "On the other
hand, the social context of deliberation can make a large difference, and
under certain conditions, group polarization need not occur. The nature of
the deliberative process, and the characteristics of the deliberating participants, can matter a great deal" (188). Interestingly, he highlights Fishkin's
Deliberative Opinion Poll as a type of deliberation that may not lead to
polarization (193–95). Among the factors that could possibly explain this,
he lists: (1) participants do not vote; (2) random sampling insures a more
diverse population; (3) deliberators listen to a balanced panel of experts; (4)
moderators play a key roll in the deliberations; and (5) participants receive
a set of balanced written materials. In a later treatment Sunstein and his
colleagues David Schkade and Reid Hastie reject the second possibility by
arguing that internal diversity before deliberation does not affect polarization (2007, 935), leaving balanced information, moderators, and nonvot-
ing as the factors most likely to mitigate against polarization effects. Yet
while these factors may contribute to the blunting of polarization, neither
Sunstein and his colleagues nor Fishkin and his give a clear indication of
the why these factors may mitigate against polarization. I contend that the
process of empathy, at least in part, can help us explain why deliberation
does not necessarily lead to group polarization.

Empathy and Individual Biases: Behavioral, Moral,
and Motivational Attributions

Early research in social psychology suggested that people tend to attach
different influences to their own behavior than to the behavior of others
(for example, Nisbett et al. 1973). Actors often attribute their own behaviors
to situational factors, those uncontrollable influences surrounding the circumstances in which they find themselves. When observers evaluate the
behavior of people they observe, however, they tend to ascribe it to the
personal and controllable dispositions those others have.[1] Thus, there are
biases in the way people tend to look at the influences that affect what

---

1. In some of the literature scholars now refer to the personal dispositions as internal factors and the situational factors as external factors. I prefer and will use the modifiers "personal" and "situational" because I find them to be more descriptively interesting.

they or others do; researchers call this a behavioral attribution bias. Social psychologists have expanded on the early research in this area in some interesting ways. The tendency of actors to attribute their own behavior to situational factors appears to depend upon the success or failure of that behavior. Studies have shown that actors tend to attribute their successful behaviors to their own dispositions and their unsuccessful behaviors to situational factors (see Gould and Sigall 1977 for a review). For example, students will attribute a successful exam to their hard work or intelligence (personal dispositions), while they will attribute failure on an exam to the difficulty of the test, the unfairness of the instructor, or the fact that they had to work too late the night before (situational factors). Observers, on the other hand, tend to generally conclude that others' behaviors are purely due to dispositional factors, so that an observer will attribute another student's failing a test almost exclusively to the student's personal dispositions or behavior and not to the student's situation. Another interesting extension of this finding has applied it to in-groups and out-groups (see Tarrant and North 2004, 161–63, for a review of this literature). Members of in-groups tend to attribute the group's positive behaviors to the characteristics of the group and its own negative behaviors to other factors. Interestingly, most research appears to indicate that there is not necessarily an opposite derogation of the out-group, though studies examining specific individuals of an out-group do demonstrate some derogation (Tarrant and North 2004).

The presence of behavioral attribution bias alone should concern deliberative theorists, but two additional studies of bias ought to raise this concern to an even higher level. Dennis Krebs and Philip Laird (1998) have shown that actors are more likely to make exculpatory judgments about their own norm-violating behavior than about the moral transgressions others commit. On the political side, Glenn Reeder and others (2005) examine the effects of bias, not on attributions for influences on behavior, but rather on what motivates behavior. What distinguishes their research, and what makes it most important for deliberative theorists, is that they specifically examined how this works in relation to political perceptions. In three studies they looked at the motivations people attributed to President Bush and their fellow citizens for going to war in Iraq, while in a fourth they examined the motivations subjects attributed to their fellow citizens for their positions on gay marriage and abortion, issues which often come up in discussions about the implications of deliberative democratic theory. The results indicate that people have a "tendency to attribute relatively negative motives to others whose attitudinal positions differ from" their own (Reeder et al. 2005, 1507). Those who are strongly concerned about an issue show an even greater tendency toward this bias. "Highly involved respondents were wary of the hidden motives in the opposition and tended to doubt that the opposition was aware of its own motives" (1508). Those who disagree about an issue, and especially those who strongly disagree, not only have differences of opinions about the facts of the issue or the approach that will be best in addressing the issue, they also perceive entirely different normative motivations in the actions of the other side.

The presence of these various biases should clearly concern theorists of deliberative democracy. If participants in deliberation tend to perceive the sources of their own behavior, as well as their own successes and failures, differently than they view the behavior of others, it is highly unlikely that deliberation can embody the equal consideration and mutual agreement necessary for successful, legitimate democratic collective decision-making. Adding in both moral evaluative and motivational attribution biases, especially since the latter tend to strongly affect people who disagree on exactly those issues that deliberative theory attempts to address, exacerbates the difficulty of reaching mutual agreement even further. Habermas, for example, writes that "communicative freedom exists only between actors who, adopting a performative attitude, want to reach an understanding with one another about something and expect one another to take positions on reciprocally raised validity claims" (1996a, 119). If interlocutors do not view the basic reasons for their respective behaviors similarly, if they tend to judge those who are least like them by stronger moral standards than they judge themselves or those closest to them, and if they attribute unethical and strategic motives to those with whom they disagree, one can hardly imagine how it would be possible for them to give each other equal consideration, reach any sort of mutual understanding, or be able to reciprocally address validity claims. While some may argue that Habermas's theory of communicative rationality is too exacting, since he bases it on the mutual and rational testing of validity claims and it thus includes fairly strong epistemic requirements, the threats of attribution biases also ought to concern other deliberative theorists.

Rawls and Gutmann and Thompson, for example, rest much of their deliberative theory on the concept of public reason. In deliberating, citizens must "publicly appeal to reasons that are shared or could be shared, by their fellow citizens, and if they take into account these same kinds of reasons presented by similarly motivated citizens, then they are engaged in a process that by its nature aims at a justifiable resolution of disagreement"

(Gutmann and Thompson 1996, 25). The difficulty that arises with attribution bias is that citizens may have completely different views of people's behaviors in any given case. As an example, the reasons why some people are poor and others wealthy will likely be very important in deciding policies that affect income distribution. Findings on behavioral attribution bias indicate that a wealthy lawyer will likely view her own economic success arising from her own dispositions, such as hard work and intelligence, while she will likely view the economic failure of others as being due to their dispositions, such as lack of effort or ability. In contrast, a poor laborer will likely attribute his lack of economic success to situations, such as having attended poor schools or facing overwhelming problems in life, while he will likely attribute the success of the wealthy to their life situations, such as coming from a wealthy family or getting the lucky breaks in life that eluded him. Even if they are committed to giving "public reasons," the simple fact that people may not even be able to agree on why things are the way they are will likely significantly reduce the prospects that they will give each other equal consideration or reach any sort of mutually justifiable, and therefore legitimate, agreement.

Let us assume, though, that citizens can agree about why certain situations exist, and yet they still disagree about what ought to be done about them. Gutmann and Thompson acknowledge that citizens will not always reach justifiable agreement, and in the face of this "deliberative disagreement," they suggest that citizens follow the principle of moral accommodation. Moral accommodation embodies equal consideration by requiring that democratic decision-making embody the value of mutual respect, which citizens can uphold by following the principles of civic integrity (integrity in speech, action, and principle) and civic magnanimity (acknowledgment of the moral status of opposing views) (Gutmann and Thompson 1996, 79–91). Attribution bias again raises serious questions about the possibility of deliberation achieving these requirements. The empirical evidence indicates that citizens could commit themselves wholeheartedly to following civic integrity, and yet their fellow citizens could just as wholeheartedly perceive their opponents as having no integrity and camouflaging the real reasons for the proposal. Opponents not only may disagree on what counts as a public reason, it may be impossible for them to see any reason given by opponents as being other than private, self-interested, and morally suspect. The possibility is slim that citizens who perceive their opponents in this manner will sincerely acknowledge the moral status of their opponents' views and give those opponents equal consideration, or even if they think that they are doing so, that their opponents will accept such acknowl-edgment as sincere. That those who are most actively engaged in political issues are the most likely to display this kind of bias leads to further skep-ticism that citizens will perceive deliberation as guided by either civic in-tegrity or civic magnanimity, and if this perception is lacking, it is hard to see how deliberation can succeed. Without overcoming attribution biases, citizens can hardly "aspire to a kind of political reasoning that is mutually justifiable" (52).

It is even hard to see how these citizens could meet the less stringent re-quirements of James Bohman's version of deliberative democracy. Bohman argues that deliberators ought to "modify their conflicting interpretations of the [common] framework so that each can recognize the other's moral values and standards as part of it. The framework is then common enough for each party to continue to cooperate and deliberate with the other" (1996, 91). Such modifications are unlikely to occur in the presence of behavioral and moti-vational attribution biases and inequitable moral evaluation. Motivational attribution bias threatens even Bohman's limited goal of a willingness to continue cooperation and deliberation since opponents will tend to perceive each other as motivated by hidden or unethical agendas, decreasing the likelihood that they will be willing to cooperate and continue deliberation.

Different attributions for behavior create a gulf between the perceptions of actors and observers, a gulf that should concern deliberative democrats. Subsequent research suggests, however, that the empathic process can help close this gap. Dennis Regan and Judith Totten (1975) found that giving people affective role-taking instructions could affect this general tendency for actors and observers to make different behavioral attributions. When an experimental manipulation asked observers to pay attention to what a target was feeling, observers tended to make attributions for the target that were relatively more situational than dispositional; inducing subjects to engage in the affective side of the empathic process led them to see a target's behavior more from the target's own perspective. Many researchers have replicated these findings regarding the ability of affective role-taking instruc-tions to make observers' behavioral attributions much more actor-like (for example, Archer et al. 1979, Betancourt 1990, Galper 1976, and Wegner and Finstuen 1977).[2] Robert Gould and Harold Sigall (1977) also establish

---

2. Michael Storms (1973) discovered that simply reversing point of view through the use of videotaping and replaying a conversation can have the same effect. This suggests that Robert Goodin's argument for the use of film (among other arts) as a way of inducing people to em-pathize and engage in internal-reflective deliberation is not without warrant (2003, 178–83).

the effect of the empathic process on behavioral attributions for successful and unsuccessful behaviors. Subjects induced to affectively empathize
with a target tended to make attributions for the target's behavior similar to
those made by actors about their own behavior (more dispositional for successful behavior and more situational for unsuccessful behavior). As Davis
summarizes, this research indicates that affective role-taking instructions
"lead observers to offer causal attributions which resemble those typically
found among actors" (1994, 96). There is good evidence, then, that instructing people to pay attention to others' feelings will decrease biases they have
regarding those others.

Valerie Melburg and others (1984) reach similar conclusions, though
they maintain that asking subjects to pay attention only to the feelings of
the target is insufficient to produce the effect. They argue that role-playing,
which induces subjects to take the broader perspective of the target, is necessary for changes in observers' attributions of others' behaviors. To test
this, they created three instruction sets for the observers: one asked subjects simply to observe the target's behavior carefully (observation only), a
second followed Gould and Sigall (1977) in asking subjects to empathize
with the target's feelings and reactions (empathy), and the third specifically
told subjects to empathize with the target's feelings but not the target's
intellectual reactions (purified empathy) (Melburg et al. 1984, 204). While
the "purified" empathy instruction did not really distinguish between reactive and parallel empathy, it clearly steered subjects away from a broader
role taking. The data indicate that neither the observation alone nor purified empathy enabled subjects to overcome their attribution biases; only
subjects asked to engage in empathy in the broad sense of paying attention
to the targets' feelings and reactions demonstrated lower levels of bias. The
implication of these results is that previous research, while seemingly con-
fining itself to testing a purely affective mode of empathy, actually tested
empathy in a broader, role-taking sense. These findings support the multidimensional process model of empathy by indicating that both affective
and cognitive sensitivity to others is what helps individuals overcome their
biased perceptions of others' motivations and behaviors.

In addition to indicating the importance of an empathic process involving both affect and cognition, research on attribution biases also points
us toward an understanding of the mechanisms involved in that process.
Since simply observing others, and even paying specific attention only to
their feelings, does not induce people to alter their attribution biases, we
have good evidence that the empathic mechanism of role taking is central

to overcoming such biases. Only activating a purposeful, broad process of role taking can lead to the reduction of biases that can impair effective deliberation. While the data cited to this point cannot fully explain why this is the case, other research points us in what I believe is the right direction. Gerald Sande, George Goethals, and Christine Radloff (1988), though they did not study empathy or the success/failure differentiation, offer one of the more interesting explanations for the original finding of a difference in behavioral attributions. They found that actors tend to see themselves, as well as others who are close to or well liked by them, as having both more and opposing traits. Actors see themselves as versatile, complex, and multifaceted; they do not see one specific trait as being dominant in any given behavior, and thus, the situations in which they find themselves bring forth different traits depending upon the circumstances. The empirical evidence supports the hypothesis that instructing people to be sensitive to others' thoughts and feelings will increase the probability that they will come to see others as more multifaceted and complex, and because of this, be less biased in their attributional judgments. This hypothesis also fits well with the models of affective intelligence and motivated reasoning highlighted earlier. The affective intelligence model indicates that people generally rely upon the disposition system "when the political environment presents familiar friends and foes" (Wolak and Marcus 2007, 189), while the motivated reasoning model suggests that people react to "all political leaders, groups, issues, symbols, and ideas" based upon an affective "evaluative tally" drawn from previous experiences that "comes automatically and inescapably to mind upon presentation of the associated object, thereby signaling its affective coloration" (Lodge and Taber 2005, 456). Both the disposition system's evaluations of the environment and the affective tally serve to simplify our reactions to political stimuli by giving them a coherent, unidimensional character. Specifically instructing people to engage in a process of role taking that asks them to pay attention to the thoughts and feelings of others will increase the likelihood that they will perceive even distant others as multifaceted and complex and thereby interrupt the simplifying processes of the disposition system or the affective tally. Though there is no guarantee that the information search and deeper appraisal that can arise from this interruption will always result in a different evaluation of the political stimuli, research on behavioral attributions at least intimates that the evaluations will be less simplistic. While we cannot know everything about everyone, if we rely primarily on simplistic explanations of others' personalities and behaviors, while viewing ourselves and those close to us as multifaceted and complex, the chances are quite slim that we can reach mutual understanding in deliberation. An intersubjective agreement among deliberators, or even a common framework on which to premise future cooperation, requires that we view others' personalities and behaviors as being as complex as our own. Overcoming judgment biases requires that deliberators engage in a broad process of role taking in which they pay attention, not just to others' thoughts and arguments, but to their feelings as well.

Empathy and Out-Groups

A second area that is important for understanding the role of the empathic process in deliberative democracy comes from a growing literature demonstrating a relationship between empathy and intergroup relations.[3] While the studies on behavioral attributions focus primarily on instructing subjects to engage in role taking of some sort, studies on intergroup relations examine additional components of the process model of empathy including reactive affect, parallel affect, and empathic predispositions. The research in this area demonstrates a generally consistent relationship between the process of empathy and out-group evaluation, but the relationship also appears to be rather complex. Researchers have posited many different constructs to explain the relationship between the process of empathy and positive changes in out-group evaluations.

Like the research on behavioral attributions, several studies on intergroup relations have demonstrated that role-taking instructions can positively affect out-group evaluations. Mark Davis and others (1996) found that giving subjects affective role-taking instructions increased the likelihood that people would ascribe traits to a member of a stigmatized group similar to the traits they ascribed to themselves, especially positive traits. This effect occurred whether the role-taking instructions asked subjects to focus on how the out-group member felt (imagine other) or how they would feel in the out-group member's place (imagine self). Subjects instructed to be objective and not pay attention to the stigmatized group member's

---

3. In this section I focus on intergroup relations and perceptions of out-groups or stigmatized groups. Davis (1994, 100–102) reports various studies that examine the relationship between empathy and liking others, but the conclusions from these studies are mixed, and I believe that "liking" specific others as defined in that literature is less important to democratic deliberation than the intergroup attitudes I discuss in this section.

feelings, though, did not demonstrate the same tendency. While Davis and others utilized affective role-taking instructions, Adam Galinsky and Gordon Moskowitz (2000) examined the effects of more general perspective-taking instructions. They instructed subjects to "imagine a day in the life of this individual as if you were that person, looking at the world through his eyes and walking through the world in his shoes" (2000, 711). The results indicate that general perspective taking can increase positive out-group evaluations and decrease stereotyping over a greater period of time than stereotype suppression instructions, and it does so without creating the hypersensitivity to stereotypes that often accompany stereotype suppression. This evidence indicates that both affective role-taking and general role-taking instructions can increase positive perceptions of stigmatized groups.

Other studies have investigated the relationship between different facets of empathy and out-group evaluations in more depth. Batson, Polycarpou, and others (1997) employed "listening-perspective" instructions to test the effects of empathy on attitudes toward three stigmatized groups: AIDS sufferers, the homeless, and murderers. They measured empathy as reactive affect with subjects' self-reported feelings about the target using six adjectives: sympathetic, compassionate, soft-hearted, warm, tender, and moved. Their results indicate that in all three experiments subjects given the perspective-taking instructions had significantly higher reactive affective empathy toward the specific experimental targets (a woman with AIDS, a homeless man, and a convicted murderer) than those given instructions to take an "objective" view. For AIDS sufferers and the homeless, these positive affective responses to the individual targets generally led to more positive attitudes toward the stigmatized groups of which the targets were members.[4] The effect of perspective-taking instructions was not as strong in the "convicted murderers" experiment, though even in this case, subjects in this condition reported more positive general feelings toward convicted murders in general, and the specific experimental target in particular. This attitude change was more durable than expected. Subjects were interviewed one to two weeks after the experiment; those who had been given "empathy-inducing" instructions still showed more positive attitudes toward the stigmatized group than the "objective" group. Using a similar procedure, Batson and others (2002) discovered that affective perspective-taking instructions increased affective

---

4. One exception occurred in the AIDS experiment. In addition to testing empathy, the researchers manipulated whether the target was "responsible" for her situation. Women who found out that the target acquired AIDS by having unprotected sex showed a defensive derogation of the target that limited the effects of the reactive affective empathy.

reactive empathy toward a target member of a stigmatized group, in this case drug users. This increase in positive reactive affect in turn led to an increased likelihood of helping a member of the stigmatized group by increasing positive attitudes toward the group as a whole. The effect, though diminished, remained significant even when the experimenters indicated that the target was fictional. These studies indicate that paying attention to the feelings of a member of a stigmatized group can increase positive emotions toward that individual, which, in turn, can increase positive attitudes toward the stigmatized group as a whole.

Theresa Vescio, Gretchen Sechrist, and Matthew Paolucci (2003) also examined whether affective perspective-taking instructions and reactive affective empathy can have a positive effect on attitudes toward an outgroup. They were also interested in whether this effect is more important than stereotype suppression strategies, and what role behavioral attribution bias might have in the process. After researchers gave subjects either "imagine other" affective perspective-taking or "objective focus" instructions, and cither a stereotype confirming or disconfirming treatment, subjects then watched an audio interview segment in which an African American discussed difficulties experienced as a result of his out-group membership. The data indicate that the stereotype confirming or disconfirming treatment did affect subsequent stereotype endorsement. Irrespective of this stereotype effect, subjects given affective perspective-taking instructions showed higher "pro-black" attitudes than those told to remain objective, though there was no difference between the groups on "antiblack" attitudes. They then tested the mediating effects of reactive affective empathy, measured with the same adjectives (sympathetic, compassionate, warm-hearted, tender, and moved) and behavioral attribution biases that Batson and others (2002) had used. Unlike previous studies, the results here indicate that "situational attributions were a stronger mediator than [reactive affective] empathy and accounted for the majority of the variance in the relation between perspective taking and intergroup attitudes" (Vescio, Sechrist, and Paolucci 2003, 467).

Krystina Finlay and Walter Stephan (2000) not only investigated role-taking instructions and reactive affect, they also tested the effects of parallel affective reactions and simply reading material about a discriminatory incident (see also Stephan and Finlay 1999). They gave subjects "imagine self" or "imagine other" affective role-taking instructions, or "observation only" instructions, and then had them read one of two firsthand accounts of a discriminatory incident. Since all subjects were Anglo American, they read an account by either an African American who had experienced discrimination within the United States or an Anglo American who had experienced discrimination while attending a university in Hong Kong. They also included a baseline control group that did not receive instructions or read the scenarios. In addition to the instructional sets, Finlay and Stephen measured reactive affective empathy with the adjectives compassion, sympathy, and understanding, and parallel affective empathy with the adjectives anger, annoyance, hostility, discomfort, and disgust.[5] Finlay and Stephan found no differences between the "imagine self" and "imagine other" instructions, so their subsequent analysis combined these groups into one. They discovered that there were no significant effects on reactive affect (compassion, sympathy, and understanding), but there were important effects on the parallel affect measures (anger, annoyance, hostility, discomfort, and disgust). Those who read about discrimination against an African American had more negative feelings toward Anglo Americans than those who read about discrimination against an Anglo American in Hong Kong. In addition, those given the affective role-taking instructions showed less negative attitudes toward African Americans than those given the "observation only" instructions. These parallel affective reactions led to slightly more positive evaluations of the African Americans, the out-group, but more interesting, they led to significantly lower evaluations of Anglo Americans, the in-group. Only those given the "observation only" instructions and then asked to read about discrimination against an Anglo American retained significant differences in their evaluations of in-group and out-group, and in fact, they did not differ significantly from the baseline control group. Either having subjects read a firsthand account of discrimination by an African American or giving subjects affective role-taking instructions eliminated differences between in-group and out-group evaluations. There are several important implications of this research. First, it supports previous findings that affective role-taking instructions can positively affect out-group evaluations. Second, it indicates that such instructions may not always be necessary, given that the affectively loaded firsthand accounts of discrimination induced even those given "observation only" instructions to have more balanced evaluations of in-groups and out-groups. Finally, it indicates that there may be

5. Finlay and Stephan (2000) included indications of these feelings within the text of the self-reports, thus justifying them as parallel affective reactions. It is important to remember that these are only parallel because they are the emotions the text specifically mentioned. These may sometimes qualify as reactive affective reactions, for example, if I respond in anger when I see someone else treated in ways I believe are unjust even if that person herself shows no signs of anger.

times where parallel affective reactions of anger, annoyance, hostility, discomfort, and disgust can change attitudes toward in-groups and out-groups, at least under certain circumstances.

In addition to studies focusing on empathy-inducing instructions of some form, several studies have examined the effects of empathic predispositions on out-group evaluations. These studies tend to focus on two subscales from Davis's Interpersonal Reactivity Index (IRI) (Davis 1980, 1983a). The perspective-taking subscale measures people's self-reported tendency to look at things from others' points of view, and the empathic-concern subscale taps into people's self-reported inclination to have tender and concerned feelings for others in need. One study found that respondents who scored high on the perspective-taking subscale, when asked to evaluate the 1979 seizure of the American embassy in Iran, were "significantly less likely to offer harsh and punitive evaluations of Iran, and . . . also more likely to assign the United States some share of the responsibility for the circumstances leading up to the seizure" (Davis 1994, 102). A second study, in which the researcher posited homosexuals and AIDS sufferers as the out-groups, concluded that higher dispositional scores on both perspective taking and empathic concern "were significantly associated with more favorable attitudes toward both homosexuals and AIDS sufferers" (102). In both cases, predispositions to engage in the empathic process led individuals to have more open evaluations of out-groups.

Beyond role-taking instructions and empathic predispositions, researchers have proposed several factors that may mediate between the empathic process and out-group evaluations. Adam Galinsky and Gillian Ku (2004) argue that a person's self-esteem may have a moderating effect. In two experiments they showed that both chronic and induced high self-esteem increased the positive effects of general perspective-taking instructions on out-group evaluation. Sheri Levy, Antonio Freitas, and Peter Salovey (2002) posit that a key factor relating perspective taking, empathic concern, and helping out-groups is the degree to which observers construe action in abstract terms. Subjects who see others' actions more abstractly perceive greater similarity among persons within and across groups, are more capable of taking the perspective of and feeling empathic concern for others, and are more likely to help others; all of these findings hold whether those others are members of stigmatized or nonstigmatized groups. Though the research I have outlined demonstrates a relationship between empathy and out-group evaluation, the relationship appears to be rather complex. Researchers have posited that affective role-taking instructions, general role-taking instructions, reactive affect, parallel affect, changes in behavioral attributions, self-esteem, abstract action construal, and simply reading about discrimination against out-groups can all have positive effects on out-group evaluations. The one consistent finding, however, is that the process of empathy, in all its complexity, increases the likelihood that people will have less negative, or even more positive, evaluations of out-groups.

While the studies cited so far have examined general attitudes, one study examined the relationship between an empathic predisposition and deliberation. Diana Mutz (2002) studied the relationship between Davis's perspective-taking subscale and subjects' openness to contrary opinions during deliberation. She concludes that for "those high in perspective-taking ability, mean levels of tolerance were higher when subjects were exposed to rationales for dissonant views. However, among those low in perspective-taking ability, tolerance levels were lower when subjects were exposed to dissonant views, although the higher variance among this group makes this a suggestive, though not significant difference" (121). The tentative conclusion from Mutz's research is that people with higher predispositions for perspective taking are, at the least, more consistently open to opinions that conflict with their own.

This research relating empathy and out-groups provides persuasive evidence that the empathic process is vital if deliberative democracy is to function as envisioned by theorists and give equal consideration to all. One of the key components of deliberative democracy is reciprocity. "The ideal of reciprocity," Robert George argues, "is realized in practice when, or to the extent that, citizens understand and accept the obligation to justify their positions to those fellow citizens who reasonably disagree" (1999, 189). Reciprocity requires citizens committed to finding "fair terms of social cooperation; it cannot reach those who refuse to press their public claims in terms accessible to their fellow citizens" (Gutmann and Thompson 1996, 55). Deliberative democracy requires that interlocutors remain open to the experiences and positions of others, especially others that society usually stigmatizes. As James Bohman notes, "Minorities in particular have difficulty receiving uptake in deliberation, because they also suffer from persistent social inequalities" (1996, 105). The empirical evidence indicates that various aspects of the empathic process can induce citizens to be open to the experiences and views of others, including those marginalized by society. Without the process of empathy, it is highly unlikely that citizens will demonstrate the toleration, mutual respect, reciprocity, and openness toward others vital for a deliberative democracy to fulfill its promise of equal consideration that is central to giving collective decisions their legitimacy.

Altruism and Helping Behavior

I do not believe that deliberative democracy requires altruistic or helping-oriented citizens, though citizens who tended to help their fellow citizens might produce positive benefits. Even if one wanted to argue that these were necessities, the evidence on the links among empathy, altruism, and helping behavior are highly contested. The original impetus for this field of research was Batson's empathy-induced altruism hypothesis, for which numerous experiments have provided support (see Batson 1991 for a review). Recently, though, other researchers have questioned the interpretation of these results. In an interesting and direct exchange, these two camps debated whether helping behavior was due to empathy-induced altruism or self-other merging (Cialdini et al. 1997; Batson, Sager, et al. 1997; Neuberg et al. 1997; Batson 1997). Jon Maner and others (2002) employ structural equation models and conclude that after controlling for nonaltruistic motivation, especially a measure of the subject's feeling of "oneness" with the target, the impact of empathic concern (reactive empathy) on helping behavior disappears. Despite the unsettled questions in these debates, there are findings in this literature that are important for our understanding of the relationship between empathy and deliberative democracy.

The first findings concern experiments involving prisoner's dilemma games. Previous research has shown that players in a prisoner's dilemma game are more likely to cooperate if there is some communication between them prior to engaging in the game (see, for example, Orbell, Van de Kragt, and Dawes 1988); this gives indirect evidence that empathizing may importantly influence the way people approach conflict situations. More direct evidence comes from two studies that examine the role of affective role-taking instructions on a prisoner's dilemma game. C. Daniel Batson and Tecia Moran (1999) find that altruism induced by affective role-taking instructions increased the likelihood of cooperation across two different framings of the prisoner's dilemma game, a business frame and a social frame.[6] Batson

---

6. I find it interesting that, absent empathy induction, the business frame led to less cooperation than the social frame. This should be of interest to deliberative democrats, for to my knowledge there has been little theoretical or empirical examination of the way in which framing occurs in the deliberative process.

and Nadia Ahmad (2001) conclude that altruism induced by affective role-taking instructions increases cooperation even in cases where the target of empathy has already defected, although not as much as in cases where the target of empathy has not defected. In both studies, the researchers also found that the subjects' self-reported levels of reactive affective empathy mediated the experimental manipulation's effect by increasing the likelihood of cooperation; this demonstrates that the affective role-taking instructions alone were not key to the outcomes. Whether or not reactive affective empathizing results in altruism is not important for my discussion; what is important is to observe that affective role-taking instructions and self-reported reactive affect can increase cooperation in even highly conflictual situations.

Deliberative democracy relies upon citizens to engage with each other in a cooperative manner. While the analogy to the prisoner's dilemma game is not exact, I believe that deliberative democracy and prisoner's dilemma games are sufficiently alike to support the claim that empathizing will likely encourage citizen cooperation, and thereby, a successfully functioning deliberative democracy. It is undeniable that conflict is an inherent part of any political process, deliberative or not, but deliberative democracy posits mutual cooperation and equal consideration as keys to legitimately dealing with such conflict. As Benhabib articulates, the procedures of democracy themselves provide the basis for mutual cooperation: "Democratic procedures have to convince, even under conditions when one's interests as an individual or group are negatively affected, that the conditions of mutual cooperation are still legitimate. Procedures can be regarded as methods for articulating, sifting through, and weighing conflicting interests. . . . Proceduralist models of democracy allow the articulation of conflicts of interests under conditions of social cooperation mutually acceptable to all" (1996, 73). Yet are procedures alone enough? If participants in deliberation are not predisposed toward the cooperation necessary for reaching a reasoned agreement, or at least induced to go in this direction, deliberative democratic procedures cannot function. The process of empathy can help bridge this gap between participant's commitments and the procedures of deliberation by encouraging citizens to enter deliberation with a cooperative attitude toward their fellow interlocutors. Without such a cooperative attitude, no matter how well structured the procedures, the threat of impasse and breakdown looms large.

While these findings offer evidence that the empathic process can help a deliberative democracy function properly, a second set of findings provides a cautionary note about empathy. Batson, Batson, and others (1995) argue that empathy-induced altruism can actually conflict with the common good. In an allocation of scarce resources, subjects could choose to allocate in ways that benefited themselves, the group as a whole, or specific others; those subjects in whom researchers induced empathy tended to allocate more to the target of empathy, even though this meant harming others in the group. Batson and others (1999) went further and developed an experiment that showed that both self-interested egoism and empathy-induced altruism can threaten the common good. The evidence also demonstrates that requiring subjects to make allocations in public reduced the self-interested egoists' tendencies to give themselves more than others did, but empathy-induced altruists still tended to benefit the targets of empathy to the detriment of the group as a whole. Both these experiments involved a relatively benign resource (raffle tickets), but Batson, Klein, and others (1995) utilized experimental manipulations with more serious resources in studying the effects of empathy-induced altruism on justice. In one experiment, subjects decided whether or not they would move a needy child ahead of other needy children on a waiting list for help, even though subjects knew that the list ranked children based upon their needs, the threat to their health, and how long they had been on the list.[7] The findings consistently indicate that subjects in the empathy condition tended to favor the targets of empathy, even when subjects reported that they recognized their actions were unjust (unfair) and perceived themselves to be acting less morally than those in the control condition did.[8] These experiments demonstrate that inducing people to empathize can lead them to be partial toward the object of empathy, even if that partiality may harm others.

Such partiality is clearly contrary to the needs of a deliberative democracy, especially the need for equal consideration. In describing deliberative democracy in legislative practice, Habermas states that "one can understand the complex validity claim of legal norms as the claim, on the one hand, to compromise competing interests in a manner compatible with the common good and, on the other hand, to bring universalistic principles of justice into the horizon of the specific form of life of a particular community" (1996b, 25). If empathizing leads citizens to ignore both the common

---

7. Subjects were not aware that the target of empathy and the other children were fictional.

8. There are some problems with the instructions for the experiment and the measures for these findings, as the instructions and measures appear to frame justice, morality, and fairness as impartiality. Subjects would have been hard pressed in this situation to claim that they acted justly or morally after having just shown partiality; still, I think the findings are illuminating.

good and principles of justice, it just might mitigate against the very philosophical underpinnings that recommend deliberative democracy as a superior alternative to other forms of democracy. It is important to note, however, that in each of these experiments the researchers induced subjects to empathize with only *one* of the others involved. Not only did the researchers not induce the subject to empathize with all others, in every experiment the subjects knew only vague and limited information about those other than the target of empathy. Instead of being an argument against deliberative democracy, I would argue that these findings bolster the case in favor of a more open, more inclusive deliberative democratic process. In an aggregative democratic process, citizens are going to know or be close to only a limited number of their fellow citizens; unless they must engage with others with whom they are unfamiliar, they are unlikely to give equal consideration except to those who are close to them. Deliberative democracy aims to overcome this bias by making these unknown others more present, for example, through face-to-face deliberations, or, as Goodin argues, through media such as film and literature. Inducing citizens to empathize with more of their fellow citizens will make them less likely to violate justice. Still, these findings suggest that deliberative democrats must be vigilant in insuring that excluded others are present, either literally or figuratively, in deliberations. There is a constant need to prevent selective inclusion in the deliberative process (see Goodin 2003, 194–208). Without doing so, a deliberative democracy is unlikely to achieve the equal consideration necessary for collective decisions to remain legitimate.

Reciprocity and the Commitment to Continued Deliberation

In addition to the empirical research generated by others, my colleague Adam Kanter and I also conducted an experimental study to examine the empirical effects of empathy. We found that the levels of empathic predispositions within deliberative groups can have positive effects on several measures of reciprocity and a commitment to continued deliberation, even when we controlled for participants who were winners and losers at the end of the deliberative process.

As I have already shown, reciprocity is one of the key concepts in deliberative theory. Habermas (1996b) argues that deliberation is a process of reciprocal recognition, implied by the very nature of politics itself, wherein individuals who compose society come together to do good for everyone.

For Rawls, reciprocity defines the way in which we must deliberate by specifying that "our exercise of political power is proper only when we sincerely believe that the reasons we offer for our political action may reasonably be accepted by other citizens as a justification of those actions" (1996, xlvi). For both theorists, when people deliberate, they do not simply put ideas on display but actually have *reciprocal* discussions among affected parties. Reciprocity is thus one of the most important ways in which deliberation embodies democracy's promise of equal respect. Gutmann and Thompson have the most developed concept of reciprocity, positing it as one of deliberative democracy's foundational principles (1996, 52–94). In the face of deliberative disagreement, reciprocity invokes principles that they call "principles of accommodation" (79–91), which they derive from the value of mutual respect that "lies at the core of reciprocity and deliberation in a democracy" (79). Mutual respect "requires a favorable attitude toward, and constructive interaction with, the persons with whom one disagrees" (79); and arising out of mutual respect are two principles of accommodation: civic integrity and civic magnanimity. Civic magnanimity "calls on citizens and officials to acknowledge the moral status of the positions they oppose" (82) and has three components: acknowledgment in speech of the moral status of others' positions, open-mindedness to others' positions, and the seeking of rationales that minimize the rejection of others' positions (an "economy of moral disagreement"). Thus, reciprocity requires that citizens, even and especially when they disagree with their fellow citizens, recognize, acknowledge, remain open to, and accommodate the arguments put forward in deliberation by others as moral positions. In our experimental work, we focused on mutual respect in the broader sense and the open-mindedness and economy of moral disagreement components of civic magnanimity as representative of the concept of reciprocity.[9]

Bohman also argues that deliberation should lead to moral compromises in which citizens "modify their conflicting interpretations of the [common] framework so that each can recognize the other's moral values and standards as part of it" (1996, 91). Yet unlike some other theories of deliberation, Bohman's does not require consensus on the substance of such compromises. Habermas, for example, argues that "the democratic principle

9. The first principle of civic magnanimity, civic integrity, requires consistency in speech, consistency between speech and action, and integrity of principle, and while it may be possible to construct empirical measures of these, we chose to focus on those concepts that we could confidently measure within our experimental methodology. Despite our efforts, we were also unable to measure the first component of civic magnanimity: acknowledgment of others' positions as moral.

states that only those statutes may claim legitimacy that can meet with the assent (*Zustimmung*) of *all* citizens in the discursive process of legislation that in turn has been legally constituted" (1996a, 110; emphasis added). In contrast to this strong notion of a substantive consensus, Bohman argues that reasons given in deliberation are legitimate "when they are convincing enough to motivate each citizen, even a dissenter, to continue to cooperate in deliberation even after the decision has been made" (1996, 35). Thus, the criterion for determining deliberation's success is not whether citizens reach consensus based upon the same reasons, but whether they agree to *continue deliberation* even when they are on the losing end of a decision.

The studies cited earlier indicate the strong probability that the empathic process (in both its cognitive and affective dimensions) can buttress reciprocity and a commitment to continued deliberation by affecting out-group evaluations. Open-mindedness and sensitivity to others are psychological attitudes that mutual respect and civic magnanimity inherently require; citizens who show little positive regard for out-groups will be very unlikely to meet deliberation's exacting requirements for reciprocity. These attitudes would also seem to be a minimal requirement for a commitment to continued deliberation. In one description of the deliberative process, Bohman posits that "novel interpretations signify the success of a dialogue, measured in the uptake of other points of view and reasons into speakers' own interpretations of the ongoing course of discussion" (1996, 58). A deliberative process in which different groups do not display an openness to one another is one in which there is likely to be a breakdown in communication, and in the end, very few participants are likely to commit to continue deliberating in such an environment. It seems impossible to expect the uptake Bohman requires if citizens do not demonstrate open-mindedness and sensitivity to each other. Based upon the empirical data, we believe that the process of empathy will likely increase the chances that deliberators will exhibit reciprocity and a commitment to continued deliberation. The process model provides several variables for testing this hypothesis, and since several studies I have cited point to the importance of empathic dispositions, we decided to examine whether the levels of predispositions to empathy within a group would positively affect reciprocity and a commitment to continued deliberation.

Though we hypothesized that group empathy levels can positively affect deliberation, research indicates that winning and losing can also have a strong impact on political attitudes. Being on the winning or losing side in an election can affect attitudes such as political efficacy (Clarke and Acock 1989) and political trust (Anderson and LoTempio 2002). In a broader, comparative study of the effects of electoral success, Christopher Anderson and others concluded that "being the political majority generally translates into more positive attitudes toward government, while losers tend to exhibit significantly more negative attitudes toward the political system" (2005, 183). While they discovered evidence that this effect can vary across countries and over time, the general trend they found was that losers, especially consistent losers, view democratic systems as less legitimate. In a more specific study of deliberation, I also found that losing had a negative effect on collective decision acceptance in a one-shot deliberative experiment (Morrell 1999). This evidence strongly supports the conjecture that winning and losing will have a significant effect on participants' evaluations of deliberation. Thus, in addition to testing group empathy levels, we also controlled for whether subjects won or lost during the deliberation.

We chose an experimental research design that would allow us to examine the effects of both group levels of empathic predispositions and winning and losing on citizens' perceptions of reciprocity and their commitment to continued deliberation. Our test examined what we call *deliberative decision-making*, in which winning and losing might be a factor in participants' perceptions of the process. It would have been impossible to find "real life" examples of deliberative decision-making for which we could randomly assign participants in order to test the effects of group empathy levels, and thus, an experimental method was the most methodologically sound choice. We gave subjects a pretest, and immediately following this, gave each subject reading material including essays and Web sites supporting both sides of the issue. Using the results of the pretest, we assigned subjects to groups with stratification based upon their predispositions to empathy, gender, and position on the issue. We measured subjects' predispositions to empathy by adding subjects' scores on Davis's IRI empathic-concern and perspective-taking subscales (see Davis 1983a and 1983b). We created two experimental groups (low empathy and high empathy) and one control group by randomly assigning subjects based upon their IRI scores such that members of the low and high empathy groups were below or above the median empathy score for their stratification set determined by gender and issue position, while the control group had subjects both above and below the median. Though the control group participated in deliberation, they were not subject to the experimental manipulation on group empathy level. They represented, instead, what a random distribution of subjects would create on the group empathy level variable, and we thus used them to compare the relative effects of *high* or *low* group empathy on deliberation. The week after the pretest, subjects engaged in deliberations led by randomly assigned moderators. After the deliberation, moderators passed out and collected secret ballots, tallied the results, announced the winning side, and administered the posttest surveys.

We included several indexes of the variables associated with reciprocity and commitment to continued deliberation to test our hypotheses. The first index we generated measures the value of mutual respect that lies at the core of reciprocity. The open-mindedness index measures whether subjects perceived group members as truly open to other's arguments, and whether subjects acknowledged the possibility that others had something positive to contribute. This index operationalizes the open-mindedness component of Gutmann and Thompson's concept of civic magnanimity. To measure the economy of moral disagreement, the third component of civic magnanimity (Gutmann and Thompson 1996, 84–85), we used an index I developed in an earlier study (see Morrell 2003). The traditional measure of external political efficacy focuses on citizens' perceptions of the political system's responsiveness to their input (see Craig, Niemi, and Silver 1990); we adapted this to deliberation by creating a situation-specific external efficacy index, which measures whether subjects felt that they had a say in what the group decided and whether the other group members cared about what they thought. To measure participants' willingness to continue deliberation, we used the enjoyment index developed in studies of strategic decision-making (see Schweiger, Sandberg, and Ragan 1986; Schweiger, Sandberg, and Rechner 1989; and Schwenk and Cosier 1993); this index measures the degree to which subjects enjoyed the deliberative experience and are willing to work with the same group in the future. Table 1 provides a summary of our indexes and the concepts and principles they measure. We hypothesized that, for all indexes, the high empathy group would have higher average scores than the control group, which would have higher average scores than the low empathy group. We also hypothesized that winners would have higher scores on average than losers for all indexes.

To test our conjectures, we ran ordinary least squares regressions with each index as the dependent variable and independent variables for winning and losing and dichotomous dummy variables for the low and high empathy groups. To control for the possibility that individual predispositions for empathic concern or perspective taking might be the real cause of any effects we might find, we entered these as separate control variables. We present the results from our analysis for each index, as well as a measure that aggregates the other four indexes into one, in table 2.

Table 1   Measures of reciprocity and commitment to continued deliberation

Concept	Principle	Index
Reciprocity	Mutual respect	Mutual respect[a]
Reciprocity	Civic magnanimity I: Open-mindedness	Open-mindedness[b]
Reciprocity	Civic magnanimity II: Economy of moral disagreement	Situation-specific external efficacy[c]
Commitment to continued deliberation		Enjoyment[d]

NOTE: All measures used items with a response scale range of 1 to 7 from strongly agree to strongly disagree, except for the situation-specific external efficacy index, which used items with a scale range of 1 to 5 from strongly agree to strongly disagree to make it comparable to other surveys. Items are coded so that higher scores indicate more positive evaluations.
[a] Mutual respect index (range 3 to 21)
I felt that the other group members did not accept me as part of the group.
The other group members respected my views on the issue we discussed.
Most of the conflict in our group focused on the issue itself.
[b] Open-mindedness index (range 3 to 21)
I found myself annoyed with other group members.
The other group members were closed-minded. They wouldn't fully consider all points of view.
The other group members seemed to argue a point just for the sake of argument.
[c] Situation-specific external efficacy index (range 2 to 10)
People like me had no say about what the group did when deciding the issues discussed.
I don't think other members of the group cared much what people like me thought.
[d] Enjoyment index (range 2 to 14)
I would be willing to work with this group on other projects in the future.
Working with my group was an enjoyable experience.

The data confirm that winning or losing was a significant independent variable in our models. Winning had a highly statistically and substantively significant positive effect on participants' perceptions of open-mindedness and their commitment to continued deliberation. Being on the winning side at the end of deliberation, controlling for all other variables, increased perceptions of open-mindedness by 3.3 on an index with a range of 18 (+18.3 percent of the possible difference), and increased enjoyment by 1.56 on an index that had a range of 12 (+13 percent of the possible difference). Winning also had a substantively significant positive effect on the economy of moral disagreement as measured by the situation-specific external efficacy index, creating an increase of 0.94 on an index with range of 8 (+11.8 percent). The only index for which winning or losing did not have a significant effect was mutual respect.

While winning or losing was important, the high empathy group variable also had significant positive effects. The most statistically significant

Table 2   OLS regression of deliberation evaluation indexes for group empathy experiment

	Mutual respect	Open-mindedness	Situation-specific external efficacy	Enjoyment	Aggregate evaluations of deliberation
Winning/losing	1.00	3.30[b]	0.94[a]	1.56[b]	3.40[b]
	(0.67)	(0.95)	(0.39)	(0.58)	(0.98)
Low group empathy	1.16	0.20	1.02[a]	0.87	3.25
	(0.74)	(1.05)	(0.43)	(0.64)	(2.16)
High group empathy	1.25	2.44[a]	0.93[a]	2.08[b]	6.69[b]
	(0.75)	(1.07)	(0.44)	(0.65)	(2.20)
Empathic concern	0.03	−0.17	−0.04	0.00	−0.18
	(0.08)	(0.11)	(0.05)	(0.07)	(0.23)
Perspective taking	0.03	−0.09	0.02	0.02	−0.02
	(0.08)	(0.12)	(0.05)	(0.07)	(0.24)
N	97	97	97	97	97
Adjusted r^2	0.03	0.11	0.10	0.15	0.16

NOTE: Entries represent unstandardized ordinary least-squares regression coefficients. Standard errors in parentheses.

[a] $p < .05$

[b] $p < .01$

effect of the high empathy group was on participants' commitment to continued deliberation. Being in the high empathy group resulted in a 2.08 increase on the enjoyment index, which represents 17.3 percent of the possible difference. For both open-mindedness and the economy of moral disagreement, the high empathy group variable had statistically significant effects, with substantive increases of 2.44 (13.5 percent) and 0.93 (11.6 percent) respectively. It also approached having a significant effect on perceptions of mutual respect. Statistically significant at the .10 level, being in the high empathy group generated a 1.25 point increase on the mutual respect index (8.7 percent of the possible difference).

There are several other notable results in Table 2. First, participants in the low empathy group did not, as hypothesized, demonstrate lower evaluations of the deliberation than those in the control group on any of the indexes. In fact, being in the low empathy group had a slightly more positive effect on the situation-specific external efficacy index than either being in the high empathy group or winning the vote. Statistically significant at the .05 level, the low empathy group variable increased perceptions of the economy of moral disagreement by 1.02 points (12.8 percent of possible difference), controlling for all other variables. We also note that the control variables for predispositions to empathy (empathic concern and perspective taking) did not have any significant affects.

Finally, we wanted to create a measure that looked at the overall evaluations that subjects had of the deliberative process. To produce this measure, we aggregated the other four indexes into one evaluative score and ran our model using it as the dependent variable. As the results indicate, winning or losing and being in the high empathy group both had statistically and substantively significant effects on the aggregate measure. Whether citizens win or lose during deliberative decision-making has an important effect on their evaluations of the deliberative process, but even controlling for this effect, when citizens who have high predispositions to empathy deliberate together they grade the process much more positively than citizens in mixed or low empathy groups.

Our results lead to several important conclusions on the relationships among empathic predispositions, winning or losing, and citizens' perceptions of deliberation. For the economy of moral disagreement, the first component of civic magnanimity, the results for the situation-specific external efficacy index are unclear. While both winning and high group empathy had positive effects on external efficacy low group empathy had a similar effect. One could argue that we did not effectively measure perceptions of the economy of moral disagreement, but given the measures we chose to employ, we conclude that winning and being in a group that is homogeneous on empathy levels (whether high or low) had similar positive effects on participants perceptions of their impact on the deliberative decision. We need further research to determine what factors might contribute to a deliberative process in which those who disagree on moral issues are more likely to work together to find as much common ground as possible, but our data have little clear to say about this component of civic magnanimity.

Interpreting the results for open-mindedness, the other component of civic magnanimity, is much easier. As we hypothesized, winners were more likely than losers to perceive that the deliberation was open-minded. Winning was not the only important factor here, however, as high group empathy had a significant effect on the open-mindedness index. Our experiment provides evidence that group levels of empathic predispositions, even after controlling for the effects of winning or losing and individual empathic predispositions, can increase the probability that citizens will perceive deliberation as open-minded, and through this, contribute to improving the deliberative process.

Mutual respect was the only index on which winning or losing did not have an effect. High group empathy was the only factor that had a significant and positive impact on mutual respect. Groups composed of citizens who have a tendency to both see others' viewpoints and feel concerned for those others are more likely to engage in deliberation they perceive as characterized by mutual respect. Since mutual respect is such an important component of reciprocity, this supports the claim that group empathic predispositions are an important factor if we are to achieve the kinds of deliberation advocated by political theorists.

We now turn to Bohman's requirement that citizens make a commitment to continued deliberation even if their own position does not win in deliberation. The data indicate that winning had positive and significant effects on the enjoyment index. This is not highly surprising, as we might expect those who win on a vote to indicate greater enjoyment of the decision-making process and a greater willingness to continue deliberations in the future. The enjoyment index asks respondents whether they enjoyed working with their group and whether they would be willing to work with the group again in the future. As such, it clearly measures what Bohman requires. Members of the high empathy group, even after controlling for the effects of winning and losing, scored higher on this measure on average than members of the control or low empathy groups. The high empathy variable even had a greater substantive impact on this index than winning or losing. Thus, our data provide good evidence that although winning and losing are important, the levels of predispositions to empathy within deliberating groups are a significant factor in determining whether citizens, even when they lose, will commit themselves to a continued process of deliberation.

Implications of Empirical Research

The empirical research I have surveyed supports several conclusions about the effects the process of empathy can have on deliberative democracy. Most important, it appears highly likely that we need citizens to engage in the process of empathy if deliberative democracy is to function properly. In order to decrease biases and polarization, and increase cooperation and reciprocity, deliberators must demonstrate predispositions to both perspective taking and empathic concern, and the deliberative democratic system must somehow encourage citizens to act on those predispositions. Without the process of empathy, deliberation is highly unlikely to embody the equal consideration necessary for legitimate democratic decision-making. Based upon the process model and the empirical literature, there seem to be two basic options on this point.[10] The first, as I have argued elsewhere in a broader context, is that we ought to include empathy as part of democratic education (Morrell 2007). In doing so we can aim at increasing citizens' predispositions for empathy, specifically for perspective taking and empathic concern, so that they will be more likely to take into account the perspectives of their fellow deliberators. While giving citizens predispositions for empathy does not guarantee that they will actually engage in the process of empathy during deliberation, it significantly increases the likelihood that this will happen.

A second option is to try to induce empathy in the deliberative democratic system itself. One possible approach to this is to follow Goodin's recommendations regarding internal-reflective deliberation. It is possible that through presentations in literature, film, and other arts that we can encourage citizens to be empathetically sensitive, and thus, consider how public policies and laws affect those who are not immediately present. The advantage of this approach is that it appears much more practical than attempting to induce empathy by having all (or even most) citizens in a large-scale society actually meet face-to-face with each other. The policy implications of this approach may include public funding for libraries and the arts, moves to increase the representativeness of the arts, and moves toward more social mixing (see Goodin 2003, 189–92). While we could debate which specific public policies will support this form of "deliberation within," it is likely that it would stimulate citizens to empathize with more of their fellow citizens. The empirical research on empathy suggests a second, related approach for both "deliberation within" and face-to-face deliberation. Moderators could specifically instruct citizens engaged in deliberation to pay attention to the feelings and perspectives of their fellow citizens, and we could use public rhetoric that specifically promotes this as the proper approach citizens should take to public questions. This may seem facile, and citizens could easily ignore the instructions, but if we could get citizens to take such admonitions seriously, it would go a long way toward encouraging citizens to engage in the process of empathy. Supplementing deliberative theories with a democratic education for empathy, an increase in

10. Though early childhood experiences also affect people's capacity to empathize, I do not believe this offers us a clear option for addressing the need for empathy in deliberation (see Hoffman 2000).

funding for the arts that could induce greater empathy in citizens, and the encouragement of deliberative forums that include moderators who specifically ask citizens to engage in empathy, improves the persuasiveness of those theories. Yet I believe we need more to do more than simply supplement deliberative theory. I will show why this is the case by examining the critics of deliberative democratic theory, but in defending deliberation against their charges, I will demonstrate that we need to entirely recast deliberative theory by placing the empathic process at the heart of deliberation. This is the only way for us to insure that democracy can move toward fulfilling its promise to give all citizens equal consideration and still allow for legitimate democratic decisions.

6

DELIBERATIVE DEMOCRACY AND ITS CRITICS

The empirical evidence indicates that the process of empathy is necessary if deliberative democracy is going to function as conceived in the core deliberative theories. Without empathizing citizens, deliberative democracy will likely be no more than a talkative form of aggregative democracy. Yet there is an alternative, further-reaching conclusion suggested by this evidence: constructing a theory of deliberative democracy with the process model of empathy in view requires a shift in our thinking about the purpose of deliberation and its connection to democratic legitimacy. Deliberation is necessary to move closer to a more equal consideration of all citizens in a democratic society, and it can serve as a necessary component of democratic legitimacy, but only if we no longer conceive of deliberation as focused solely on argumentation and justification. In order to demonstrate this, I will examine how the process model of empathy can help deliberative theory respond to the challenges raised by its critics in novel ways that strengthen the persuasiveness of the deliberative model. Such an approach makes clear that we must alter or reject some of the positions previous deliberative theorists have taken on the issues of rationality and the forms of legitimate communication in deliberation, legitimacy and the role of consent in democracy, and inclusion and the path toward impartiality in democratic judgment.

Affect, Cognition, and Reason

As I have already noted, one of the primary criticisms of deliberative theories is that they misconceive the relationships among affect, cognition, and reason. Political psychologists and political theorists argue that deliberative theorists inaccurately conceive of reason as a cognitive process that is or should be generally affect-free. Although speaking about evaluations of candidates, David Redlawsk sums up this position nicely: "Political scientists who prefer voters as affect-free calculators who coolly consider candidates and make even-handed evaluations if simply given enough information miss a critical piece of the puzzle. Affect counts. We can no more process political information without being aware of how it makes us feel than we can make reasoned candidate choices with no information at all" (2002, 1041). While some deliberative theorists have shown a greater openness to affect, we still must clarify the import of integrating affect, cognition, and reason in deliberation. The process model can assist us in doing so.

The Centrality of Affect in Political Reasoning

In Chapter 1 I highlighted the two most prominent theories in political psychology that address the relationships among affect, cognition, and reason in political judgment. The affective intelligence theory (Marcus 2000, 2002, 2003; Marcus, Neuman, and MacKuen 2000; Wolak and Marcus 2007) posits that two brain systems constantly monitor stimuli: the disposition and surveillance systems. The disposition system evaluates behavior to determine its success and is central to the formation of habits. Over a period of time the disposition system marks stimuli and situations in such a way that it can provide feedback on our habitual behavior. When we encounter familiar sensory input for which the disposition system has already determined the appropriate response, it monitors our behavior and responds with positive or negative feedback. We rely upon these habitual responses in order to function, and they apply to politics just as to other inputs: "We rely on proven habits to decide whether to listen to political rhetoric or dismiss it, to react warmly or coldly to political appeal" (Marcus 2002, 72). The disposition system relies upon an affective marker in its functioning, and the most prominent is enthusiasm. Successful behaviors elicit enthusiasm, but so too does the appearance of political objects that the disposition system connects with positive habits. In contrast, the disposition system reacts by dampening down enthusiasm for unsuccessful behaviors, and can even react with anger or loathing in the presence of political objects that it assesses negatively. A political "friend" can release positive feelings and enthusiasm, a political "enemy" negative feelings and even anger.

The surveillance system, in contrast, monitors our current plan of action with an eye toward the expected outcome in the environment, and compares those expectations with the input from the sensory streams entering the brain. If there is some discord between expectations and environment, the surveillance system interrupts ongoing behavior and shifts awareness to that which is novel or threatening in the environment. It leads us to take account of our environment by gathering information and reflecting on how to respond. As with the disposition system, the surveillance system relies upon an affective marker, in this case anxiety. Thus, it is only when the surveillance system activates anxiety that we begin to deliberate (Marcus 2002, 116).

Marcus applies the theory of affective intelligence to criticize certain expectations of democratic citizens. Emotions such as enthusiasm and anxiety are important to the way citizens respond to the political system, and democratic theorists who conceive of citizens as rational, unemotional decision makers misperceive how human beings function. Habits marked by enthusiasm allow us to navigate in a complex society, and they can also reinforce positive behaviors necessary in a democratic society. Yet the disposition system is also important in learning new habits beneficial to a democratic society, something that would be impossible without emotion. Anxiety is required if we ever want citizens to engage in deliberation regarding their political world. Citizens' abilities to feel anxiety is what can persuade them "to set aside [their] familiar views and to reflect on what is now required" (Marcus 2002, 140). The expectation that citizens will respond to every political issue with deliberation is unrealistic. They will remain inattentive and rely upon habits for most issues, a strategy that allows them to function; and yet when the surveillance system reacts with anxiety to a situation, people become exactly the kind of deliberating citizens democratic theorists desire. Marcus acknowledges that emotion is not always a positive force in democratic society. Habits tend to be conservative and parochial, and the disposition system can encourage a search for disconfirming information in the face of a challenge to our ingrained habits. The disposition system can even come to rely on the destructive emotion of loathing in reaction to political stimuli (Marcus 2002, chap. 7). People tend to be uncomfortable with anxiety. Marcus's point, though, is not to valorize emotion over deliberation. Rather, he maintains that recognizing how human beings function is vital for democratic theorists because it will allow "a more vibrant and complex intermeshing of thought and feeling" and give us "a sounder understanding of how democracy is possible and how political deliberation can be foundationally anchored in our natures rather than merely impelled by institutional imposition and constraint" (147).

Political psychologists defending the "hot cognition" hypothesis make similar arguments (see, for example, Lodge and Taber 2000 and 2005; Lodge, Taber, and Weber 2006; and Redlawsk 2002). Hot cognition is a component of the motivated political reasoning theory. The basic assumption of the theory is that affect permeates all thinking and reasoning. "Affect imbues the judgment process from start to finish—from the encoding of information, its retrieval and comprehension, to its expression as a preference or choice" (Lodge and Taber 2005, 456). Over time people construct evaluative tallies of objects, including political objects, that "appear to reflect a summing up of one's prior evaluations, a distillation of the evaluative implications of most if not all relevant information one has been exposed to" (476). Since these evaluative tallies respond to all of the information people encounter, they involve a coupling of "affect and cognition in long-term memory" (456). Hot cognition enters the picture whenever people must respond to some political stimuli. In ways similar to the disposition system in affective intelligence, the brain will automatically respond with the appropriate affective markers whenever people encounter stimuli for which an evaluative tally exists: positive affect if the tally is positive and negative if negative.[1]

The problem for democratic theory is that automatic affective reactions by citizens may have deleterious consequences. Citizens will often be biased in their reactions to political stimuli (Redlawsk 2002). "They are apt to see congruent arguments as inherently stronger than those which are attitudinally incongruent; they spend time and cognitive resources counter-arguing the points that challenge their priors; they seek to insulate themselves from challenging information by actively searching out congruent information" (Lodge and Taber 2005, 456). As we have seen, this can lead to polarization, especially among citizens with strong attitudes, and holds true even for citizens trying to be "impartial." "Even when motivated to be even-handed, 'to leave their feelings aside,' people find it near impossible to view political policy arguments dispassionately (on gun control, affirmative action, federal support for the arts, etc.)" (476). Since all human beings are structured to engage in motivated reasoning, it is a fact of political life that most citizens most of the time will fall prey to this bias. "Thus, we

---

1. There are at least two important differences between motivated reasoning and affective intelligence. Motivated reasoning does not contain a parallel to the surveillance system and it does not specify discrete emotional valences (e.g., enthusiasm, loathing, anxiety) as affective intelligence theory does. Neither difference is that important to the argument I am developing here.

cannot really hope to avoid every bias affect brings. At best, by understanding the nature of these biases we can devise ways to correct for them" (Redlawsk 2002, 1041).

Despite these negative findings, there are a few rays of hope for deliberative theorists in the studies of hot cognition. Lodge and Taber highlight that the hot cognition hypothesis supports the idea "that people internalize simple summary evaluations, formed spontaneously as part of an online evaluation process, as they encounter political information. Once formed, such running tallies (or more accurately, links) provide a ready-made liking heuristic to guide future behavior" (Lodge and Taber 2005, 476). Since these tallies register nearly all information people encounter, they actually provide a high information source for decision-making. Citizens are not simply responding irrationally and haphazardly to the political world, but are using heuristic devices based upon a wealth of information. David Redlawsk also finds that people who are memory processors—those who generally withhold evaluations until they have to make a decision—tend to react a bit differently than others. While they demonstrate the same bias as others of searching out information primarily on the candidates that they like, they are also more apt to modify their prior affect based upon negative information on those candidates (Redlawsk 2002, 1040–41). This indicates that the evaluative tallies may be amenable to change over time in the face of contrary information, at least for memory processors. Despite these caveats, the main challenge of the hot cognition hypothesis—that most citizens most of the time will have automatic, affective reactions to political stimuli rather than deliberating about their response—remains.

Affective intelligence and motivated reasoning theories challenge democratic theories by focusing on the interconnections among affect, cognition, and reason. The challenge is thus primarily to any theory of democracy that conceives of citizens as primarily rational, reasonable, or impartial decision makers and which tries to marginalize the importance of affect in political judgment. If people usually (affective intelligence) or always (motivated reasoning) respond to political phenomena with unconscious affect, then the prospects for deliberation of the kind required by deliberative theory appear minimal. It would appear that only in novel or unexpected political situations, on what political scientists would call issues that are not salient, could we expect citizens to engage in anything like deliberation. What is most important is that democratic theory must account for the fact that when human beings use their judgment, they do so by relying upon an interrelated system of affect and cognition.

Political psychologists are not the only ones who claim that deliberative theory focuses too much on a cognitive understanding of judgment and ignores the role of affect. Lynn Sanders criticizes deliberative theory for its tendency to exclude anything but rational appeals to common interests. "Arguing that democratic discussion should be rational, moderate, and not selfish implicitly excludes public talk that is impassioned, extreme, and the product of particular interests" (Sanders 1997, 370). While she does not reject deliberation per se, she argues that any alternative deliberative theory ought to "avoid stated or implicit requirements that talk be only rational and moderate, or that the only perspectives worth attending to are perspectives that illuminate what is common" (370). Young rejects the "opposition between mind and body, reason and emotion" (1996, 124). She argues that deliberative theory, to the extent that it privileges "a standard of allegedly dispassionate, unsituated, neutral reason," is exclusionary, and "the ideal of disembodied and disembedded reason that it presupposes is a fiction" (2000, 63). Mansbridge notes that "emotions always include some form of appraisal and evaluation, and reason can proceed only rarely without emotional commitment, if only an emotional commitment to the process of reasoning" (1999, 225–26). Political theorists such as Sanders, Young, and Mansbridge demonstrate concerns similar to those the theories of affective intelligence and motivated reasoning raise, though they do so more within the democratic theory tradition.

Giving Affect Its Place: Deliberation and Empathy

I believe that deliberative theory can answer the criticisms of both political psychologists and political theorists by relying upon the process model of empathy. Though many deliberative theorists have moved past conceiving of citizens as purely rational agents, as we saw in Chapter 4, many still lean heavily toward a conceptualization of deliberation focused primarily upon rational or reasonable argumentation that is often silent or only barely audible on the question of affect. What we can learn from the criticisms of political psychologists and political theorists is that only on a misguided understanding of "rational" can we justify categorizing affect as biased or illegitimate and therefore unavailable to deliberators. Understanding this will require a shift in our understanding of deliberation itself.

Affective intelligence theory and motivated reasoning theory both speak to the role of affect in political judgment. In the affective intelligence theory, the disposition system reacts to familiar objects with the appropriate affective markers based upon past experience; under the motivated reasoning theory, people build up a set of evaluative tallies that guide the brain's response to familiar objects. In both cases what guides people's unconscious reactions is past experience, yet neither theory discusses in much depth what leads people to evaluate these past experiences in the way they do. Affective intelligence speaks of the success or failure of previous experience leading to habits, yet how people define "success" or "failure" must certainly vary, especially in relation to the political world. Motivated reasoning speaks of evaluative tallies, but the criteria people utilize to create these must also vary. Before people ever get to the point of automatic, affective reaction to political objects, they must encounter and form judgments about them (or objects like them), a process informed by a mixture of their feelings and thoughts. The process model indicates that those who empathize will be more open to others as they develop their habits and create their evaluative tallies than those who do not empathize. Thus, the process of empathy can lead to automatic affective reactions that will already have built in more deliberation, reflection, and openness to others.

Beyond the development of habits and evaluative tallies, as Redlawsk finds, some human beings attenuate the biases arising from their automatic affective responses because they do not make final evaluations until they have to make decisions. In doing so, they show a greater likelihood to incorporate information contrary to their initial reactions into their final judgments. While there is no empirical evidence yet directly connecting empathy to memory processors, the similarity between the evidence Redlawsk finds and that cited in Chapter 4 on attribution biases, out-group evaluations, and reciprocity leads me to conclude that citizens who empathize are more likely to make judgments in a way that attenuates the biasing effects of their immediate affective reactions. Though there is no requirement that they revise their predeliberation judgments, at its heart deliberative theory relies upon people being at least open to doing so. The evidence indicates that empathy can play an important role in making sure that this is the case.

Finally, empathy has something to say about the role of anxiety in inducing deliberation. In their studies, defenders of the affective intelligence theory focus primarily on the surveillance system's use of anxiety as the catalyst that induces citizens to gather and consider more information when evaluating presidential candidates. Motivated reasoning does not discuss the role of anxiety in inducing deliberation, I believe, because of its reliance upon prior evaluation, something that people do not do in a situation of anxiety. The reason is because such situations, by definition, involve objects that are unfamiliar or threatening. Yet what makes something seem unfamiliar or unthreatening, or to put it colloquially, "worth a second look," will vary from person to person. People who are more open to the process of empathy are also more likely to view things in complex terms, and thus, to see situations that may seem familiar as unfamiliar (though probably not as threatening). This may induce "anxiety" of a sort, but certainly an anxious reaction to something perceived as threatening is different than a curious reaction to something perceived as novel. Theorists of affective intelligence already note that people are uncomfortable with that which causes anxiety, but it is likely that they are not as uncomfortable with that which arouses their curiosity. Citizens open to the process of empathy, because they will likely perceive more situations as less settled by particular habits or evaluative tallies, and are more likely to display curiosity in response to these "unfamiliar" objects, are also more likely to engage in deliberation. This is not to say that they will do so continuously, for as Marcus points out it is unlikely and implausible to expect every citizen to deliberate on every issue all the time, but citizens predisposed to empathy or induced to empathize will be more likely to deliberate on important issues rather than rely predominately upon parochial habits or settled evaluative tallies.

If citizens who empathize are more likely to develop habits and evaluative tallies that are more open to others, to be open to information that contradicts their predeliberative judgments, to see more political objects as unfamiliar or novel, and to respond to those objects with curiosity and deliberation, then empathy must play a necessary role in deliberation. Yet as we have already seen, these effects are most likely to occur if we conceive of empathy as a multidimensional process involving both cognition and affect. One way in which we can acknowledge this is to follow theorists such as Sanders, Young, and Mansbridge in opening up a place in deliberation for the affective utterances that are necessary to empathy. As the process model indicates, empathy does not always occur at a highly cognitive level, though it can. Deliberation itself can become the place where the empathic process occurs, but this requires deliberative theory to accept more than just "reasonable" or "rational" utterances in deliberation, without at the same time excluding such utterances. Deliberation must give space to forms of communication that will increase the chances that participants will engage in the process of empathy.

Rhetoric, Greeting, Narrative, and Testimony

Several theorists have suggested that we might incorporate affect more fully into the deliberative process by admitting communicative modes such as rhetoric, greeting, narrative, and testimony. Young writes: "Because rhetoric is an aspect of all discourse, the temptation should be resisted to base a theory of deliberative democracy on a notion of non-rhetorical speech that is coolly and purely argumentative" (2000, 64). Beyond just arguing that rhetoric is necessarily a part of political discourse, Young maintains that it can fulfill three important deliberative purposes. It can move issues onto the agenda for deliberation, fashion claims and arguments for the audience at hand, and move people from reason to judgments (66–70). Excluding affect-laden rhetoric or figurative speech, she maintains, would undermine the process of deliberation itself by inhibiting these three functions. The problem is that Young appears to actually limit the role of rhetoric to bringing attention to an issue, framing an argument, and motivating people to act. For her rhetoric is the way in which people present themselves, rather than the content of the presentation. While Young rejects the dichotomy between emotion and reason (1996, 124), I do not believe she understands fully how rhetoric overcomes this dichotomy. At one point she contrasts "making assertions and giving reasons" with additional modes of communication, including rhetoric (2000, 77). In responding to Benhabib's criticism that alternative modes of communication have no place in public reason and are irrational, arbitrary, and capricious, Young says that she aims "to describe the political functions of these modes of communication . . . as accompanying rather than alternatives to argument. They give generalized reason orientation and body" (78–79). In the end, Young accepts the dichotomy between rhetoric (including emotional appeal) and argumentation (giving public reasons), and in doing so, undermines her own stated position.

Young also argues for the inclusion of greeting and narrative in democratic politics. She defines greeting, which she also calls public acknowledgment, as "communicative political gestures through which those who have conflicts aim to solve problems, *recognize* others as included in the discussion, especially those with whom they differ in opinion, interest, or social location" (2000, 61). While she recognizes that "gestures of acknowledgment are often pro forma and superficial," and that "less powerful groups often must struggle for recognition over and over," she maintains that absent the "moment of greeting . . . no discussion can take place at all, because the parties refuse to face one another as dialogue partners" (61–62). Thus, the presence or absence of greeting can serve as a critical tool for assessing whether deliberation is inclusive or exclusionary. Young also argues for "political" narrative as an appropriate mode of communication in democratic deliberations. She defines political narrative as different because people engage in it "not primarily to entertain or reveal" themselves, "but to make a point—to demonstrate, describe, explain, or justify something to others in an ongoing political discussion" (72). Political narrative can serve democratic discussion in five ways: (1) by allowing those who suffer injustice to reveal their plight when they cannot do so under the prevailing discourse; (2) by giving local publics—those smaller publics or enclaves within the larger public political sphere—a means for articulating their affinities and collective identities; (3) by providing a means for people to gain a better understanding of the experiences of those in different social situations and by combating flawed understandings of unsupported generalities people bring to deliberation; (4) by revealing the sources of peoples' values, priorities, or cultural meanings that would not appear in traditional argumentation; and (5) by enlarging the thought of speakers and listeners such that they look at issues in a way that takes account of the perspectives of others (72–77). Narrative, thus, can help to "foster understanding among members of a polity with very different experience or assumptions about what is important" (71). Only once people come to understand one another can they begin to engage in meaningful discussion and debate, and narrative allows them to reach the place where they can then engage in meaningful argument.

Sanders makes a parallel argument when she states that testimony, something similar to narrative, can be an important part of public discourse. Like Young, she posits that democratic discussion can open up citizens to the perspective of others: "Instead of aiming for a common discussion, democrats might adopt a more fundamental goal: to try to ensure that those who are usually left out of public discussions learn to speak whether their perspectives are common or not, and those who usually dominate learn to hear the perspectives of others" (1997, 373). One way to achieve this exchange of perspectives is by allowing people to engage in testimony, putting forward their own particular stories, whether or not those stories reflect something more generalizable. "Testimony might be a model that allows for the expression of different perspectives rather than seeking what's common. The contrast between the pursuit of commonality, and the simpler aim to include and represent a fuller range of critical voices, is at the core of the difference between deliberation and testimony" (371). The need for testimony arises because the inequalities that exist in the United States preclude effective deliberation. Sanders writes that "the current state of American politics is sufficiently exclusive, sufficiently afflicted by patterns of dominance, so that evenhanded group deliberations are unlikely" (371). Before we can expect a deliberative democracy to function, it is important to overcome injustices and exclusions; otherwise, deliberation will simply reinforce already existing hierarchies. Sanders position is unique in arguing that instead of incorporating affective modes of communication into deliberation, democracy (at least in the United States) requires that we begin first with other modes of communication that will allow the opening up of perspectives.

Deliberative Theorists on Rhetoric, Greeting, Narrative, and Testimony

In response to these criticisms, some deliberative democrats address the role of rhetoric, greeting, narrative, and testimony in deliberation. Benhabib argues that greeting, rhetoric, and storytelling "may have a place within the *informally structured process of everyday communication among individuals who share a cultural and historical lifeworld*" (1996, 82–83; emphasis in original). These forms, however, cannot "become the public language of institutions and legislatures in a democracy" (83). She maintains that Young's "attempt to transform the language of the rule of law into a more partial, affective, and situated mode of communication would have the consequence of introducing arbitrariness," "create capriciousness," and eliminate the role of impartial reason in deliberation (83). Her position is somewhat surprising given her criticism of Rawls's and Habermas's reliance upon the generalized rather than the concrete other. Yet if we take into account the Arendtian influence on Benhabib, with its call for an enlarged mentality in the Kantian sense and the rejection of empathy, we can see how she can criticize Rawls, Habermas, and Young. People must pay attention to the concrete other, but must do so without relying upon forms of communication that interfere with their ability to adopt an enlarged, yet impartial, viewpoint. I believe that Benhabib's response too easily accepts the dichotomy between reason and emotion, and between the particular and the general, which I have already argued we must reject.

As Gutmann and Thompson point out, critics who focus upon affective communicative modes—they specifically mention Sanders—assume a dichotomy between passion and reason that deliberative democrats should reject (2004, 50). They maintain that "passionate rhetoric can be as justifiable as logical demonstration" and recognize "the legitimacy of modes of persuasion in politics that combine reason and passion" (51). Yet as Krause points out, "in the paragraphs that follow it becomes clear that Gutmann and Thompson see affect as a potential motivational support for deliberation but not as a constitutive feature of deliberation itself and not as a source of normativity" (2006, 7). They never fully develop how deliberation can more fully accommodate alternative modes of communication that combine reason and passion, and thus it is difficult to assess their theory from this perspective. I think they remain open to these forms, but their focus on reason giving too easily mutes the importance of affect in the deliberative process. Bohman also demonstrates an openness to alternative forms of communication: "Nor should deliberative theories be considered one-sidedly rationalistic. Many different 'self-governing capacities' are necessary if citizens are to participate effectively in public deliberation and dialogue, including understanding, imagining, valuing, desiring, storytelling, and the use of rhetoric and argumentation" (1996, 7). The purpose of deliberation in Bohman's dialogic theory is the exchange of reasons that aim "to produce claims that are wide enough in scope and sufficiently justified to be accountable to an indefinite public of fellow citizens" (57). In this model, the success of deliberation relies upon "uptake," in which citizens not only understand others' perspectives but also incorporate those perspectives and reinterpret their own. Uptake can occur through various mechanisms that seem to rely upon or parallel the alternative forms of communication: making explicit what is latent in common understandings, shared institutions, and ongoing activities; the exchange of biographical and historical experiences; applying norms to specific situations; the dialectic between abstract ideals and concrete proposals; and perspective taking (59–64). Yet the point of these mechanisms is to "promote deliberation on reasons addressed to others, who are expected to respond in dialogue" (59). Though I believe he is open to alternative forms of communication, Bohman never explains exactly how they might work in deliberation, and his focus on public reason, though it is a wider view of public reason than either Rawls's or Habermas's, still tends to ignore the importance of these affective forms of communication to the deliberative process.

Unlike those who develop only a limited response to the critiques of Young and Sanders, Dryzek specifically addresses the role of alternative forms of communication such as greeting, rhetoric, narrative, and testimony in deliberation. He recognizes that these forms and argumentation are not mutually exclusive, but he argues that we should only conditionally admit any form of communication into deliberation. In order to be deliberatively legitimate, all forms of communication must meet two tests: they must not involve coercion or threat of coercion, and they must connect the particular to the general (Dryzek 2000, 68).[2] Dryzek argues that storytelling and testimony are coercive when group norms constrain what stories are acceptable, yet he never teases out the implications of this claim. I would maintain that he is correct, but the result should be that storytelling or testimony ought to be completely open in deliberation. Defenders of narrative and testimony often write as if these forms of communication are disproportionately the purview of marginalized groups, or that they ought to use storytelling as an effective tool to fight unjust power relations. This approach tends to unnecessarily essentialize these forms of communication as "alternative" or "marginalized," and gives the impression that they are only legitimate if used by certain marginalized groups. This is not to say that narrative and testimony cannot be effective tools in deliberation (and even combating injustice), rather that deliberative theory should not hint at the legitimacy of restricting the use of testimony and storytelling to certain groups. As Young and Sanders argue, narrative and testimony can be a key mechanism whereby people gain an understanding of other perspectives, but they can only do so if all citizens can testify or tell their stories so that all others have a chance of gaining understanding. Dryzek at least implies how narrative and testimony might become coercive by resisting this possibility through the exclusion of certain stories or storytellers.

Regarding his second criterion, Dryzek claims that "if an individual's story is purely about that individual then there is no political point in hearing it" (2000, 69). Instead, stories must resonate with individuals who do not share the storyteller's situation. "Thus a truly effective story about a particular repression will also involve implicit appeal to more universal standards" (69). Acceptable narrative or testimony must be able to show how particular stories cause listeners to reflect upon "more general standards of human dignity" rather than identify with the individuals or groups who are the stories' subjects. Since the process of empathy requires that people have at least some overlap in experiences or feelings, I agree with Dryzek, but terms such as "universal" or "general" standards concern me

---

2. In a recent work John Dryzek adds a third test that communication must be capable of inducing reflection (2005, 224). Since he does not explain how this test applies to alternative forms of communication, I will focus on the two he develops here. This new test, though, matches closely with the kind of criteria for which I argue later.

for several reasons. As I argued in Chapter 4, I agree with Benhabib that deliberation cannot always be about the "generalized" other. At least one goal in narrative or storytelling is to open people up to other perspectives and experiences; this does not always require that the experiences themselves are generalizable or universal. For example, many white people tend to have few experiences analogous to living as a black person in a racist society, and in this respect, the experience of blacks is not generalizable. The way white people may come to understand this experience is through a combination of hearing the personal narratives of blacks and reflecting on their own emotional experiences. They may have never felt humiliation because of the color of their skin, but they have certainly felt the pain of humiliation in other contexts. The generalizable aspect that is important is not the experience itself but the underlying emotions that allow empathy to occur. As I noted in Chapter 5, Batson and his colleagues have given evidence that inducing empathic concern for an individual of a stigmatized group can increase positive attitudes toward that group as a whole (Batson, Polycarpou et al. 1997). The experimental manipulation they used was to play a recording of the particular individual telling his or her story; thus, having a person listen to the narrative of another can encourage them to reflect on the situations faced by particular individuals and the groups of which they are a part. It is not simply the universal standards of human dignity that lead people to alter their attitudes and perceptions of others, but also the connections to universal human emotions revealed by empathy. If similar emotional experiences can count as "universal" or "general" standards for Dryzek, then our positions are not far apart, and yet I remain concerned regarding this criterion.

Even when the process of empathy allows people to understand one another, it still may not lead them to agree on particular issues. If narrative or testimony opens people up to other perspectives, even if they do not then agree with those perspectives, then narrative and testimony can serve an important function by clarifying what different people believe is at stake in deliberation. For example, those opposed to same-sex marriage may never agree that it should be legal, but they may reach a better understanding of what is at stake in the issue after listening to the narratives of same-sex couples and the difficulties they face in society. Requiring that narratives or storytelling automatically reflect universal or general standards might prevent this very basic level of understanding from occurring. I am also concerned that this criterion would tend to lead to the exclusion of important communications. Barriers to listening attentively to others who are not like us already exist, and I am unsure how we can determine beforehand which narratives will connect to common values or experiences, or to put it another way, which contributions to deliberation will enhance the chances that empathy will occur. It would be impossible to distinguish which contributions violate Dryzek's criterion except in hindsight, so placing *a priori* restrictions on individual narratives or stories in deliberation risks excluding communication that can promote equal consideration. Finally, there is a tension between the need for communications that resonate with something that is common and the important contribution communications can make by introducing something that is novel in a way that may induce empathy. Before novel communications occur, we would be hard pressed to predict what might open up these new ways of seeing things. In the end, I believe that very few people would offer communications in deliberation that do not at least attempt to articulate something that is common or that they believe should be generally accessible. The danger in imposing a condition before deliberation is that we might exclude communications that do not appear to rely upon common values or experiences because we cannot yet conceive of them in these ways (a tendency highlighted by the theories of affective intelligence and motivated reasoning that I discuss). It is true that narratives and stories need to connect up with something that is generally accessible for the process model of empathy to function within deliberation, but we must be very cautious in interpreting and applying a criterion such as the one suggested by Dryzek lest we exclude exactly those kinds of communications that will allow empathy to occur.

Dryzek spends little time discussing greeting other than to point out that sometimes it can be coercive; for example, the use of a traditional Maori greeting by the New Zealand national rugby team intended to intimidate opponents (2000, 69). Greeting can also fail to connect the particular to the general if people use it as a means of exclusion (for example, a secret handshake), though Young certainly takes this into account in her defense of the practice. I agree with her that an analysis of greeting can provide a critical tool for indicating inclusion and exclusion, though Dryzek is correct that greeting can also serve alternative purposes. The difficulty is that what some people might see as an inclusive form of greeting or acknowledgment (a strong, warm handshake, say), others might perceive as a means for intimidation. They are both correct that we ought to view how greeting can work in a positive way to include others, though I believe we should focus on the degree to which such greeting supports or interferes with the process of empathy.

Regarding rhetoric, rather than banish it to the realm of strategic action, Dryzek argues that the use of emotional appeal in rhetoric can be "consistent with the orientation of communicative action to reciprocal understanding" (2000, 52). He maintains that "rhetoric plays an important role in deliberating across difference, as well across the boundary between the state and public sphere" (167), and that "good rhetoric on behalf of the disadvantaged can induce a sense of the need for redress on the part of the powerful" (70). People can subject emotions "to rational justification," and since they can be coercive, "in the end [rhetoric] must answer to reason" (52–53). Interestingly, he also argues that rhetoric, by definition, "must *always* fail in its capacity to connect the particular with the general" (70; emphasis added). Yet "good" rhetoric can be effective in making appeals across different perspectives and enable the transmission of public opinion developed in the public sphere to the state. Rhetoric that achieves these aims is legitimate in deliberation. Here Dryzek appears to follow Young in cataloguing the importance of rhetoric in raising items to the agenda and in giving a voice to the marginalized. As I have already posited, however, I think they both limit rhetoric in ways that are unpersuasive. Dryzek appears to accept the notion that since rhetoric appeals to people's emotions, it is only important in motivating action or bringing items to others' attentions. These limitations rely upon a limited notion of the relationships among affect, cognition, and reason. Human reason depends upon a mixture of thinking and feeling, and rhetoric can be an important and legitimate influence on human judgment. Dryzek is absolutely correct that we ought to avoid coercive rhetoric, but I believe he is incorrect that it *must* connect the particular to the general or that it can *never* do so. Rhetoric can help people in understanding others, even when it does not persuade them; it can also present people with "reasons" for adopting or rejecting a position during deliberation. While people may "think" that they ought to condemn genocide, certainly they also "feel" that they should do so. A more persuasive account of the role of rhetoric in democratic deliberation must take account of the multidimensional nature of human judgment in ways that neither the deliberative democrats nor critics such as Young and Sanders do. As an alternative view on rhetoric, some critics of deliberation rely upon the understanding of rhetoric found in classical sources such as Cicero and Aristotle.

The Classical Rhetoricians

Gary Remer criticizes deliberative democrats for neglecting the role of rhetoric in democracy. Relying primarily upon Cicero, he distinguishes between conversation and oratory, positing that the latter is an essential component of politics. "Because political speech is public and directed primarily toward the masses, Cicero believed that emotional appeals were necessary, and deliberative oratory made use of such appeals" (Remer 1999, 52). Oratory is important to politics because Cicero and the other classical rhetoricians recognize, unlike deliberative democrats, "that human beings are complex creatures—rational and emotional—and must be addressed as such" (54). Rhetorical oratory is the means by which a speaker can address both the emotional and the rational in humans, and since politics inevitably involves large groups of people, emotional appeals will always be a part of any democracy. Oratory is as legitimate a model of political discourse as conversation, which Remer demonstrates in his analysis of the debate in Massachusetts over the ratification of the Constitution (2000). While his findings indicate that the oratorical model better captures this particular case, he does not go so far as to claim that conversation is an illegitimate model of deliberation. Rather, he raises "doubts about reasoned conversation as the only legitimate exemplar of deliberation" and confirms "the oratorical perspective as a valid (if not uniquely legitimate) approach to political deliberation" (2000, 69). Rather than posit rhetorical oratory as more legitimate than conversation, Remer offers it as a possible alternative to the conversational model he attributes to deliberative democrats.

Despite his defense of rhetoric and its concomitant reliance upon affect, Remer argues that "it is misleading to portray rhetoric as one-sidedly grounded on emotional appeals. Classical rhetoricians concerned themselves with the moral ends of the appeals, and were even ambivalent about the goal of moving passions" (1999, 55). Rhetorical oratory is legitimate, not only because it captures the actual practices of deliberation, but also because it concerns itself with the moral uses of appeals. Orators rely upon a balance of "rational" and "emotional" appeals in order to achieve the just ends toward which they strive. Though Remer does not accept some of Cicero's elitist tendencies, the rhetorical oratory model of deliberation recognizes that "the distinction between speaker and audience cannot be made to vanish," but even though speakers and listeners are not equal, it is the listeners that must deliberate and decide (57–58). While this model may not reflect the kind of rational political discourse deliberative democrats desire, he argues that it still represents a legitimate way in which people can participate in a democracy. Remer's account of rhetoric certainly moves beyond that offered by deliberative democrats, and yet I believe that the alternative he offers still tends to accept the dichotomy between the rational and the emotional. Although Cicero attends to the rational and the emotional in his discussions of both oratory and conversation, because of the nature of mass politics, as Remer himself points out, "Cicero even advises the orator to prefer emotion to reason" (42). We are left with a choice of oratorical rhetoric, which relies primarily on emotional appeals, and rational conversation, which the masses are not equipped to pursue. On this understanding, there is thus still a dichotomy between reason and emotion that does not help us explain the importance of empathy to deliberation.

Several theorists have relied upon Aristotle, rather than Cicero, to argue for the role of rhetoric in democracy and deliberation.[3] Bryan Garsten defends the role of persuasion in democratic politics, and in doing so, gives a more persuasive account of how affect and cognition might interact in deliberation. Instead of focusing on deliberation as an exercise in justification, he posits that deliberation is a means for inducing citizens to engage in judgment. Aristotle demonstrates "how speech that invokes particular and personal forms of knowledge and emotion can draw citizens into exercising their capacity for judgment" (Garsten 2006, 192). Without appealing to people's concrete situations, deliberation can never effectively induce the kind of judgment necessary in our political world. It is only based upon people's experiences that they can "create the intricate structures of belief and emotion" that allow them to engage in judgment, and thus, only deliberation that involves people's particular goods can spur them "to draw upon those structures and produce judgments" (128). This does not indicate that people's particular attachments are intractable. Echoing the arguments put forward by the theories of affective intelligence and motivated reasoning, Garsten posits that judgment relies upon something like habits or evaluative tallies people derive from their experiences, yet he also argues that people adjust these over time. "The activity of judgment is therefore one in which we adjust certain commitments in light of others. Over time, such adjustments give to our beliefs and emotions a certain structure, producing hierarchies of criteria to which we turn, consciously or unconsciously, when evaluating new situations" (192). Deliberation holds out the possibility that people can influence each other's criteria, but the only way it can do so is through what Garsten calls the "politics of persuasion." This inherently requires that deliberation rely upon the affective side of human experience. "Since effective deliberation aims to take advantage of the tacit knowledge each citizen has within his or her experience, and since that

3. In addition to those I specifically discuss, see also Abizadeh 2005, Bickford 1996, and O'Neill 2002.

knowledge is intricately intertwined with his emotional ties and attachments, deliberation should not aim to ground itself in a standpoint that denies the relevance of those attachments" (194). Since persuasion requires that people pay attention to the particular situations of the others engaged in dialogue, it inherently requires something like the role taking found in the process model of empathy. "The politics of persuasion asks that we look to understand the commitments, beliefs, and passions of the other side if only for the purpose of trying to bring them to our side—or, more often, for the purpose of trying to rebut their views in front of people who have no settled position of their own. . . . Trying to persuade others requires us to step outside our particular perspectives without asking us to leave our particular commitments behind" (210). For Garsten, then, deliberation inherently relies upon persuasion, and persuasion itself depends upon a mixture of affective and cognitive appeals to the particular situations of concrete individuals. Without this, citizens will never engage in the kind of judgment deliberation requires.

Bernard Yack, also drawing upon Aristotle, argues that eliminating rhetoric from public deliberation would undermine the very practice itself. Yack posits that Aristotle "seems uninterested in improving public rationality more directly by imposing constraints on deliberative rhetoric itself—for example, by means of norms that limit the kind of proofs or arguments that one can offer in public life. . . . Aristotle allows appeals to all three forms of rhetorical proof: emotion and character as well as argument" (428). While Aristotle argues for eliminating partial emotional appeals in the adjudication of legal cases, doing so in political deliberation leads to problems: "For [Aristotle] argues that people who, like the third parties we ask to adjudicate in legal cases, lack a direct interest in the result of their deliberations are willing to entertain frivolous and illogical proposals that they would reject out of hand if they thought that they would have to live with the consequences of their decisions (*Rhetoric* 1354b)" (433). Political deliberation concerns future actions and consequences, as well as an assessment of values, and thus requires that citizens allow emotion to enter into their judgment, despite the risks. "But deliberation about what serves the common advantage requires a living reason, reasoning informed by the emotions that interest us in the consequences of our decisions" (433).

In recognizing the key role emotion plays in human judgment and deliberation, Garsten and Yack provide us with a persuasive beginning for how we might incorporate rhetoric into a convincing theory of deliberation. Yet they both recognize that there are risks involved in doing so. Garsten notes that since persuasion is a central aspect of democratic life, demagogy is always a threat (2006, 200). Yack observes that rhetoric must appeal to an audience, and if that audience is "ignorant and disorderly . . . even the most admirable and trustworthy speakers will have to lower their sights in order to persuade" (2006, 427). Further, since people must remain open to persuasion, they will be "vulnerable to the possibility of being carried away against [their] interests and better judgment by the eloquence of public speakers" (427–28). While the importance of emotions to human judgment requires that people accept the risks that those emotions may mislead them (433), both Yack and Garsten offer solutions to mitigate those risks. Garsten defends the Madisonian republican system as institutionalized in the Constitution as the way to tame judgment (2006, 199–209). Yack believes that Aristotle "would have no objection" to practices such as "divided legislatures, complex and time-consuming processes of constitutional amendment, and simple requirements that legislation be read and debated more than once" (2006, 428).

While I would not reject such precautions out of hand, they do not address the underlying issue of why rhetoric may mislead. The underlying problem is not that emotions may mislead people, but that public speakers may use techniques of persuasion that induce them to concentrate on certain thoughts and emotions to the exclusion of others. As Young notes, however, "People can also be deceived or manipulated by argumentative discourse" (2000, 79). Human beings cannot help but rely upon a mixture of affect and cognition in reasoning about how they want to act, and the threat that demagogy poses is that it can skew this process either through emotional appeals or manipulative logic. Institutions that slow down decision-making are important because they may make it more likely that people will examine *all* their thoughts and feelings and not just those prevailing at any given moment. These institutions also may increase the likelihood that the *majority* will recognize the thoughts and feelings of the *minority*. The underlying threat posed by demagogy is that citizens will engage in a decision-making process that is neither self-aware nor empathic, and if republican institutions make self-awareness and empathy more likely, they serve a purpose. The answer to the threat posed by demagogy is not to banish affective appeals from public deliberation or diminish their importance; rather, deliberative democracy must examine institutions and practices with a critical eye to insure that they make citizens more self-aware and empathic. Recognizing the importance of rhetoric for deliberation gives us a good understanding of the interconnections among affect, cognition, and reason and provides a better understanding of how a deliberative democracy will likely function than those theories that rely upon unrealistic, cognitive understandings of rationality. Yet if we want a deliberative democracy that gives equal consideration to all, and thus supports legitimate collective decision-making, we must recognize that rhetoric can only contribute positively if it supports the process of empathy rather than impeding it.[4]

Beyond Agonism

Difference democrats such as Young and classicists such as Remer, Yack, and Garsten are not the only theorists who criticize deliberative democrats' positions on rhetoric.[5] Robert Ivie also takes various deliberative democrats to task—specifically Bessette, Gutmann and Thompson, and Bohman—for arguing that rhetoric is an illegitimate form of democratic discourse, but he does so from a more postmodern perspective. Given his approach, he provides a nice transition to a discussion of another group of theorists critical of deliberative democracy: agonistic democrats.

Ivie contrasts what he calls the "rhetorical republic" with the "liberal republic." "Democratic deliberation in a rhetorical republic is different than its counterpart in a liberal republic. It is robust and distempered, and open instead of contained" (1998, 495). Deliberation should not be, as it is in the liberal republic, a process of justification based in a limited conception of reason: "The aim of rhetorical deliberation and democratic politics is not the quixotic, even tragic, quest to locate the common good in universal truth derived from pure reason" (499). Instead, democracy is the politics of community that aims at the creation of meaning through the collaboration of "advocate and audience, who depend upon one another as mutually accountable co-agents of political meaning and action" and "construct appearances into judgments of political contingencies in order to arrive at practical decisions on questions of public policy" (499). This politics of community, rather than requiring a limitation of rhetoric, inherently relies upon it, and deliberative democrats fail to recognize this. By putting rhetoric and deliberation in contention, Bessette cannot recognize the need for a "robust and open rhetorical deliberation that privileges the public as

4. For several further perspectives on the role of rhetoric in democracy, see Fontana, Nederman, and Remer 2004.
5. I have adapted the title for this section from Dryzek 2005.

audience and relational agent participating in a sophisticated act of reasoning about contingencies and particulars" (496). Gutmann and Thompson remain constrained by their notion of "rational deliberation among constitutionally constrained citizens in civil society and government institutions under a regime of representative government" (497). For Bohman, "Rhetoric remains problematic as a mode of strategic, justificatory rationality, or public advocacy, unless it somehow produces the unlikely result of dialogical uptake" (498). Instead of eschewing rhetoric as detrimental to the justificatory processes required of democracy, Ivie argues that scholars ought to conceptualize democratic deliberation as rhetoric and engage in critiques of actual democratic practice in order to challenge and renegotiate received notions of the community itself (502–3).

Thus Ivie defines democratic deliberation as "a robust practice of actively addressing and identifying with diverse others enough to achieve a working community of interests" (1998, 503). It is clear that the main target of his critique is not deliberative democracy per se, but liberal democracy in whatever guise it appears. He sees in liberal democracy a distrust of the *demos* as the "Other," and in the deliberative theories he criticizes, he finds the imposition of a predetermined notion of reason that marginalizes and imposes. Rhetorical democracy, in contrast, does not rely upon "a restricted elite code that makes audiences captive to a cultural hegemony" but "is open to different and new interpretations of appearances" (499). This openness applies not only to domestic politics, but to the international arena as well: "Reinforcing the bonds between rhetorical practice and democratic deliberation, I believe, is an important dynamic in political communities capable of courting the internal Other sufficiently to reduce exaggerated fears of the external Other" (503). Since it is more open both internally and externally, democratic deliberation on the model of the rhetorical republic "is more friendly to difference and conducive to peace . . . than is deliberative democracy in the liberal tradition" (502).

Setting aside whether Ivie accurately represents the positions taken by Bessette, Gutmann and Thompson, and Bohman, I believe that Ivie's defense of the "rhetorical republic" is unpersuasive. Deliberative theory should certainly be more open to rhetoric than many of its defenders are, but to posit that rhetoric alone is what deliberation requires is either incorrect or uses the term "rhetoric" in a way very different from anyone I have discussed so far. Ivie cites Thomas B. Farrell (1993) as giving a "revised Aristotelian conception of political rhetoric," which "brings us closer to the understanding of democratic deliberation as a robust practice and nudges us nearer to overcoming our ingrained fear of the *demos*" (Ivie 1998, 499). Rhetoric is "argument in the service of judgment" that does not "confuse reason with logic," is "responsive to the problem of alienation and exile," and is "a partisan but permeable and egalitarian 'mode of participatory reflection on cultural norms' which, through the invitation of the enthymeme, allows audiences to persuade themselves" (499). Ivie never indicates how rhetoric on his understanding can lead to judgment while still being egalitarian and avoiding alienation and exile. While the rhetorical republic may remain more open and flexible, and while scholars "could do far worse than participate theoretically and critically in rhetorical enactment of democratic culture" (503), Ivie's argument provides little guidance on how this type of deliberation might achieve its stated aims. If politics, as he claims, resides "in the realm of the scramble, marked by fallibility and struggle," is it advisable to simply rely "on the critic's comic voice to prevent us from pursuing any single version of truth or vision of beauty all the way to the end of the line, over the edge, and into the abyss" (499). Rhetoric can certainly be open and flexible, but it also poses dangers, as we have seen, something Ivie does not acknowledge. Communicative forms other than rhetoric—such as narrative, testimony, and argument—can also serve openness and critique. We need some criteria by which to evaluate whether these different forms of political communication, including rhetoric, however we define it, serve the democratic ends of equal consideration and legitimate decision-making. As should be clear by now, I believe that the process of empathy provides that criteria, and while much of what Ivie posits is congruent with the need for empathy, his concentration on rejecting liberal reason in favor of open criticism can only take us so far.

While Ivie criticizes liberal deliberative democracy from a postmodern perspective for its reliance on "pure" forms of rationality and reason, several other theorists criticize deliberative democracy from a postmodern perspective for trying to remove the "political" from politics.[6] Chantal Mouffe defends what she calls her conception of agonistic pluralism. She begins by explaining that claims to legitimate power have purely pragmatic grounds: "a) if any power has been able to impose itself, it is because it has been recognized as legitimate in some quarters; and b) if legitimacy is not based in

6. While there are several variants of agonism, I follow Dryzek in focusing on Chantal Mouffe because "she explicitly advocates agonism against deliberative democracy in plural societies" (Dryzek 2005, 220). For further descriptions of agonism and its implications, see Connolly 1991, Deveaux 1999, Goi 2005, Honig 1993, Martin 2005, Schaap 2006, and Villa 1992.

an a prioristic ground, it is because it is based in some form of successful power" (1999, 753). Deliberative democracy cannot recognize this because it eliminates power from argumentation and grounds legitimacy in pure rationality. Instead of trying to eliminate power as deliberative democrats wish to do, democracies must be able "to constitute forms of power that are compatible with democratic values" (753). In order to explain how this is possible, she draws on the work of Carl Schmitt to make a distinction between "the political" and "politics." The political is "the dimension of antagonism that is inherent in all human society, antagonism that can take many different forms and can emerge in diverse social relations" (754). Politics is the practices, discourses, and institutions that seek to establish a certain order and organize human coexistence, and these are always potentially conflictual because the political affects politics. Agonistic pluralism can help make sure that the antagonistic nature of the political does not overwhelm politics.

Agonistic pluralism recognizes that politics will always contain we/they distinctions along with their potential for conflict, but it maintains that this is a necessary condition of political life. Politics depends upon the mobilization of people to action, and mobilization depends, in turn, upon passions. Mouffe defines passions as "the various affective forces which are at the origin of collective forms of identifications" (2005, 24), and thus, mobilization depends upon the very we/they distinctions that threaten conflict. "Mobilization requires politicization, but politicization cannot exist without the production of a conflictual representation of the world, with opposed camps with which people can identify, thereby allowing for passions to be mobilized politically within the spectrum of the democratic process" (24–25). Not giving a political outlet to the passions arising from we/they distinctions risks "that the democratic confrontation will therefore be replaced by a confrontation between essentialist forms of identification or nonnegotiable moral values" (30). For example, Mouffe argues that the attempt to eliminate political conflict in liberal democracies in Europe helps explain the appeal of right-wing populist parties (69). Democratic politics must not attempt to "eliminate passions nor to relegate them to the private sphere in order to render rational consensus possible," but it must "mobilize those passions towards the promotion of democratic designs" (Mouffe 1999, 755–56).

While conflict is an inherent part of politics, in order for it "to be accepted as legitimate," it "needs to take a form that does not destroy the political association" (Mouffe 2005, 20). Agonism attempts to create a democratic politics that draws "the we/they distinction in a way which is compatible with the recognition of the pluralism which is constitutive of modern democracy" (14). To help explain how this might be possible, Mouffe distinguishes between enemies and adversaries. When conflict involves enemies, "the we/they confrontation is visualized as a moral one between good and evil, the opponent can be perceived only as an enemy to be destroyed and this is not conducive to an agonistic treatment" (5). Agonism aims at putting forward an alternative conceptualization of conflict as between adversaries in which there "is a we/they relation where the conflicting parties, although acknowledging that there is no rational solution to their conflict, nevertheless recognize the legitimacy of their opponents" (20). What allows this type of relationship is that adversaries "have in common a shared adhesion to the ethico-political principles of democracy" such as liberty and equality, though they still may disagree on how to interpret and implement those principles (Mouffe 1999, 755). An agonistic democracy must make room for dissent, because its survival depends on collective identities forming around clearly differentiated positions, yet it must also rely upon a commitment to basic ethico-political principles that allow it to function. "A democratic society requires the allegiance of its citizens to a set of shared ethico-political principles, usually spelled out in a constitution and embodied in a legal framework, and it cannot allow the coexistence of conflicting principles of legitimacy in its midst" (Mouffe 2005, 122). Beyond this basic requirement for turning enemies into adversaries, agonism argues that conflict is both an inherent part of democratic politics, and the basis of its very existence.

The problem is that liberal democratic theory, including the deliberative variety, is incapable of addressing these questions. At a general level, neither the aggregative nor the deliberative model can "acknowledge the role of 'passions' as one of the main moving forces in the field of politics and finds itself disarmed when faced with its diverse manifestations" (Mouffe 2005, 24). Instead of trying to limit democratic politics "to establishing compromises among interests or values or to deliberation about the common good," a theory of democracy must "have a real purchase on people's desires and fantasies" and "mobilize passions towards democratic designs"; thus, "democratic politics must have a partisan character" (6). Rather than an entirely cooperative enterprise as most liberals desire, agnostic pluralism combines both collaboration and conflict, yet it does so for the very purpose of sustaining democracy. To be more specific, Mouffe criticizes Habermas's theory for assuming the universal validity of Western liberal constitutional democracy. "The enforced universalization of the Western model, instead of bringing peace and prosperity, will lead to ever bloodier reactions on the part of those whose cultures and ways of life are being destroyed by this process" (86–87). She also argues that the epistemic nature of democratic will-formation in Habermas's theory will result in the imposition of a hegemonic understanding of what it means to be rational. While criticizing Habermas's universalizing and hegemonic tendencies, Mouffe does believe in some limits. She argues that "contrary to some post-modern thinkers who envisage a pluralism without any frontiers, I do not believe that a democratic pluralist politics should consider as legitimate all the demands formulated in a given society" (120). A democracy can exclude those who put into question its basic institutions as legitimate, those who reject the ethico-political values necessary to transform antagonism into agonism, but Mouffe is quick to point out that this exclusion is political, not moral. Here Mouffe briefly addresses Rawls because this suggestion sounds very similar to Rawls's idea of the reasonable. She maintains that Rawls "pretends that such a discrimination is grounded in rationality and moral-ity, while I claim that the drawing of the frontier between the legitimate and illegitimate is always a political decision, and that it should therefore always remain open to contestation" (121). For Mouffe, then, deliberative theorists' reliance on moral or rational positions that attempt to eliminate conflict and passions eviscerate the very conditions necessary for a well-functioning democratic society.

One deliberative theorist has responded directly to Mouffe's position: John Dryzek. While Dryzek accepts the need to transform antagonism into at least more civilized engagement, he has three disagreements with her theory. First, he argues that Mouffe paradoxically wants people's core iden-tities to energize agonistic exchange because they are the source of passion, and yet "if identities themselves are highlighted, exchange is more likely to freeze identities than convert them" (Dryzek 2005, 221). Instead of focus-ing on identities, exchange should focus on the specific needs of the individ-uals or groups. If "individuals can listen to each others' stories, they might at least accept one another's specific needs—which can be reconciled, even when value systems and identities cannot" (221). Second, he argues that his version of discursive democracy provides a space for contestation that is not as "dispassionate and reasoned" as Mouffe's image of deliberative democracy might imply. He provides this by defending a public sphere sep-arate from formal political institutions in which there is a contestation of discourses. Third, he argues that "Mouffe's interpretation of the main task of democracy has no obvious place for collective decision-making and resolution of social problems" (221). Agonism focuses on decision-making in order to argue for the need for more contestation. Dryzek argues that democracy can "combine critical engagement and collective decision" if it differentiates between the independent public sphere as the place of con-testation that has loose ties to formal political institutions that are the sites of collective decision-making.

Dryzek's criticisms of Mouffe have merit. He is correct that contestation around core identities is more likely to lead to intransigence and antago-nism than to agonism, but I believe Mouffe recognizes this. In her latest work she defends the need to retain the *political* identities of left/right as the focus of we/they distinctions so that people do not channel their passion through other essentialist identities or non-negotiable moral posi-tions. Dryzek is also correct that his discursive theory, with its focus on a contestation of discourses within the public sphere, does not fit the stereo-typical image many critics attribute to deliberative democracy of a dispas-sionate, reasonable, reasoned debate. As we have seen, the only tests he requires forms of communication to meet are that they are not coercive, connect the particular to the general, and are capable of inducing reflection. I have already indicated why I disagree with the general/particular test, and I believe Mouffe would raise similar objections, but this does not deny that discursive democracy allows more open contestation than other theories of deliberation. Finally, I agree with Dryzek that agonism often pays little attention to the decision-making process within a democracy, and his solu-tion of decoupling the purposes of the public sphere from formal political institutions is promising.[7]

Though I generally agree with Dryzek's criticisms of Mouffe, I believe that he misses one fundamental critique of the agonistic pluralism model. The political most certainly involves conflict and contestation, and any attempt to eliminate it completely raises the possibility of oppression, exclu-sion, and hegemonic blindness—as agonists recognize. By conceptualizing democratic legitimacy as consensus (or near consensus), rational agree-ment, reasonable agreement, or other forms of a rationally constructed public will, many deliberative theories at least tend toward exclusion and the evisceration of politics. Yet this does not mean that politics must *always* be about contestation. People may agree about some goal that they want to achieve, and yet they still must coordinate to achieve this goal; this is poli-tics. People may confront a new issue or problem that is unclear, and they

---

7. Of course, Habermas (1996a) and others do this as well.

may engage in a discussion to examine the various sides of the issue; this is politics. It is even possible that people may eventually overcome their disagreement, for example, by agreeing that citizens have the right to vote regardless of gender, and even if the agreement comes about at the end of a process of contestation, the very possibility of agreement is also itself politics. While certain theories of deliberation may drift toward exclusion and repression by highlighting rationality and consensus, agonism tends to drift toward the reification of conflict as the only option available in democratic politics. Democratic politics must work toward allowing agonistic contestation between adversaries in order to prevent an all-out fight between enemies, but it must also be open to the possibility that people can overcome their antagonisms and reach agreement under noncoercive, nonrepressive conditions.

One possibility for allowing both agonism and agreement is to combine agonism and deliberation within one system. Dryzek does this by his differentiation between the public sphere and the state. Simona Goi also argues for a combined approach of opening agonistic spaces alongside deliberative ones. Combining agonism and deliberation "secures an opportunity to voice alternative standpoints and to make sure that they are heard in all their distinctive 'otherness'" (Goi 2005, 80; emphasis in original). Yet there is a slight difference in tone between her approach and Dryzek's. She maintains that disagreements often arise because of gaps between people's lifeworlds. "This gap cannot be bridged simply by forcing participants in deliberation to limit their arguments to the commonly shared rational premises of communication, as this denies dissenting voices recognition of their perspectives and identities *on their own terms*" (80; emphasis in original). Goi appears more open than Dryzek to allowing people to voice their own perspectives on their own terms regardless of whether those terms can connect the particular to the general. Combining agonism and deliberation appears promising, but there remains one vital question that even Dryzek highlights. Even if democracy should not eliminate conflict, it is important that the conflict does not degenerate into antagonism; this requires that democratic citizens display a particular attitude toward one another (agonism) or meet certain criteria in communicating (discursive democracy). Dryzek points out that agonism "is vulnerable to questions about where exactly the required attitude should come from, especially where groups asserting identity themselves feature hierarchy and repression" (2005, 221). Monique Deveaux makes a similar argument that "agonistic democrats have done little to defend the link between agonism and greater respect for citizens' moral, religious and cultural differences" (1999, 5). Some agonists seem to assume that a more open process will allow more agonistic contestation, but Deveaux points out that this is only a possibility. What is necessary is the stronger claim that an agonistic system could actually foster inclusion and mutual respect, but this claim "will remain an ineffectual bit of rhetoric in the absence of clearer ideas about how (or indeed whether) we can formalize such inclusion and recognition" (14). What both Dryzek and agonistic democrats miss, I want to argue, is that the way we can combine both respectful contestation and the possibility for cooperation and legitimate decision-making is by placing the process of empathy at the heart of democratic politics. Political contestation among citizens who engage in the process of empathy can be adversarial and respectful without requiring a totalizing notion of rationality. It is not only open to a variety of affective and cognitive forms of communication, it requires them, and also provides a criterion by which we can judge whether or not forms of communication are legitimate that itself does not rely upon a particular moral or rational foundation. While allowing for disagreement and contestation, it retains the possibility for cooperation and agreement. A deliberative theory that places the process of empathy at its core opens the possibility for equal consideration without threatening legitimacy by eviscerating the differences among people identified by agonists.

7

EMPATHY AND DEMOCRACY

Democracy needs the process of empathy. At the end of Chapter 5 I argued that deliberative theories, in order to address the empirical evidence, had to take the empathic process more seriously. The theoretical critiques surveyed in the previous chapter, though, make even more serious claims about the viability of deliberative democracy. The most persuasive way to answer those claims is to adopt a new model of deliberation that gives empathy a central place in democracy. Even more important, adopting a model of deliberative democracy that incorporates the process of empathy will allow me to demonstrate how democracy can make legitimate collective decisions while fulfilling its promise to give equal consideration to all citizens. In constructing this new deliberative theory, I will draw upon the most persuasive aspects of other theories and combine them with the process model developed in Chapter 3. The process of empathy is not a sufficient condition for democracy, but it is undoubtedly a necessary one.

Deliberation, Reflective Consideration, and Empathy

Before defining what deliberation would mean under a model of deliberative democracy that takes empathy seriously, I want to highlight the background features within which such a model will function. I make these claims as assertions, and even though I believe they are defensible assertions, I will not defend them here because I believe that anyone who disagrees with them will never find my model persuasive. First, democracies must function in a world characterized by a pluralism of values, identities, beliefs, experiences, and what Rawls calls conceptions of the good. I believe that this is a "fact" as Rawls claims (1996, 36), though it is not inherent only to liberal societies. While the degree of pluralism may vary, an examination of history demonstrates clearly that people living together are never going to agree about many important questions in life and are going to have different perspectives on the world. In some places and in some periods, people may not have had the opportunity or will to express their perspectives, but this does not deny that disagreements existed. We should not limit this fact, as Rawls does, to the claim that there are a variety of "reasonable" comprehensive conceptions of the good. While this may be likely as Rawls defines it, it is unfruitful and unnecessary to predetermine what values, beliefs, conceptions of the good, and opinions are "reasonable." It is unfruitful because it risks the imposition of a narrowly tailored conception of reasonable, and it is unnecessary because democratic practice itself can reveal the unreasonable without predetermining it. Second, we live in a world without an infallible authority to which people can appeal to resolve their differences, similar to Habermas's postmetaphysical thinking in ethics. There is no book, god, science, or nature that can provide unerring guidance for people in resolving political differences. This does not arise out of the fact of pluralism, but is a condition of the world that has always existed, even if some denied it in the past and some do so today. Finally, everyone in a society deserves equal consideration whenever the society engages in collective decision-making. This does not mean that every decision will result in the satisfaction of everyone's desires and interests, but decisions must always take those desires or interests into account somehow. Any democracy faces the problem of how to make collective decisions in the face of the fact of pluralism, the lack of an infallible arbiter of differences, and the need to give citizens equal consideration.

Empathy and Defining Deliberation

My argument is that democracy can deal with this problem by defining democracy as deliberation that puts empathy at its heart, but this requires that we begin by defining deliberation. As Chapter 2 made clear, deliberative theorists disagree on many points about what constitutes deliberation, but there are some general definitions with which most deliberative democrats would agree. John Gastil and Laura Black "advance a broad, yet flexible definition of deliberation" in which people "carefully examine a problem and arrive at a well-reasoned solution after a period of inclusive, respectful consideration of diverse points of view" (Gastil and Black 2008, 2). Bessette defines deliberation similarly "as *reasoning on the merits of public policy* in which the participants seriously consider substantive information and arguments and seek to decide individually and to persuade each other as to what constitutes good public policy" (1994, 46; emphasis in original). Chambers defines deliberation generally as "debate and discussion aimed at producing reasonable, well-informed opinions in which participants are willing to revise preferences in light of discussion, new information, and claims made by fellow participants" (2003, 309). What we see in these three definitions is that people *contemplate* (examine, seriously consider) an *object* (public policy, problem) by engaging in *communicative exchange* (persuasion, debate, and discussion) that allows them to reach a *reflective* (well-reasoned, reasonable, well-informed) *decision* on the object through an *inclusive* (inclusive, respectful) process in which people are *open* to (willing to revise) the influence of others. By definition, deliberation must involve contemplation of an object, and because of democracy's requirement for equal consideration, such contemplation must be inclusive. While deliberation does not necessarily involve communicative exchange—we can individually deliberate without communicative exchange as Rousseau prescribes—theorists now generally accept communicative exchange as part of any definition of deliberative democracy. So far, I define deliberation as a process in which people contemplate a political object by engaging in a communicative exchange that is inclusive. The questions remaining are what it means for deliberation to be reflective, and whether deliberation must always aim at making a decision.

The use of terms like "reasonable" and "well-reasoned" (or in other definitions "rational") risks the exclusion of different forms of communication, especially those that are affective, and the imposition of particular ways of considering the object. Deliberation must be "reflective" in the sense that people seriously consider all the information gained during communicative exchange, and this may be what "reasonable" and "well-reasoned" mean to some theorists, but given the history and connotations of words such as "reasonable" and "well-reasoned," it is best to avoid those terms. As we have seen, even terms such as "reflective" and "well-informed" tend to connote "cool" or nonaffective consideration of an object. As an alternative description less likely to pose these risks, I will describe deliberation as an *attentive* process. Instead of focusing on decision-making, I want to follow Stephanie Burkhalter, John Gastil, and Todd Kelshaw in highlighting the side of deliberation that they describe as its "dialogic component." This component allows a "careful analysis of problems and solutions" and "makes discussion more democratic" (Burkhalter, Gastil, and Kelshaw 2002, 411).

Deliberation leads to better analysis by "tapping into previously unrealized or unacknowledged perspectives within a group" that "brings different epistemologies to bear on a common problem," and it is more democratic because it opens "up conversation about alternative ways of speaking and knowing" (411). Attentive deliberation includes careful analysis of an object and an openness to alternative ways of speaking and knowing, but it does not require a final decision, and as I will argue, oftentimes should not do so. As I noted at the end of Chapter 5, the pressure of winning and losing can have deleterious effects on deliberation. The threat of these effects is the reason that Fishkin and his colleagues, as well as many other "real world" examples of deliberation,[1] never require their participants to come to a group decision. As Burkhalter, Gastil, and Kelshaw note, "Not all deliberative forums require decisions, and in some cases it is inappropriate to make a decision, such as when the group has no authority, when a decision would be premature, or when a group decision would conflict with a larger decision-making process" (2002, 404). Since deliberative democracy inherently requires collective decision-making, deliberation must eventually lead to collective decisions, but as Dryzek and Habermas note, decision-making and deliberation can occur at different sites and in different ways within the larger democratic system. Thus, deliberation does not require decision-making in every instance.

Given these considerations, I preliminarily define deliberation as a practice in which people contemplate a political object (viz., an issue, policy, or candidate) by engaging in an inclusive, attentive communicative exchange. For this practice to function, people must also empathize, and the process model of empathy can explain why. For deliberation to be truly inclusive, it must not only give everyone the opportunity to engage in the communicative exchange, it must also insure that everyone's input receives full consideration. The empirical evidence demonstrates that empathic predispositions and engaging people in role taking—both affective and cognitive—overcome biases and prejudices that would seriously interfere with this possibility of full consideration. Evidence also shows that empathic predispositions are likely to reinforce the attitudes of reciprocity and mutual respect that are vital for deliberative inclusion. Without the process of empathy, therefore, deliberation will be less inclusive.

1. I am referring to deliberative groups such as the National Issues Forums (http://www .nifi.org/index.aspx), citizens' juries, the Deliberative Democracy Consortium (http://www .deliberative-democracy.net/), and Everyday Democracy (http://www.everyday-democracy.org/ en/index.aspx).

The empathic process is also important for attentiveness. Attentiveness requires that participants pay attention to information presented in deliberation, but "information" not only includes what we might call facts about the world; it must also include the thoughts and feelings others have regarding the political object. Attentiveness requires a free flow of communication of all types, not just "rational" argumentation, generalized views about human society, positions on the "common good," or communication that can link the particular to the general. As Burkhalter, Gastil, and Kelshaw explain, "Arguments need not always be framed in terms of the public good. Sometimes it is better simply to begin by hearing how individual participants view a public issue in terms of their own self-interest. When participants speak from their own experience and in terms of their own interests, other participants can more easily recognize real differences in background and identity" (2002, 409). Deliberation must admit all forms of communication, at least provisionally, including communication types that are affective or particular; only thus can participants see concrete others in ways that insure that deliberation is truly attentive. The process of empathy may play only a limited role in the communication of certain factual information, but it is vital for communicating the information about others that deliberation requires. The process of empathy can occur through several mechanisms that do not necessarily require communicative exchange, but most of them—including direct association, language-mediated associations, elaborated cognitive networks, and even role taking—can occur through such exchange. Communicative exchange has the added benefit that it allows people to make corrections in their misperceptions of how other people are thinking and feeling. Finally, the empathic process is important to attentiveness because of the possibility of empathic concern. While it is not necessary for participants to have strong feelings of concern for their fellow deliberators in order to be attentive, at least some level of valuing others—what Habermas calls solidarity—will make it more likely that people will pay attention to each other's inputs in deliberation. This requires that people listen carefully to one another: "Consideration begins with careful listening that is attentive both to the content of a speaker's words and the speaker's larger perspective or experience" (Gastil and Black 2008, 4; see also Kessel 2003). Evidence also indicates that valuing others increases both perspective taking and empathic concern (Batson et al. 2007). Without at least some empathic concern for their fellows, participants in deliberation are unlikely to listen to one another in this manner.

Having demonstrated empathy's centrality to deliberation, we can now provide a final definition: deliberation is a practice in which people contemplate a political object by engaging in an inclusive, attentive communicative exchange that promotes the exchange of information and the process of empathy. This definition aligns with what researchers often find in actual deliberations. Francesca Polletta finds in her case study of post 9/11 online public discussions about what to do with the World Trade Center site that "more than democratic theorists have recognized, people 'just talk' in deliberative forums in ways that help to clarify their opinions, consider alternatives, and work toward compromise" (2008, 17). Janusz Reykowski and his colleagues reached a similar conclusion in their study of Polish parents' deliberation about sex education in schools. They found that "collective rational analysis of the issues" did not occur often in the deliberation, but rather, "the large part of the participants' activities consisted in sharing opinions, information, and experience" and expressing "their agreement or disagreement with the opinions of the others" (2006, 343). Deliberation between citizens often involves the kind of attentive communicative exchange my definition of deliberation captures, but another study demonstrates that affect is a central part of this.

Jane Mansbridge, Janette Hartz-Karp, Matthew Amengual, and John Gastil studied how a group of professional facilitators coded videotapes of ten small group deliberations on public issues from six different organizations in the United States. Regarding the role of affect, the researchers "conclude that the facilitators coding these deliberations welcomed the expression of emotion—even 'passion'—when it provided insight, engaged the participants, or even brought 'focus' back to the proceedings. . . . The coders positively valued emotions that elicited new ideas and perspectives for consideration" (Mansbridge et al. 2006, 20). While they do not mention empathy in their findings, the expression of emotion allowed for a more inclusive, attentive process in deliberation, and I would conjecture that this is because of the process of empathy. Anecdotal evidence for this comes from some of the professional facilitators' comments: "One facilitator coded as 'good' the way the 'increasing passion' in the participants' comments led to a 'deeper level of group discussion.' Another found that 'the injection of emotion into the discussion makes for greater introspection on the part of the other participants. This is evidence[d] by their body language and the tenor of their response to [the person talking].' Several other coders shared this positive assessment of emotion-laden expression leading to deeper deliberation" (19). These studies demonstrate that when people actually get together and deliberate, they usually engage in communicative exchanges, including affective expressions, which focus on being attentive and inclusive. While none of the studies examined empathy, they provide strong indirect evidence that my definition of deliberation captures what often happens in actual deliberative exchanges and that empathy can contribute to more reflective deliberation.

Critics of Empathy's Role in Deliberation

In opposition to the definition I have developed here, there are some scholars who argue that empathy is either not desirable or not possible in deliberation. I noted how Benhabib, following Arendt, rejects "empathy" in favor of a Kantian "enlarged mentality." Benhabib limits the definition of empathy to feeling for or with another, which equates with the reactive affective response of empathic concern (feeling for) and a general parallel affective response (feeling with) in the process model. Her definition of enlarged mentality approximates role taking in the process model, though it does so only partially. She limits role taking to the projection of the self into the situation of the other and looking at that situation from one's own perspective. Overall, then, Benhabib rejects the importance of most aspects of the process model of empathy for deliberation. Young also questions the role of empathy in deliberation, but for different reasons than Benhabib. Young worries that empathy may lead participants to impose upon others by projecting their own feelings onto others rather than really understanding them. When people "put themselves in the position of a person in a wheelchair, they do not imagine the point of view of others; rather, they project on to those others their own fears and fantasies about themselves" (Young 2001, 209). Young believes that attempts at empathy by participants are more likely to be detrimental than helpful, and she encourages participants to just accept what others say without trying to imagine their point of view. Burkhalter, Gastil, and Kelshaw (2002) seem to go even further than Young by being skeptical about the very possibility of the process of empathy occurring, though they maintain that people still ought to try to empathize. They begin by arguing that "it is strictly impossible to put oneself in another's position" (409) because seeing the world through another's eyes or standing in another's shoes requires people "to shed their own cultural and historical experiences," something that is both impossible and absurd (408). Yet in their description of the dialogic components of deliberation, they cite Rogers in positing that "a deliberative participant

EMPATHY AND DEMOCRACY 165

who fails to understand another's viewpoint, even after careful reflection, employs empathy" (409). They say that the reason attempting to empathize is important, despite its impossibility, is because "it is helpful to refocus attention from the content of the other's argument to the individual person" (409). Even though the empathy will never really occur as described in the process model, an imaginative effort to perceive others can help participants recognize the differences that separate them. These theorists, therefore, reject the full process model of empathy I have developed because it is unnecessary (Benhabib), detrimental (Young), or impossible in reality (Burkhalter, Gastil, and Kelshaw).

It should come as no surprise that I do not agree that empathy is impossible. Though Burkhalter, Gastil, and Kelshaw support attempts by participants to empathize, and their claim that empathy is impossible may be strictly ontologically correct—one can never fully put oneself in the shoes of another—the incommensurability of human experience is not nearly as strong as they indicate. A large body of empirical evidence in psychology and neuroscience indicate that humans can engage in the process of empathy. Jean Decety and Philip Jackson, for example, write, "Humans have the capacity to intentionally adopt the subjective perspective of others by putting themselves into other people's shoes and imagining what they feel. Such a capacity requires that one mentally simulate the other's perspective using one's own neural machinery" (2006, 55). This ability does require that people share experiences that are similar enough so that there can be some matching between them, but the experiences do not have to be exactly the same. Even though people may react to different situations differently, human experiences such as joy, pain, desire, frustration, excitement, and regret provide fertile ground for the possibility of empathy. While there will be times when it may be difficult for some people to empathize with others, empathy is not impossible or absurd. Participants in deliberation should not attempt to empathize only in order to recognize the differences in background and identity that separate them, though this certainly may happen; they must engage in the process of empathy in order to gain an understanding of various perspectives that will then allow them to give those perspectives equal consideration in collective decision-making.

It should also come as no surprise that I do not believe empathy is either undesirable or detrimental. Benhabib's and Young's criticisms draw upon a distinction between self and other. For Benhabib, people should view the other's world from the self's perspective; for Young, this is exactly the danger from empathy. Social psychologists have recognized some of the issues surrounding the self/other distinction in empathy research (see, for example, Batson 1997; Batson, Sager, et al. 1997; Cialdini et al. 1997; and Davis et al. 1996). Studies using role-taking instructions have dealt with this issue by distinguishing between "imagine self" and "imagine other" instructions (see, for example, Batson, Early, and Salvarani 1997). These studies show that that "imagine other" instructions result in more consistently positive results in terms of out-group evaluation and bias reduction. Given the importance of these findings for deliberation, Benhabib's admonition to only employ an Arendtian "enlarged mentality" is not persuasive. If participants in deliberation only attempt to view the situations of their fellows from their own perspective, they are not giving others the consideration required by deliberative theory. In one study, for example, subjects who imagined how they would feel after watching another in pain had strong feelings of personal distress, while those who imagined what the other was feeling reported more feelings of empathic concern (Decety and Lamm 2006, 1160). If participants simply imagine how they would feel in another's place, they tend to focus on their own concerns rather than understanding the concerns of the other. Citizens must strive to understand how others see their positions from their perspectives; only by doing so will democratic citizens reduce the biases they tend to have and give others the equal consideration necessary for legitimate collective decision-making.

Recent work in neuroscience that further demonstrates the importance of the self/other distinction in the process of empathy helps address the concerns regarding projection raised by Young. This research demonstrates that people rely upon overlapping neural circuits when understanding how others think and feel. Decety and Jackson write, "There is strong evidence that, in the domain of emotion processing and empathic understanding, people use the same neural circuits for themselves and for others. These circuits provide a functional bridge between first-person and third-person information, which paves the way for intersubjective transactions between self and others. These circuits can also be activated when one adopts the perspective of the other" (2006, 57). Studies confirm this overlap or bridge in neural mechanisms for both affective empathy (see, for example, Decety 2007; Decety and Jackson 2004; Decety and Lamm 2006; Decety and Moriguchi 2007; Lamm, Batson, and Decety 2007; and Ruby and Decety 2004) and a cognitive understanding of others (see, for example, Decety and Grèzes 2006 and Decety and Sommerville 2003).[2] Yet beyond these

2. I believe that this work makes too strong a distinction between cognition and affect in the empathic process, but given the consistent findings in both areas, this does not undermine the argument I am making here.

bridging neural mechanisms, both affective empathy and a cognitive under-standing of others require people to distinguish clearly between themselves and the other. Human empathy and perspective taking rely upon "both a shared neural network between self and other representations (involving the amygdala in a social–emotional context) for mutual understanding" and a set of neural regions that account "for the distinction between self and other representations (somatosensory cortex, frontopolar cortex, right inferior parietal cortex), irrespective of the processing domain, preventing the confusion that could derive from the shared network" (Ruby and Decety 2004). In the human brain, the process of empathy, in both its affective and cognitive aspects, requires that people maintain a healthy distinction between themselves and others that will mitigate against the possibility of projection that Young fears.

I do not wish to claim that projection would never be a threat in deliber-ation that puts an emphasis on the process of empathy, but there is good evidence that empathizing does not necessarily lead to the kind of projec-tion that Young fears. Instead of leading to a rejection of empathy, her anecdote regarding the person in the wheelchair highlights the importance of the process model of empathy. As the model indicates, the empathic process can have negative effects such as personal distress or empathic overarousal. The deliberative process must work to insure that neither these negative effects nor projection occur by encouraging participants to fully imagine others' affective and cognitive perspectives rather than impos-ing their own. Deliberation also provides a corrective to the possibility of projection, something nondeliberative forms of democracy lack. It is much more likely for people to carry incorrect assumptions about others if they never have to engage in a discussion with them. An attentive, communica-tive exchange among citizens committed to the process of empathy is the best cure for the kind of projection Young fears.

The Process Model of Empathy and the Limits of Communication

Though empathy is necessary for deliberation to function, and because of this we must provisionally allow all forms of communication, there are lim-its that the process model does set. Mansbridge and others demonstrate in their coding study that professional facilitators praise the role of affective utterances that deepen deliberation, but not all affective utterances do this. The facilitators "found emotion unproductive when it made participants feel "defensive or angry" and when it kept them from "consider[ing] others' views" or explaining the reasons behind their position," and they "negatively valued emotions that in various ways seemed to close down communication" (Mansbridge et al. 2006, 20). As Dryzek argues, deliberation should provisionally admit any communication—including greeting, rhetoric, storytelling, narrative, and argument, but perhaps also poetry, exegesis, film, and fiction—but submit that communication to only one test: does it advance the process of inclusive, attentive deliberation that promotes the process of empathy?

While some forms of communication may impede the flow of "factual" information necessary for attentive deliberation, the most likely impediment to inclusive, attentive deliberation will be those moments of communication that interfere with the process of empathy. The empathy test encompasses Dryzek's test of noncoercive speech, for certainly coercive speech would impede both empathy and the free flow of other information. It also approximates his test that communication induces reflection, though I believe that my test may define reflection slightly more broadly than his does. Where he and I part ways is his requirement that communication connect the particular with the general. I certainly understand why he wants this as a test for deliberative communication, but I believe that participants in deliberation can benefit from a communicative exchange even if it focuses on particular needs and interests. I think that oftentimes such exchanges will connect the particular with something more general, but this is not necessary. There may even be times when such communication, such as an individual's story, may not immediately connect with more general issues under discussion, but in the future such connections may become visible. Provisionally admitting forms of communication, as long as they aid in the empathic process, allow for this possibility.

Beyond even Dryzek's tests, the requirement that communications advance the process of empathy also says something about inclusion. In Chapter 5 I pointed to empirical evidence that demonstrates that empathy, if one-sided, may actually decrease just actions, and the process model also points out that the similarity between a target and an observer can have an effect on the empathic process. While some might see this as a point against empathy, the empirical data show that this already occurs and leads to biases. Deliberation that encourages the empathic process is the only way to overcome this already occurring problem. These points highlight the need for balance in deliberation. This does not mean that all communications must be balanced, and my argument to this point indicates that people should be able to communicate from their own perspectives. Yet communicative exchange in deliberation must strive for an overall balance of perspectives, including affective perspectives. The deliberative opinion poll, for example, provides all participants with a balanced packet of information before deliberation, usually brings in a balanced panel of experts during deliberation, and trains facilitators to work to insure that all participants get a chance to speak. I would suggest that deliberative institutions could augment this practice even further by including a set of balanced narratives in the information packets given to participants. What the test for communication demonstrates ultimately is that a deliberative democracy must work to insure that—both at the macro, systemic level and in micro, face-to-face, deliberative exercises—communication represents the variety of views found in society. Only by doing so will deliberation embody the process of empathy that is necessary to give all citizens equal consideration.

Legitimacy, Justification, and Manin's Challenge

Defining deliberation as a practice in which people contemplate a political object by engaging in an inclusive, attentive communicative exchange that promotes the exchange of information and the process of empathy allows deliberative theory to address criticisms that deliberation illegitimately excludes certain forms of communication, especially those with affective content. It does so without linking those forms only to certain groups, such as minorities, and it provides a criterion by which we can judge when communication is deliberatively legitimate. Thus, a deliberative theory that takes empathy seriously leads to a more equal consideration of all affected by decisions. Yet democracy still involves making collective decisions that must be legitimate, and so now I turn to the questions of how deliberation with a focus on empathy can support democratic legitimacy.

The Problem of Justification

While some critics may exaggerate deliberative democrats' positions, underlying many deliberative theories is the need to justify democratic decisions through pubic reason or within a rationally constituted legal system. As Chambers notes, while "consensus need not be the ultimate aim of deliberation, and participants are expected to pursue their interests, an overarching interest in the legitimacy of outcomes (understood as justification to all affected) ideally characterizes deliberation" (2003, 309). Even granting that consensus need not be the *ultimate* aim of deliberation, thus moving deliberative theories away from something like Rousseau's general will, the focus on justification as the basis of legitimacy requires that participants in deliberation move toward something like a general belief that they have discovered what is justifiable to all. For Rawls, public reason requires a citizen to deliberate "within a framework of what he or she sincerely regards as the most reasonable conception of justice, a conception that expresses political values that others, as free and equal citizens might also reasonably be expected to endorse" (1997, 773). His proviso expands this view of public reasons in that it allows people to rely upon their comprehensive conceptions of the good to make arguments, but at some indeterminate point in the future they must be able to justify their position by reference to the same political values they believe other reasonable citizens should accept. Even if there is no actual consensus, Rawls's theory assumes that those who rely upon a political conception of justice sincerely believe that conception to be the one that all reasonable citizens should reasonably accept.

Habermas's theory of deliberative democracy is less clear because of his shift away from discourse ethics with its clear universalization principle. As I noted in Chapter 2, he shifts from an individual or group level of analysis to look at the social level of the institutionalized processes of deliberation and decision-making. Yet he remains wedded to a principle of legitimacy that requires all laws to "meet with the assent (*Zustimmung*) of all citizens in a discursive process of legislation that in turn has been legally constituted" (Habermas 1996a, 110). Democratic deliberation may admit, in addition to moral reasoning, legal and ethical reasoning, but in the end there must still be a process of rational public opinion- and will-formation. The requirement to justify our positions to others through argumentation, as I have noted, requires that we take a generalized perspective. Citizens must go beyond just the pursuit of their own interests in exercising their communicative liberties, and must look toward the common good by taking "the perspective of participants who are engaged in the process of reaching understanding about the rules for their life in common" (1996a, 461; emphasis in original). Both Rawls and Habermas move beyond Rousseau in requiring the citizens interact with and take seriously their fellow citizens, but in the end, people justify their use of democratic power by reference to what they believe is the most reasonable or most rationally justifiable position on the political question at hand.

As we have seen, both political psychologists and political theorists raise important questions about using justification in the sense of reasonable or rational defensibility as the basis of democratic legitimacy. Even if legitimacy does not rely upon a general will, if the core of justification is reasons that all could (or should) accept, the better argument, or the common good, then its very possibility relies upon the removal of aspects of human existence that might prevent finding these general or common bases. For many deliberative theorists, affect falls into the category of something that is purely subjective and cannot reach the level of generalization necessary for agreement. Beyond even affect, any particular aspect of a person's life raises the possibility of not being able to find commonality. Yet any move away from the particular to finding something common to all is problematic. The theories of affective intelligence and motivated reasoning highlight the fact that human beings do not reason without reference to their emotions. Political theorists who defend rhetoric and persuasion also demonstrate how political reasoning relies upon the affective side of human experience. If affect is not generalizable, then there is an inherent contradiction between trying to find reasons or arguments acceptable to all and the very way in which people actually reason. Agonistic democrats point out that the very move toward requiring reasons all could or should accept as the basis of justification tends toward an evisceration of difference and the imposition of particular ways of thinking about the world. While agonists overemphasize the necessity of conflict and exaggerate the degree to which deliberative theories impose certain notions of rationality and reasonableness, the spirit of their critique is valid. I understand why many deliberative democrats argue that people should only act upon what they deem are generally justifiable reasons, but people who believe they have found such reasons are likely to be less sensitive to others and the possibility that they are mistaken in their beliefs. While they might not completely ignore others, they can "justify" acting contrary to the interests of others as long as they are defending what they see as "justice" or the "common good." Rather than acknowledge that their decision is their own, they perceive it as what all would or should decide. By definition, anyone who disagrees must be unreasonable, irrational, or at the least, mistaken about what justice or the common good requires. Basing democratic legitimacy in this kind of justification, therefore, is problematic because it cannot account for how human beings actually reason and threatens the very openness and equality it aims to embody.

Manin's Challenge

This brings us back to Manin's challenge to deliberative theory. In Chapter 2 I showed how Manin criticizes the notion of legitimacy as justification in a way similar to the agonists. Pointing out that consensus on important political questions is highly unlikely, Manin questions whether any process can achieve the kind of rational justification theorists like Rawls and Habermas expect. There are shortcomings in Manin's interpretations of Rawls and Habermas, but he raises an important point. There is a sense in which deliberative theory in its various guises seems to confer upon the majority will "all the attributes of unanimous will" (Manin 1987, 342), at least on a provisional basis. Yet Manin himself appears to mirror the later incarnations of deliberative theory when he posits that "between the *rational* object of universal agreement and the *arbitrary* lies the domain of the *reasonable* and *justifiable,* that is, the domain of propositions that are likely to convince, by means of arguments whose conclusion is not incontestable, the greater part of an audience made up of all the citizens" (363; emphasis in original). What distinguishes his position is that he does not say that the reasonable and justifiable represent what *all* could or should reasonably accept or what *all* could or should find justifiable; instead, they represent what *a majority* of citizens do find reasonable and justifiable. That a majority finds a decision reasonable and justifiable may indicate that it is not arbitrary, but it does not give it any special status as representative of a more general will, even provisionally. What provides legitimacy is that the decision occurs only after a process of deliberation that meets certain conditions: there are genuine alternatives, deliberation is before the universal audience of citizens, the majority is subject to dismissal at regular intervals, and there are guarantees of basic rights and liberties. It is deliberation itself, not the fact that a majority believes that the decision rests upon public reason or the force of the better argument, that provides democratic legitimacy.

Manin's position highlights the importance of the process of deliberation, rather than its aim, as the source of legitimacy. Yack makes a similar point when he writes, "It is important at the outset to emphasize that, contrary to much of the recent literature on deliberative democracy, political deliberation is not a form of collective decision-making. Political deliberation informs and prepares collective decisions by helping individual citizens determine which collective action to support" (2006, 419–20). As I noted in Chapter 2, deliberative democrats recognize this point by delineating certain conditions as necessary for deliberation and acknowledging the importance of the cultural and background conditions in which deliberation occurs. They do so, however, in order to confer a "reasonable" or "rational" justificatory status on the decision the majority eventually makes following deliberation. They remain caught in the problems of this approach I have already identified. Instead of justification on this understanding, we ought to follow Manin and Yack, as well as theorists such as Fishkin and Bessette, by grounding democratic legitimacy in deliberation itself. Yet the conditions for deliberation these theorists identify, though necessary, are not enough. Democratic legitimacy requires the process of empathy.

Empathy and Democratic Legitimacy

The process of empathy is necessary for democratic legitimacy because it insures that majorities will make decisions with a better knowledge of what those decisions mean. It does so in several ways. First, it gives a place to both cognition and affect in deliberation. Affect is a part of human reasoning, and democracy requires that people reason together. Deliberation that incorporates the empathic process allows them to reason together in a way that gives affect its proper place. People who empathize not only understand the logical arguments of those with whom they disagree, they will gain a better knowledge of the thoughts and feelings that inform those arguments. For example, people who are pro-choice may understand on a logical level why pharmacists who believe that contraception is against God's law, and who do not want to violate God's law, would not want to dispense contraception. Conversely, these pharmacists could logically understand why people who do believe that contraception is a legitimate health product, and who believe that pharmacists should dispense legitimate health products, would want pharmacists to dispense contraception. Just understanding the logic of these views, however, is not enough for democratic legitimacy. Unless those who are pro-choice understand what the pharmacists think and feel about dispensing contraception, and unless the pharmacists understand how those who disagree with them think and feel about not having access to contraception, any decision on the issue will only be partially informed. This does not mean that if those who disagree engage in empathy, they will overcome their disagreement. As Meyers points out, while empathy requires some "basic concern for the other," it does not have to lead to agreeing with "the other's point of view" or "endorsing the other's state of mind" (1993, 25).

What empathy promotes is not necessarily agreement, but understanding the impacts a decision will have on others. This understanding reduces the threat that people can justify to themselves the legitimacy of a decision that ignores others. A majority that enacts a policy exempting Catholic hospitals from providing rape victims with emergency contraception could justify their decision with the argument that the principle of freedom of religious expression outweighs all other values involved in the issue. A majority that enacts a policy requiring all hospitals to provide rape victims with emergency contraception could justify their decision based upon the claim that the separation of church and state requires that religious doctrine should not dictate public health policy in this area. Both majorities could draw upon generally recognized political values and arguments they believe that others could accept in ways that allow them to rationalize ignoring the minorities' thoughts and feelings on the issue. If they engage in empathy, however, it will be much more difficult for them to ignore the fact that their decisions will have profound effects upon those with whom they disagree.

By inducing majorities to acknowledge the impacts of their decisions on others more fully, the process of empathy will have an effect on democratic decision-making. The majorities may make the same decisions, but knowing that they are imposing their own beliefs and feelings on others, I believe, will more often lead to something like what Gutmann and Thompson call "moral accommodation" (1996, 79–91): decisions that attempt to take into account as many views as possible. For example, a law could exempt Catholic hospitals from dispensing emergency contraception to rape victims, but require that in all rape cases someone else is available to do so, perhaps by giving emergency medical technicians or rape counselors the necessary authority and responsibility. Similarly, a law could exempt pharmacists who object on moral grounds from having to dispense contraception while making sure that people had alternative ways to access contraception that would be no more burdensome than if the pharmacist did dispense it. Some may find such decisions unpalatable and satisfying to no one, but if they result from an attentive deliberative process, they will be more legitimate, at least provisionally. Decision-making does not conclude the deliberative process, and future deliberations may yield changes in views and perspectives that lead to alternative resolutions of differences. Yet even after engaging in a deliberative process that induces the empathic process, there will certainly be issues for which there is little if any room for accommodation, or for which the majority is not willing to accommodate the minority. The majority may still decide the issue the way it prefers. If an attentive deliberation that induces the process of empathy precedes the decisions, however, the majority will do so with a fuller knowledge that it is imposing its decision on those who disagree, however it justifies its decision.

There is another possibility, though, that the empathic model of deliberation provides that is lacking in other models. A deliberative democracy that incorporates empathy, in both its affective and cognitive aspects, may serve interlocutors by allowing them to achieve what Albrecht Wellmer calls the "elimination of nonsense" (1991, 196–99). Knowing that their decision will ignore the thoughts and feelings of others may give majorities pause, and if no accommodationist position is available, perhaps they will be less likely to act (or not act) in ways that affect others negatively. This elimination of nonsense would be no small feat, and if it occurred, it would demonstrate that empathy is a vital component of deliberative democracy. Some might question whether this tendency might increase people's ambivalence to a point that paralyzes democratic decision-making. If empathy becomes too strong, people may hold back from reaching a decision when the majority realizes that a minority will "lose" and have to accept defeat. Yet in most circumstances, I believe this is not a problem, but rather a positive benefit of empathy. One of the reasons why deliberation is important on any understanding is that it requires people to reflect upon the decisions they are making.

Human history gives ample evidence that majorities are much more likely to act in a way that ignores or marginalizes minorities, even after reflection. Requiring that deliberative reflection include empathy will make it more likely that majorities are conscious of how their actions affect minorities, and if this leads to hesitation by majorities, in most cases this will be a positive development. Yet empathy also requires minorities to empathize with majorities, and so it does not ask that one side sacrifice more than the other. Empathy may also lead minorities to realize more keenly what they are asking for when they claim that the majority should not decide as they intend. If, after a fully attentive deliberative process in which both the majority and the minority empathize with one another, the two sides cannot find a position of accommodation and the majority cannot bring itself to impose its decision on the minority, I believe that in most cases the decision not to act will be the most legitimate. While there may be a few instances in which a majority's failure to act will indisputably be harmful, such cases would be very rare and would not undermine the general argument I am presenting here. If the evidence is so clear, it is hardly likely that the majority will fail to decide, but even in such cases they will only decide after acknowledging the full import of the decision for all involved. Most of human history demonstrates that democracies ought to be more concerned about majorities acting self-interestedly in ways contrary to the interests of the minority rather than about majorities failing to act when they should. The theory of deliberative democracy I have developed shows the proper concern in this area by working to eliminate the tendency of majorities to act without giving equal consideration to all through the incorporation of the process of empathy into democratic decision-making.

Given the positive effects the process of empathy can have, as well as what I demonstrated in the previous section about it reducing barriers to equal consideration, I can now define democratic legitimacy for the model. A democratic decision is legitimate to the extent that the majority decides only after a process of deliberation that gives all citizens the opportunity to engage in a full exchange of perspectives and induces them to empathize with one another. This definition sets up the ideal conditions for legitimate decision-making, and most democratic decisions will occur without meeting the ideal in full. This is true, however, of every theory of democracy. The real world often violates even minimalist democratic theories that only require the guarantee of equal basic rights such as voting. My use of the phrase "to the extent that" indicates that legitimacy is a continuum along which democratic decisions will fall. The more the deliberation that precedes a decision includes all citizens in a free exchange of perspectives and induces them to empathize with one another, the more legitimate it will be. This can serve as the guide for critique of actually existing practices of democracy. Yet the real world immediately raises several issues regarding the feasibility of this definition of legitimacy.

Empathy and the Feasibility of Deliberative Democracy

The Problem of Economy

Critics have raised several concerns regarding the feasibility of a deliberative conception of democracy. One concern is what Dryzek calls the problem of economy. As Michael Walzer puts it: "Deliberation is not an activity for the demos. I don't mean that ordinary men and women don't have the capacity to reason, only that 100 million of them, or even 1 million or 100,000 can't plausibly 'reason together'" (1999, 68). While Walzer conceives of deliberation as a way of thinking that is "quiet, reflective, open to a wide range of evidence, respectful of different views," a conceptualization that I have already rejected, his point remains: in a polity of any size, it is impossible for all citizens to deliberate together. Dryzek elucidates and rejects several responses to the problem of economy. The first is to restrict deliberation "to a small number of occasions when popular deliberation can occur," yet he believes that this cannot really overcome the economy problem and finds it odd to base democratic legitimacy on such limited moments (2001, 653). The second solution he cites "is somehow to restrict the number of people involved in deliberation, making sure that the individuals who do participate be in some way representative of those who do not. There are two main ways of securing representativeness: by popular election and by random selection" (653). He rejects popular elections as unable to meet the legitimacy requirements of deliberative theory, especially as they compound legitimacy problems if elections are not deliberative. He rejects random selection for not really representing real group deliberation processes, for failing to capture what deliberation of the entire population would be like, and for delimiting the areas of deliberation (654). An alternative version of this solution is to restrict deliberation in nondemocratic ways, for example, as he sees Rawls doing. "If some people are better able to reflect than others, perhaps political philosophers and legal theorists, then they should be the ones to whom society entrusts public reason" (655). He rejects this approach because it can answer the problem of legitimacy "only to the extent that the public accepts that public reason is indeed singular and that professional experts in the exercise of public reason do indeed know best," something he seems to doubt would happen (655).

The third solution Dryzek mentions is Goodin's argument for internal-reflective deliberation in which those "who do participate in proceedings . . . call to mind the interests of those who do not participate" (2001, 655). Dryzek calls this "a kind of partial substitution of internal-individual deliberation for real interaction" (655), and even points out that some theorists make a similar argument that this allows the inclusion of nonhuman species and future generations, as well as the possibility that it could allow transnational deliberation. Dryzek rejects this approach by positing that Goodin's specific solution "presupposes that we have already restricted the number of deliberators," probably to representatives (656). Yet this exacerbates the problem of legitimacy for representatives by "asking members of the broader public to take it on trust that the deliberators really are calling to mind and internalizing broader sets of interests" (656). Public records of an institution such as a Supreme Court would allow citizens to check if this was occurring, but Dryzek argues that Goodin gives no hints of such a check.

Dryzek draws his final solution from Habermas's distinction between the informal public sphere and formal political institutions. "Legitimacy is secured by public acceptance of the procedures through which lawmaking achieves responsiveness to public opinion as formed in a broader public sphere. Public opinion is converted into communicative power as a result of the electoral process, then into administrative power via lawmaking" (Dryzek 2001, 656). Thus, only legislators need deliberate specifically on any given legislation. Dryzek argues that Habermas's model is inadequate in the face of the problem of economy because: (1) it is not clear about extra-constitutional agents of influence, focusing too often only on the legislature; (2) its focus on elections is open to rational choice critiques about the influence of voting systems on outcomes; and (3) most seriously, its proceduralism cannot account for the substance of public opinion (656–57).

Dryzek offers an alternative response to the problem of economy by drawing on Habermas's distinction between the public sphere and formal institutions but altering it to suit his purposes. He argues that democratic decisions are legitimate when they are "consistent with the constellation of discourses present in the public sphere, in the degree to which this constellation is subject to the reflective control of competent actors" (2001, 660). Public opinion represents the provisional outcome of this contestation of discourses as transmitted to formal political institutions. Dryzek maintains that he solves the economy problem "because the number of participants in deliberation is indeterminate" (663). His theory does not require any exclusion, allowing that at any given time the number of participants can vary considerably. The contestation of discourses is open to any who wish to engage in it and can occur at many different sites within the public sphere. The "indeterminacy in numbers of participants in the contestation of discourses solves the seemingly incompatible demands of deliberative economy and the need for collective decisions to secure actual popular reflective acceptance . . . discursive contestation can accept, even welcome, the participation of the many at any time" (663). Deliberative democrats must still criticize the contestation of discourses if (1) "state imperatives (related, for example, to the need to maintain the confidence of financial markets) override the constellation of discourses in determining the content of public policy"; (2) "popular discourses themselves are ideological (in the pejorative sense of specifying false necessities, perhaps even the necessity of always having to please financial markets; discourses are inescapably ideological in a more neutral sense of 'ideology')"; and (3) "the contestation of discourses is manipulated by strategy and power and not subject to reflexive control" (663). The public sphere especially allows for dispersed and competent democratic control because of the presence of networks (664–65). Networks are bottom-up organizations that arise in response to an issue of public concern, and to the extent that they engage diverse participants, their formation necessitates the equality, openness, respect, and reciprocity that deliberation requires.

Conceiving of deliberation as occurring within a system that includes an open public sphere in addition to formal political institutions is a persuasive move in helping deliberative theory address the problem of economy. Though I generally agree with Dryzek's arguments, I have several concerns. First, as Dryzek notes, the solutions he lists are not all mutually exclusive. It is possible to have representative, or even nonrepresentative, samples of people deliberate within the public sphere such as occur in deliberative opinion polls, citizens' juries, National Issues Forums, and study circles. These moments alone may not overcome the problem of economy, but they can add to the overall system's deliberative legitimacy; opportunities for such face-to-face exchanges can increase the quality of deliberation within the public sphere. Second, a reservation I have about Dryzek's approach is his reliance on a contestation of discourses as the foundation for democratic legitimacy. While such a contestation can admit as many participants as wish to engage at any given time, and thus helps overcome the problem of economy, there is still the threat that some people will be unable to engage in the deliberative process. Not everyone has the opportunities and resources to participate in the contestation of discourses, and this could lead to the kind of exclusions that threaten democratic legitimacy. While basing legitimacy on the contestation of discourses does overcome the problem of economy by shifting our view from the individual level, by doing so it may also make us less sensitive to the ways in which the contestation does not give equal consideration to all. This relates to a third concern I have with Dryzek's model.

I think that both Dryzek and Habermas tend to overestimate the extent to which there is a separation between the public sphere and formal political institutions (whether legislative or administrative). While bottom-up networks may arise within the public sphere, there are webs of interconnections among networks, public interest groups, lobbyists, political officials, fundraisers, political agencies, pundits, political consultants, and the media. Such webs threaten the opportunity for dispersed and competent democratic control by allowing narrow groups to capture and distort public sphere discourse. Though both Dryzek and Habermas recognize this, I think they underestimate the detrimental effects these webs can have on democratic decision-making. As they suggest, deliberative democrats must be critical

*ask legitimacy protocol for democratic choice
but not optimization of soc'l hlth questn*

of public sphere deliberation, and I agree completely. Public sphere deliberation is vitally important both to democratic legitimacy and overcoming the problem of economy, but we also must consider alternatives for deliberation that will connect the formal political institutions and the public sphere. Democracy needs to provide a formal site for deliberation other than among policymakers. The most viable way to achieve this is to provide for a new governmental agency whose members will deliberate before the public about important issues without having the power to implement those decisions.

My final concern with Dryzek's answer to the problem of economy is that he too easily dismisses Goodin's proposition for internal-reflective deliberation. He sees Goodin as leaning toward the use of representatives as a substitute for real deliberation, yet Goodin maintains that both "rulers" and "citizens" ought to practice democratic "deliberation within" in order to "internalize the perspectives of all the diverse interests represented within their community" (2003, 229). It is not just that citizens "trust" their representatives to deliberate with everyone's interests in mind, but every participant in the democratic system must engage in internal-reflective deliberation. Goodin argues that democratic legitimacy arises from the final vote on any decision, but "it is the preceding discussion which renders that decision a *democratically deliberative* one. . . . Internal-reflective deliberations are not a substitute for, but rather an input into, external-collective decision procedures" (192; emphasis in original). I think Dryzek's rejection of Goodin actually arises from a different understanding of democratic legitimacy. In defining legitimacy, he writes: "The essence of deliberation is generally taken to be that claims for or against collective decisions need to be justified to those subject to these decisions in terms that, given the chance to reflect, these individuals can accept" (2001, 651). The problem of economy arises because legitimacy requires that all individuals can rationally accept a decision, but Goodin's conceptualization of legitimacy is more minimalist because it only requires that everyone be given basic equal rights such as the right to vote. In this sense, Goodin does not link deliberation and democratic legitimacy directly, but instead argues that legitimate democratic decisions ought to be more deliberative.

As should be clear from the previous section, my position falls in between Dryzek's and Goodin's. I think Goodin is right that the final vote provides democratic legitimacy, but given the need for equal consideration, I also believe that the preceding discussion also contributes to a decision's democratic legitimacy. I think Dryzek is correct that public sphere deliberation can contribute to democratic legitimacy, but I do not believe that legitimacy arises from public sphere deliberation providing a "justification" of a decision that all could or should accept. Instead, public sphere deliberation contributes to legitimacy to the extent that it contributes to a process that gives all citizens the opportunity to engage in a full exchange of perspectives and induces them to empathize with one another. The process of empathy increases legitimacy because, as Goodin suggests, it allows people to reflect on others' perspectives even when they cannot engage in face-to-face deliberation with those others. It also helps overcome the problem of economy by visualizing how people might engage a large number of people without meeting them face-to-face. Rather than having to assimilate individuals or groups under discourses, deliberation that includes empathy allows people to consider the interests of many individuals and groups, even those who cannot speak—the excluded, the environment, nonhuman species, and those not yet born. I admit that in actual practice people will not be able to empathize with absolutely everyone, but in comparison to other conceptualizations of democratic legitimacy, a deliberative system that allows for the process of empathy is best situated to maximize the consideration of all perspectives before decision-making occurs. The process of empathy is the only viable way to overcome the problems of economy by making all citizens present in democratic deliberation to as great an extent as possible, yet we must not limit empathy only to formal political institutions. Deliberation both within the public sphere and in formal political bodies is legitimate to the extent that it embodies a full exchange of information and the process of empathy.

The Problems of Deliberation in Practice

The process model of empathy is also helpful in responding to concerns raised by empirical studies of deliberation (for some general reviews, see Delli Carpini, Cook, and Jacobs 2004; Mendelberg 2002; and Rosenberg 2007a). Empirical studies demonstrate that deliberation often reinforces structural inequalities (Sanders 1997, 363–65); that it can rely upon racist language that people present as universal, well-reasoned, and consonant with the common good (Mendelberg and Oleske 2000); and that it can create a false consensus by sublimating conflict (Karpowitz and Mansbridge 2005). Tali Mendelberg summarizes some of the concerns raised by empirical studies by listing the ways in which deliberative theorists must be cautious. She notes that we cannot always count on deliberative groups "to generate empathy and diminish narrow self-interest, to afford equal opportunities for participation and influence even to the powerless, to approach the discussion with a mind open to change, and to be influenced not by social pressures, unthinking commitments to social identities, or power, but by the exchange of relevant and sound reasons" (2002, 180). The news is not all bad, though. She argues that deliberation can function as deliberative theorists expect, but what is most important is that "the conditions of deliberation can matter a great deal to its success" (180). Deliberation works well for matters of "objective truth," but is likely to fail "when strong social pressures or identities exist, conflict is deep, and the matter at hand centers on values rather than facts" (180). Michael Delli Carpini, Fay Cook, and Lawrence Jacobs make a similar point in their own review of the empirical evidence: "Most important, the impact of deliberation and other forms of discursive politics is highly context dependent. It varies with the purpose of the deliberation, the subject under discussion, who participates, the connection to authoritative decision makers, the rules governing interactions, the information provided, prior beliefs, substantive outcomes, and real-world conditions" (Delli Carpini, Cook, and Jacobs 2004, 336). While empirical studies raise questions about deliberative theory, Mendelberg argues that "the role of empirical evidence in theories of deliberation should not be limited to arguments over whether a few successful deliberative exercises count as evidence for or against deliberation" (2002, 180). Instead, systemic evidence can give us insights into what can contribute to an effectively functioning deliberative democracy.

The process model of empathy provides us with the systemic evidence that reveals how to contextualize deliberation so that it can achieve its goals. Empirical studies generally conclude that actual deliberation is often not as open and egalitarian as deliberative theorists require, or that its adversarial nature prevents people from engaging in a reflective, mutually respectful exchange of ideas. My model can assist deliberative theory in answering these concerns. The process model recognizes that while empathy can occur because of deliberation, the antecedents to deliberation are also important. As I demonstrated in Chapter 5, people's predispositions to empathy can affect the ability of deliberation to embody an open, egalitarian, reflective, and mutually respectful process. The process model also demonstrates that there is an interaction between the nonaffective outcomes of reducing biases and affective outcomes of parallel and reactive affect. All too often empirical studies operationalize deliberation as the give and take of reasons in argumentation while excluding the affective side of communicative exchange; the model of deliberation I have developed demonstrates that the success of deliberation hinges on giving affect its proper place. Finally, the empirical evidence I surveyed in Chapter 5 supporting the positive non-affective outcomes in the process model highlights how empathy can provide the foundation for the other requirements in deliberation, including openness, mutual respect, and reciprocity. The process model demonstrates how deliberative theory can respond to the concerns empirical studies raise by showing, not only that empathy is important to deliberation, but also how we might incorporate a multidimensional model of empathy into a theory of deliberative democracy. The process model gives deliberative theory a criterion to evaluate the conditions necessary for successful deliberation and points us toward further hypotheses that we might test regarding these conditions.

One such hypothesis regards the importance on winning and losing in deliberation. The research I described in Chapter 5, for example, not only illuminates the importance of empathic predispositions for reciprocity, it also reveals how winning and losing can affect the quality of deliberation. In other research I have shown a similar affect of winning and losing on participants' willingness to accept collective decisions (Morrell 1999), at least in the short term. This evidence suggests that the need to win an argument interferes with some of the conditions necessary for successful deliberation. The implication is that at least some deliberation should occur under conditions that do not require a decision, and we can take advantage of the delineation between the public sphere and formal political institutions in this regard. Most theorists today acknowledge that democratic deliberation occurs on a continuum from more informal deliberation in the public sphere or civil society, what Mansbridge calls "everyday talk" (1999), to deliberation within formal political institutions. The pressure of making a final decision is much stronger in formal political institutions than in the informal public sphere, where the necessity of a final decision need only inform, but not create an undue pressure on, deliberation. The model of deliberation I propose can live with the tension between the need for a final decision and the requirement of inclusion; it can accommodate deliberation at different points along the continuum. Legislators and other policymakers may deliberate to some degree in formal political institutions, and in doing so the process of empathy remains important, but they can also be subject to the influence of, as well as participate in, more informal deliberation. In this way, deliberation influenced by the process of empathy can work through citizens' informal deliberations to influence legislators and other policymakers. It is also important to note that my own empirical research indicates that the process of empathy is important even when controlling for the pressure of having to make a decision. The final, though provisional, decisions in a deliberative democracy are highly important, and I do not want to ignore them. In many instances, however, democracy will benefit from deliberation in the public sphere that does not aim at a decision, and even within formal political institutions, the model of deliberation that places empathy at its heart suggests the need for similar moments when deliberation does not necessarily culminate in a final decision. Providing space for deliberations that do not immediately aim at final decisions will increase the chances that people will empathize with one another; this will, in turn, increase the likelihood that the collective democratic decisions that people make will give all the equal consideration that is necessary for democratic legitimacy.

Do People Even Want to Deliberate?

A final concern critics raise regarding the feasibility of deliberative democracy questions whether citizens will actually deliberate. It is interesting that both political scientists and political theorists raise such objections. I have already discussed how agonists argue that deliberative democracy does not take account of people's passions, and because of this cannot account for what motivates citizens to engage in politics. Goi extends this point by arguing that deliberative theory does not give people a reason to participate, especially if its avoidance of conflict tends to lead to the exclusion of some voices. "For [apathetic] citizens, deliberative democracy does not answer the fundamental question of why they should bother participating. When citizens feel that the decision-making apparatus of the state has already chosen to exclude their perspectives, their inclination is to retreat into the private sphere of insular communities or to resort to violence to balance the power they feel they lack before the institutions of the state" (2005, 59).

On the empirical side, in her interesting and wide-ranging study of social networks in the United States and elsewhere, Diana Mutz argues that there is a tension between the kinds of attitudes that lead to deliberation and those that lead to participation. Her evidence suggests that "within any given individual, enthusiastic participation rarely coexists with ongoing exposure to diverse political viewpoints and careful consideration of the political alternatives. Deliberation and participation, in other words, do not go hand in hand. Homogeneous and heterogeneous social contexts serve two different, yet important, purposes in this regard" (2002, 135). Mutz contrasts deliberative with participatory democracy, rather than agonistic democracy, but her point is that the heterogeneous social networks that lead to deliberative citizens cannot coexist with the homogeneous social networks that motivate those citizens engaged in politics.

Using data from another study in the United States, John Hibbing and Elizabeth Theiss-Morse argue that even if given the opportunity to participate in politics, most people would not take advantage of it. Most people do not care much about most public policies and want to avoid getting involved in politics. They would prefer a system "in which they themselves are not involved, but where they can be confident that decision makers will be motivated by a desire to serve the people" (2002, 227). With regard to deliberation in particular, Hibbing and Theiss-Morse argue that many people do not want to deliberate because either they react negatively to the conflict inherent in deliberation or they are reluctant to voice their opinions to others. They ask: "Why would thrusting people into settings where they come face-to-face with people who disagree with, and are different from, them and then requiring them to deliberate on political matters they would rather avoid make them happy, empathetic, other-regarding, and enlightened people?" (207). Instead of directly participating in or deliberating about politics (other than perhaps voting), "people want the individuals who make political decisions to be empathetic, non-self-interested decision makers" (216); citizens want what Hibbing and Theiss-Morse call "stealth democracy." Beyond simply describing what people want, Hibbing and Theiss-Morse offer concrete suggestions on how to improve democracy. They argue that certain reforms—reducing the remuneration public officials receive both officially and from special interests (though they recognize that eliminating the latter is constitutionally impossible in the United States) and campaign finance reform—may decrease the public's perception of representatives as self-interested, though it will probably do so only marginally (217–21). They consider it more important to somehow teach citizens "to accept that there is disagreement among Americans on how to resolve issues that are important to them and to accept that there is disagreement on which issues deserve to be on the political agenda in the first place" (223). People also need to understand that conflict and compromise are inherent in politics, and Hibbing and Theiss-Morse suggest that an educational curriculum that exposes "students to the range of issue interests of people across the United States and simulations illustrating the challenges of coming to an agreement in the face of divided opinion is what we need" (225). These reforms can increase people's acceptance of political conflict and increase the likelihood that they will perceive decision makers as empathetic and non-self-interested, something that will not happen if we force people to deliberate. Goi, Mutz, and Hibbing and Theiss-Morse, all in unique ways, raise concerns regarding the feasibility or desirability of deliberation.

The deliberative model I defend, by incorporating the process model of empathy as a guide for understanding and critiquing deliberative practice, can answer the challenges raised by all these scholars. Regarding the agonistic position, my model does not ignore the passions, and in fact requires that people express their passions on the issues that concern them. Without such expressions, the process of empathy would not occur, and the only limits on passionate advocacy and expression are that people do not engage in them in ways that interfere with empathy. For example, passionately demonizing others would violate the criteria of democratic legitimacy. The model also proscribes decision makers of the state from excluding certain voices from the democratic process. Through its openness and its incorporation of passion, a deliberative model that takes the process of empathy seriously does not eviscerate people's motivations to participate in politics as the agonists argue. It also can account for the tension Mutz finds between heterogeneous and homogeneous social networks. As we noted in Chapter 5, Mutz finds that people high in the predisposition for perspective taking benefit from crosscutting social networks, while those low in this predisposition actually become less open (see Mutz 2006, 83–85). Heterogeneous networks are likely to help deliberation only under the conditions the process model of empathy specifies. Even more important, her data regarding the effects of network homogeneity on participation demonstrate that the people in heterogeneous networks who tend not to participate are primarily those who are conflict avoidant (Mutz 2006, 117–23). This finding connects nicely with Hibbing and Theiss-Morse's proposition that people do not want to participate in politics because they perceive it as conflictual. Yet both of these findings, as the authors acknowledge, occur within the current political system. As Amy Gangl posits, drawing upon her experimental study of people's perceptions of legislative decision-making, "Widespread negative sentiment toward the political process does not necessarily signify rejection of difficult democratic deliberation" (2003, 136). Hibbing and Theiss-Morse suggest that educating citizens so that they understand that people disagree about politics, and how conflict and compromise are necessary to solve such disagreements, can help ameliorate people's perceptions (and misperceptions) about the political system. While Hibbing and Theiss-Morse (1996) offer their own suggestions on how such an education should occur, their identification of empathetic non-self-interested decision makers as the ideal points us toward the model I defend here, as does Mutz's findings on the effects of the predisposition to perspective taking. A democratic education for empathy would allow citizens to see that disagreements exist, but also point toward a way that democracy can deal with those disagreements beyond a "barbaric" conflict. I also believe that a deliberative democracy that incorporated the process of empathy into public deliberation and decision-making would be less likely to lead citizens to conflict-avoidant behaviors. Conflict avoidance occurs, I posit, because all too often people that are convinced of the correctness of their views, especially those who are part of homogeneous networks, ignore and intimidate those who are more timid, open, or reflective. Rather than discourage participation, a democratic system that asks people to engage in the process of empathy is more likely to provide the kind of environment that will encourage participation. It is also more likely to result in citizens perceiving the democratic system as populated by empathetic non-self-interested decision makers. A deliberative democracy that incorporates the process model allows people to express their passions, opens people up to differences and disagreements, and does not attempt to neutralize conflict, but it does so in a way that gives guidance on how democratic disagreement can exist without it spiraling into destructive and intimidating quarrel.

Empathy and the Democratic Promise

Empathy and Democratic Practice

Though I can only hint at them here, my model of deliberation, which places empathy at its heart, has several implications for democratic practice. As I noted at the end of Chapter 5, one of these is the need for empathy as a part of democratic education (see Morrell 2007 and McGregor 2004). This is especially vital given the importance of empathic predispositions to the process of empathy. Since the public educational system is the primary place in which a society can educate its citizens, it only makes sense that we would want to include empathy training as a part of civic education in public schools. Though genetic factors influence these predispositions, especially empathic concern, environmental factors are also important, especially during childhood (see Davis 1994, chap. 4, and Hoffman 2000). Educating citizens for empathic concern in the public schools during childhood is likely to have the most sustained effect on these predispositions. Martin Hoffman has some instructive suggestions on how we might achieve such a training (2000, 287–98). Yet even if it occurs later, research suggests that we can educate people for empathic predispositions (see Hatcher et al. 1994). This type of education also has an advantage over traditional civic education. Civic virtues such as tolerance, patriotism, and autonomy often lead to clashes between citizens' deeply held values and the power of the state to control public education (see, for example, Callan 2004 and Galston 1999). Empathy training does not risk the same clashes. One of the examples of empathy training in education, for example, has nothing whatsoever to do with politics, but occurs in medical training (see Raz and Fadlon 2006). A predisposition to empathy is more of a skill than a virtue, but it is a skill that, if my argument is correct, can contribute significantly to the healthy functioning of democracy.[3]

Another implication I have already noted is to follow Goodin's suggestions regarding the importance of literature, film, and other arts in supporting empathy in a democracy. The most famous example often cited regarding the importance of empathy in democracy is Harriet Beecher Stowe's *Uncle Tom's Cabin*. Policies that support a diffusion of the arts through-out society can certainly aid deliberation as empathy, though such policies must be sure to be inclusive and diverse (see Goodin 2003, 189–92). I have already noted a similar point regarding the information packets and expert panels provided to participants in deliberative forums. Including in these packets and panels balanced presentations of narratives or stories could increase the chance participants in the forums will engage in the process of empathy. A further suggestion for deliberative forums is to train facilitators and moderators to encourage citizens to pay attention not only to what others think and say, but also to what they feel. The empirical evidence demonstrates that inducing empathy either through narratives or through giving people instructions that engage them in a combined affective/cognitive role taking is the most likely to reduce biases. Deliberative forums of whatever kind, if they introduce participants to a diverse and inclusive variety of communications, if guided by moderators that encourage full role taking, and if they allow participants to deliberate without forcing them

---

3. As a possible alternative to formal education, Shawn Rosenberg argues that deliberation itself can serve "as a means of political pedagogy as well as collective decision making" that can "facilitate free and equal participation and, at the same time, foster psychological and social development" (2007b, 359). I think Rosenberg's suggestion deserves further consideration, and while I make some suggestions later on how we might achieve his goals, I can only do so briefly here.

*mutual
listening*

into making decisions, are more likely to add to democratic legitimacy by supporting attentive deliberation. Support for diverse arts programs and adjustments in deliberative forums will improve the quality of deliberation within the public sphere, yet they are not enough.

To increase the likelihood that public sphere deliberation will embody the process model of empathy, we need to improve upon wider public discourse. Deliberative theorists need to engage in a critical analysis of public discourse with an eye toward revealing the ways in which that discourse impedes attentive deliberation. Beyond assessing whether political candidates' ads are "truthful," discourse analysis must do more to identify communication that prevents a free flow of information or interferes with empathy. As examples, theorists could investigate the extent to which certain discourse demonizes others (see, for example, De Luca and Buell 2005), or they could delineate how discourse sets agendas, and thereby, excludes some voices from consideration. The need for a public discourse that increases the chances for the process of empathy to function would also require that media give more time to diverse viewpoints than they often now do. Public media that relies upon public infrastructure ought to support democratic discourse better than it often does currently. This is especially true given that many people tend to watch media that does not expose them to alternative viewpoints. While certain reasonable restrictions on how to implement this will be necessary, some form of equal time in public media could aid attentive deliberation.

Election Financing, Lobbying, and a Federal Deliberation Commission

Two final implications for democratic practice apply to legislatures themselves. First, recognizing the importance of empathy to democratic deliberation puts a new perspective on campaign finance and lobbying reform. Though often regarded as necessary to prevent corruption, or the appearance of corruption, the process model of empathy points to an even more important concern, election financing. Even if there is no quid pro quo, simply by giving greater access to certain groups and interests, lobbying and non-public campaign finance systems increase the likelihood that legislators will judge those groups and interests who have access differently than they judge others. Even the most ethical legislators may unconsciously evaluate issues involving groups that support or lobby them in more complex terms than issues raised by those who have not lobbied them or contributed financially to their campaigns. They are also more likely to perceive as important the issues in which their large financial supporters are interested.

Even if they do not vote exactly as the lobbyists or financial supporters want, they are more likely to take their positions into account when deciding which issues deserve attention and how to form compromises on those issues. Some groups and individuals have a disproportionately greater ability to contribute money to political campaigns and to engage in lobbying efforts, and because of the effects of empathy, they are inherently more likely to receive greater consideration than others. The process model reveals that the problems of campaign finance and lobbying are not corruption, or even access per se, but the distorting effects these have on the process of empathy. While banning lobbying altogether is probably not feasible, a deliberative democracy that requires empathy would likely benefit from public financing of political campaigns (or at the very least, lower limits on contributions and the banning of the practice of bundling those contributions), elimination of the provision of any benefits by lobbyists, and an extension of "revolving door" provisions that prevent politicians or political staffers from becoming lobbyists once they leave office.

The second implication regarding legislatures concerns their place as a point of deliberation. Most citizens pay little attention to most debates within legislatures or legislative committees, even those broadcast in the media (the possible exception being when a legislative committee questions a famous sports star). These public deliberations also likely have little influence on legislators' actual votes. Political theorists ranging from Edmund Burke to John Stuart Mill conceive of the legislature as the optimal site for deliberation, and though important deliberation does occur in legislatures, it often does not contribute significantly to the kind of public discourse necessary under my model of deliberation. Free-flowing deliberation within the informal public sphere is important, but a place for more formal deliberation on important political issues could contribute to democratic discourse and even influence deliberation within the public sphere. I would suggest that democracies need a government agency, which I will call the Federal Deliberation Commission (FDC), whose specific task is to engage in public deliberation on issues facing society.

The key to the FDC's ability to enhance attentive deliberation in the broader public sphere would be to make it as independent as possible from the ruling party or government at any particular time. There are many ways to achieve this, but the most important would be to staff the FDC with full-time deliberators and structure deliberations so that all deliberators would have to present all sides of an issue. To some this may sound strange, but there are scores of people prepared for this very task every year in many places throughout the world through their participation in academic debate in secondary and post-secondary schools (see "National Parliamentary Debate Association" and "World Schools Debate Championship" for examples). Participants in academic debate must both defend and oppose proposals and resolutions, often switching sides several times in one day. By requiring such preparation, academic debate encourages debaters to prepare a number of possible cases on any side of a given issue. The FDC could take the same approach by broadcasting deliberations in which staff members had to present different sides of an issue, for example, by having them switch the perspective they are defending in the middle of a one-hour broadcast. Not only would this provide balance, it also would have an effect on attentiveness. The process model of empathy points out that the similarity between a target and an observer affects whether people empathize with the target. The affective intelligence and hot cognition theories also demonstrate that people respond with unconscious affect to familiar political objects, including politicians and pundits. The results of these tendencies is that people tend to pay more attention to, and agree more often with, people like themselves or people who they believe think like themselves, regardless of the persuasiveness of the positions those people offer. Structuring FDC deliberations so that the professional deliberators would defend all sides of an issue would require those watching to pay closer attention to the deliberation rather than using shortcut cues that lead them to support or oppose a particular position because of the person offering it. This would increase the likelihood that the deliberations would contribute to a free flow of information and the process of empathy.

Since the point of these deliberations would not be to win or lose, but to enhance attentiveness, the FDC could structure them more loosely than in formal academic debate, though academic debate provides good basic guidelines such as balanced time, a cross-examination period, and alternating speeches by both sides. The media should broadcast these deliberations to the public on television and over the Internet, thus encouraging people to engage in internal-reflective deliberation. The FDC should also support face-to-face deliberative forums of groups of citizens following the public deliberation. The publicly broadcast deliberations might also spark more discussion of the issues among families, friends, and colleagues, and would almost certainly affect the public discourse on the issue. Some might question whether people would actually pay attention to FDC deliberations, but I believe that they would. If citizens believed the FDC was truly independent, then they would be more likely to see these deliberations as straightforward discussions of the issues rather than spin by self-serving politicians or special interests. Since the FDC staff would consist of professional deliberators, they would be the kind of people who could get people interested in paying attention through their oratorical skills. I can even envision a process in which the FDC encourages people to watch by asking them to vote for the best deliberator on any given night, similar to what happens for various contest shows on television. While deliberative democracy does not require eliminating legislative deliberations, establishing something like the Federal Deliberation Commission along the lines I suggest here would contribute more to enhancing the attentiveness of public deliberation that would increase the likelihood that the process of empathy will be a central component of democratic deliberation.[4]

Empathy and the Democratic Promise

While I have only been able to sketch some preliminary implications for actual democratic practice of my model of deliberative democracy, the central point of doing so is to show how this model can move us closer to fulfilling the democratic promise that when people make a collective decision backed by the force of the whole community, they will do so only after giving equal consideration to all. In contemporary mass democracies, the problem democratic theory faces is to demonstrate how people can make legitimate democratic decisions when confronted with the fact of pluralism, with its variety of views and perspectives, in the absence of a transcendent legitimate arbiter to judge these differences. Deliberative democratic theory is one plausible response to this dilemma. By requiring that decisions be properly reflective, or that decisions could meet with the agreement of all affected, deliberative theorists have begun to develop compelling theories on how to combine legitimate decision-making and equal consideration. Yet in the face of growing empirical evidence and theoretical critique, much of it involving the importance of emotions in political life and human reasoning, deliberative theory requires alterations if it is going to live up to its promise of providing a persuasive theory of democracy.

4. Ethan Leib (2004) offers another institutional option to enhance deliberation in the form of a new, popular branch of government that would operate in ways similar to James Fishkin's deliberative opinion poll but would also have actual constitutional authority. I believe Leib's proposal is innovative and interesting, and something we ought to consider. My only concern remains whether the institutional structure he proposes would lend itself to deliberations characterized by empathy or improve the discourse in the public sphere. This is the focus of my FDC proposal.

I have argued that deliberative theory needs to account better for the interrelationships among affect, cognition, and reason. This does not mean abandoning reason or eliminating the cognitive content of deliberation, but it does require modifications in deliberative theory. The process model of empathy demonstrates how deliberative theory could make these important modifications. Theorists who define deliberation as reflective consideration must recognize that reflection does not just involve the invocation of reason as a check on the passions. People ought to be able to express their emotions and passions in deliberation just as much as they ought to be able to make arguments or produce information. Theorists ought not measure good deliberation solely by examining whether participants consider all the facts or change their preferences, or whether their preferences are more rationally consistent following deliberation. Measuring reflective deliberation also requires them to gauge whether people empathized with their fellow interlocutors. If deliberation does not include the process of empathy, it is all too likely that the reflection it embodies will be exclusionary or biased and not take into consideration all who participate.

Theorists who link deliberation with reasonable or rational argumentation also must give a proper place to empathy. Since for these theorists democratic legitimacy requires justification—something like giving reasons all could accept—they make a link between legitimacy and impartiality. To embody impartiality, theorists such as Rawls and Habermas appear to incorporate reciprocal perspective taking, but they do so with abstracting moves such as the veil of ignorance or ideal role taking that interferes with the very possibility of equal consideration. There is little to no space for affect in the use of public reason or communicative rationality. Even theorists who have taken the positive first step of moving beyond Rawls and Habermas by giving some space for affective communication, such as Benhabib, Young, Bohman, and Dryzek, still tend to distinguish between affect and reason. They cannot provide a persuasive account of how a mixture of affect and cognition can inform the kind of reasoning deliberative democracy requires. A persuasive deliberative theory of democratic justification must account for affect and cognition because human beings reason using a combination of the two, and because, as the evidence from Chapter 5 demonstrates, without both the affective and cognitive components of empathy, deliberation will likely not be open, unbiased, or reciprocal.

Krause offers one way to accommodate deliberative theory with the affective turn. Drawing on Hume, Krause argues for the importance of sentiment in informing deliberation. Rightly understood, reciprocity "rests on reflective sentiment, on a form of practical reasoning that includes both cognition and affect" (Krause 2008, 173). The affective side of sentiment is important because "if I am to deliberate in a way that takes your sentiments into account, it is not enough for me to know cognitively what they are; they must also be (or become) objects of concern for me, or at least they must connect up with concerns that I have. Affective uptake is the only way that arguments about practical ends can become convincing to us" (164). Affective uptake can only occur if people are able to sympathize with others, and Krause's conceptualization of sympathy is very close to how I have defined empathy. "When sympathy is well cultivated and broadly extended, the generalized perspective of moral sentiment takes us out of ourselves in the right way; it does not demand the wholesale abandonment of our identities or an unattainable level of knowledge about the lives of others. Yet it does make our judgments more than self-referential. It causes us to register directly in our own minds and hearts the expressed (and sometimes inferred) sentiments of those affected" (163–64). Though we adduce somewhat different evidence and may have differences in our definitions of sympathy and empathy, the arguments Krause and I make are compatible; both require the recasting of deliberative theory to allow for a cognitively and affectively mixed process of sympathy or empathy in order to inform the judgments people make in deliberation. Without this, deliberation cannot provide a basis for legitimate, justified democratic decision-making that truly takes all into consideration.

Beyond this argument that deliberative theory needs modification, I have made the more ambitious case that the best way to respond to the empirical evidence from psychologists and political scientists and the theoretical arguments made by critics of deliberation is to recast the very nature of democratic legitimacy. In a pluralist society, conceptualizing legitimacy as reasonable or rational justification is unworkable because the problem of economy impedes all from agreeing on the reasons for a decision, and even if we could overcome the problem of economy, it is highly unlikely that citizens will reach a consensus on issues of importance to society. Conceptualizing legitimacy as justification also increases the danger of deliberation becoming exclusionary and dominating rather than open and reciprocal because it relies upon potentially limited conceptualizations of public reason or rationality, and because it allows majorities to rationalize their domination and exclusion. Agonistic theories are correct in this criticism of deliberative democracy, but they do not provide a persuasive alternative because they tend to reify conflict to the detriment of possible cooperation and do not adequately theorize why we should expect people to remain adversaries rather than become enemies. Rhetorical theories of persuasion are more persuasive (no pun intended) because of their incorporation of both affective and cognitive dimensions, but they too fall short by not providing clear mechanisms whereby we can delineate between legitimate persuasion and demagoguery.

The best alternative is to take a cue from Manin, though go further than he does, by recasting democratic legitimacy as a continuum that measures the degree to which majorities make decisions following a process of inclusive, attentive deliberation. Attentive deliberation not only requires reflective consideration, it also requires that participants engage in the process of empathy. Recasting democratic legitimacy requires us to rethink what deliberation means. David Ryfe proposes such an alternative: "To the extent that deliberation combines cognition (the act of making sense) with culture (the act of making meaning), it probably looks more like storytelling than argumentation" (2005, 58). While I agree that deliberation should take on more aspects that look like storytelling, storytelling alone is not what should constitute deliberation. Deliberation will include all manners of communicative exchange, including argumentation and persuasion, but the point of any exchange ought to be to facilitate an attentive deliberative process. By necessity, democratic decisions will result from majority votes, either direct or indirect, but the legitimacy of those decisions must rest on the degree to which the process that leads to them includes a variety of communication that allows for a free flow of information and the process of empathy. In the end, only by placing empathy at the heart of deliberation can democracy fulfill its promise of allowing legitimate decisions that give equal consideration to all those in a society.

REFERENCES

Abizadeh, Arash. 2002. "The Passions of the Wise: *Phronêsis*, Rhetoric, and Aristotle's Passionate Practical Deliberation." *Review of Metaphysics* 56 (2): 267–96.

Ackerman, Bruce, and James Fishkin. 2002. "Deliberation Day." *Journal of Political Philosophy* 10 (2): 129–52.

Aderman, David, and Leonard Berkowitz. 1970. "Observational Set, Empathy, and Helping." *Journal of Personality and Social Psychology* 14 (2): 141–48.

Anderson, Christopher J., André Blais, Shaun Bowler, Todd Donovan, and Ola Listhaug. 2005. *Losers' Consent: Elections and Democratic Legitimacy.* New York: Oxford University Press.

Anderson, Christopher J., and Andrew J. LoTempio. 2002. "Winning, Losing, and Political Trust in America." *British Journal of Political Science* 32 (2): 335–51.

Archer, Richard L., H. Clayton Foushee, Mark H. Davis, and David Aderman. 1979. "Emotional Empathy in a Courtroom Simulation: A Person-Situation Interaction." *Journal of Applied Social Psychology* 9 (3): 275–91.

Arendt, Hannah. 1968. "Truth and Politics." In *Between Past and Future,* enlarged edition, 227–64. New York: Penguin Books.

Barber, Benjamin R. 1984. *Strong Democracy.* Berkeley and Los Angeles: University of California Press.

Batson, C. Daniel. 1991. *The Altruism Question: Toward a Social-Psychological Answer.* Hillsdale, N.J.: Erlbaum.

———. 1997. "Self-Other Merging and the Empathy-Altruism Hypothesis: Reply to Neuberg et al. (1997)." *Journal of Personality and Social Psychology* 73 (3): 517–22.

Batson, C. Daniel, and Nadia Ahmad. 2001. "Empathy-Induced Altruism in a Prisoner's Dilemma II: What If the Target of Empathy Has Defected?" *European Journal of Social Psychology* 31 (1): 25–36.

Batson, C. Daniel, Nadia Ahmad, Jodi Yin, Steven J. Bedell, Jennifer W. Johnson, Christie M. Templin, and Aaron Whiteside. 1999. "Two Threats to the Common Good: Self-Interested Egoism and Empathy-Induced Altruism." *Personality and Social Psychology Bulletin* 25 (1): 3–16.

Batson, C. Daniel, Judy G. Batson, R. Matthew Todd, Beverly H. Brummett, Lara L. Shaw, and Carlo M. R. Aldeguer. 1995. "Empathy and the Collective Good: Caring for One of the Others in a Social Dilemma." *Journal of Personality and Social Psychology* 68:619–31.

Batson, C. Daniel, Johee Chang, Ryan Orr, and Jennifer Rowland. 2002. "Empathy, Attitudes, and Action: Can Feeling for a Member of a Stigmatized Group Motivate One to Help the Group?" *Personality and Social Psychology Bulletin* 28 (12): 1656–66.

Batson, C. Daniel, Bruce D. Duncan, Paula Ackerman, Terese Buckley, and Kimberly Birch. 1981. "Is Empathic Emotion a Source of Altruistic Motivation?" *Journal of Personality and Social Psychology* 40 (2): 290–302.

Batson, C. Daniel, Shannon Early, and Giovanni Salvarani. 1997. "Perspective Taking: Imagining How Another Feels Versus Imagining How You Would Feel." *Personality and Social Psychology Bulletin* 23 (7): 751–58.

Batson, C. Daniel, Jakob Hakansson Eklund, Valerie L. Chermok, Jennifer L. Hoyt, and Biaggio G. Ortiz. 2007. "An Additional Antecedent of Empathic Concern: Valuing the Welfare of the Person in Need." *Journal of Personality and Social Psychology* 93 (1): 65–74.

Batson, C. Daniel, Tricia R. Klein, Lori Highberger, and Laura L. Shaw. 1995. "Immorality from Empathy-Induced Altruism: When Compassion and Justice Conflict." *Journal of Personality and Social Psychology* 68 (6): 1042–54.

Batson, C. Daniel, David A. Lishner, Amy Carpenter, Luis Dulin, Sana Harjusola-Webb, E. L. Stocks, Shawna Gale, Omar Hassan, and Brenda Sampat. 2003. "'. . . As You Would Have Them Do unto You': Does Imagining Yourself in the Other's Place Stimulate Moral Action?" *Personality and Social Psychology Bulletin* 29 (9): 1190–1201.

Batson, C. Daniel, David A. Lishner, Jennifer Cook, and Stacey Sawyer. 2005. "Similarity and Nurturance: Two Possible Sources of Empathy for Strangers." *Basic and Applied Social Psychology* 27 (1): 15–25.

Batson, C. Daniel, and Tecia Moran. 1999. "Empathy-Induced Altruism in a Prisoner's Dilemma." *European Journal of Social Psychology* 29 (7): 909–24.

Batson, C. Daniel, Marina P. Polycarpou, Eddie Harmon-Jones, Heidi J. Imhoff, Erin C. Mitchener, Lori L. Bednar, Tricia R. Klein, and Lori Highberger. 1997. "Empathy and Attitudes: Can Feeling for a Member of a Stigmatized Group Improve Feelings Toward the Group?" *Journal of Personality and Social Psychology* 72 (1): 105–18.

Batson, C. Daniel, Karen Sager, Eric Garst, Misook Kang, Kostia Rubchinsky, and Karen Dawson. 1997. "Is Empathy-Induced Helping Due to Self-Other Merging?" *Journal of Personality and Social Psychology* 73 (3): 495–509.

Benhabib, Seyla. 1992. *Situating the Self.* New York: Routledge.

———. 1996. "Toward a Deliberative Model of Democratic Legitimacy." In *Democracy and Difference: Contesting Boundaries of the Political,* ed. Seyla Benhabib, 67–95. Princeton: Princeton University Press.

Berger, Seymour M. 1962. "Conditioning Through Vicarious Instigation." *Psychological Review* 69 (5): 450–66.

Bessette, Joseph M. 1980. "Deliberative Democracy: The Majority Principle in Republican Government." In *How Democratic Is the Constitution?* ed. Robert A. Goldwin and William A. Schambra, 102–16. Washington, D.C.: American Enterprise Institute.

———. 1994. *The Mild Voice of Reason.* Chicago: University of Chicago Press.

Betancourt, Hector. 1990. "An Attribution-Empathy Model of Helping Behavior: Behavioral Intentions and Judgment of Help-Giving." *Personality and Social Psychology Bulletin* 16 (3): 573–91.

Bickford, Susan. 1996. "Beyond Friendship: Aristotle on Conflict, Deliberation, and Attention." *Journal of Politics* 58 (2): 398–421.

Bohman, James. 1995. "Public Reason and Cultural Pluralism." *Political Theory* 23 (2): 253–79.

———. 1996. *Public Deliberation: Pluralism, Complexity, and Democracy.* Cambridge: MIT Press.

———. 1998. "Survey Article: The Coming of Age of Deliberative Democracy." *Journal of Political Philosophy* 6 (4): 400–425.

———. 2003. "Deliberative Toleration." *Political Theory* 31 (6): 757–79.

———. 2004. "Realizing Deliberative Democracy as a Mode of Inquiry." *Journal of Speculative Philosophy* 18 (1): 23–43.

———. 2005. "Rights, Cosmopolitanism, and Public Reason." *Philosophy and Social Criticism* 31 (7): 715–26.

Burkhalter, Stephanie, John Gastil, and Todd Kelshaw. 2002. "A Conceptual Definition and Theoretical Model of Public Deliberation in Small Face-to-Face Groups." *Communication Theory* 12 (4): 398–422.

Callan, Eamonn. 2004. "Citizenship and Education." *Annual Review of Political Science* 7:71–90.

Center for Deliberative Democracy. 2007. "Deliberative Polling®." August 16. http://cdd.stanford.edu/.

Chambers, Simone. 1995. "Discourse and Democratic Practices." In *The Cambridge Companion to Habermas*, ed. Stephen K. White. Cambridge: Cambridge University Press.

———. 1996. *Reasonable Democracy*. Ithaca: Cornell University Press.

———. 2003. "Deliberative Democratic Theory." *Annual Review of Political Science* 6:307–26.

Cialdini, Robert B., Stephanie L. Brown, Brian P. Lewis, Carol Luce, and Steven L. Neuberg. 1997. "Reinterpreting the Empathy-Altruism Relationship: When One into One Equals Oneness." *Journal of Personality and Social Psychology* 73 (3): 481–94.

Clarke, Harold D., and Alan C. Acock. 1989. "National Elections and Political Attitudes: The Case of Political Efficacy." *British Journal of Political Science* 19: 551–62.

Cohen, Joshua. [1989] 1997. "Deliberation and Democratic Legitimacy." In *Deliberative Democracy: Essays on Reason and Politics*, ed. James Bohman and William Rehg, 66–91. Cambridge: MIT Press.

———. 1996. "Procedure and Substance in Deliberative Democracy." In *Democracy and Difference*, ed. Seyla Benhabib, 95–119. Princeton: Princeton University Press.

Cohen, Joshua, and Charles F. Sabel. 2005. "Global Democracy?" *New York University Journal of International Law and Politics* 37 (4): 763–97.

Connolly, William E. 1991. *Identity/Difference: Democratic Negotiations of Political Paradox*. Ithaca: Cornell University Press.

Cooke, Maeve. 2001. "Meaning and Truth in Habermas's Pragmatics." *European Journal of Philosophy* 9:1–23.

Craig, Stephen C., Richard G. Niemi, and Glenn E. Silver. 1990. "Political Efficacy and Trust: A Report on the NES Pilot Study Items." *Political Behavior* 12:289–314.

Dagger, Richard. 1999a. "The Sandelian Republic and the Unencumbered Self." *Review of Politics* 61 (2): 181–208.

Dahl, Robert A. 1956. *A Preface to Democratic Theory*. Chicago: University of Chicago Press.

———. 1961. *Who Governs? Democracy and Power in the American City*. New Haven: Yale University Press.

———. 1989. *Democracy and Its Critics*. New Haven: Yale University Press.

———. 1999b. "Rejoinder to Michael Sandel." *Review of Politics* 61 (2): 215–17.

Damasio, Antonio R. 1994. *Descartes' Error: Emotion, Reason, and the Human Brain*. New York: Avon.

———. 1999. *The Feeling of What Happens: Body and Emotion in the Making of Consciousness*. New York: Harcourt Brace.

Davis, Mark H. 1980. "A Multidimensional Approach to Individual Differences in Empathy." *Catalog of Selected Documents in Psychology* 10:85.

———. 1983a. "Measuring Individual Differences in Empathy: Evidence for a Multidimensional Approach." *Journal of Personality and Social Psychology* 44: 113–26.

———. 1983b. "The Effects of Dispositional Empathy on Emotional Reactions and Helping: A Multidimensional Approach." *Journal of Personality* 51:167–84.

———. 1994. *Empathy: A Social Psychological Approach*. Madison, Wis.: Brown and Benchmark.

Davis, Mark H., Laura Conklin, Amy Smith, and Carol Luce. 1996. "Effects of Perspective Taking on the Cognitive Representation of Persons: A Merging of Self and Other." *Journal of Personality and Social Psychology* 70:713–26.

Decety, Jean. 2007. "A Social Cognitive Neuroscience Model of Human Empathy." In *Social Neuroscience: Integrating Biological and Psychological Explanations of Social Behavior*, ed. Eddie Harmon-Jones and Piotr Winkielman, 246–70. New York: Guilford.

Decety, Jean, and Julie Grèzes. 2006. "The Power of Simulation: Imagining One's Own and Other's Behavior." *Brain Research* 1079 (1): 4–14.

Decety, Jean, and Philip L. Jackson. 2004. "The Functional Architecture of Human Empathy." *Behavioral and Cognitive Neuroscience Reviews* 3 (2): 71–100.

———. 2006. "A Social-Neuroscience Perspective on Empathy." *Current Directions in Psychological Science* 15 (2): 54–58.

Decety, Jean, and Claus Lamm. 2006. "Human Empathy Through the Lens of Social Neuroscience." *Scientific World Journal* 6 (September): 1146–63.

Decety, Jean, and Yoshiya Moriguchi. 2007. "The Empathic Brain and Its Dysfunction in Psychiatric Populations: Implications for Intervention Across Different Clinical Conditions." *BioPsychoSocial Medicine* 1 (22): 1–21.

Decety, Jean, and Jessica A. Sommerville. 2003. "Shared Representations Between Self and Other: A Social Cognitive Neuroscience View." *Trends in Cognitive Sciences* 7 (12): 527–33.

Delli Carpini, Michael X., Fay Lomax Cook, and Lawrence R. Jacobs. 2004. "Public Deliberation, Discursive Participation, and Citizen Engagement." *Annual Review of Political Science* 7 (1): 315–44.

De Luca, Tom, and John Buell. 2005. *Liars! Cheaters! Evildoers! Demonization and the End of Civil Debate in American Politics*. New York: New York University Press.

Deveaux, Monique. 1999. "Agonism and Pluralism." *Philosophy and Social Criticism* 25 (4): 1–22.

Dodds, Agnes E., Jeanette A. Lawrence, and Jaan Valsiner. 1997. "The Personal and the Social: Mead's Theory of the 'Generalized Other.'" *Theory and Psychology* 7 (4): 483–503.

Dollard, John, and Neal E. Miller. 1950. *Personality and Psychotherapy*. New York: McGraw-Hill.

Dryzek, John S. 1990. *Discursive Democracy: Politics, Policy, and Political Science*. New York: Cambridge University Press.

———. 2000. *Deliberative Democracy and Beyond*. New York: Oxford University Press.

———. 2001. "Legitimacy and Economy in Deliberative Democracy." *Political Theory* 29 (5): 651–69.

———. 2005. "Deliberative Democracy in Divided Societies." *Political Theory* 33 (2): 218–42.

Dryzek, John S., and Valerie Braithwaite. 2000. "On the Prospects for Democratic Deliberation: Values Analysis Applied to Australian Politics." *Political Psychology* 21 (2): 241–66.

Eisenberg, Nancy, and Janet Strayer. 1987. "Critical Issues in the Study of Empathy." In *Empathy and Its Development*, ed. Nancy Eisenberg and Janet Strayer, 3–13. Cambridge: Cambridge University Press.

Farrell, Thomas B. 1993. *Norms of Rhetorical Culture*. New Haven: Yale University Press.

Finlay, Krystina A., and Walter G. Stephan. 2000. "Improving Intergroup Relations: The Effects of Empathy on Racial Attitudes." *Journal of Applied Social Psychology* 30:1720–37.

Fishkin, James S. 1991. *Democracy and Deliberation*. New Haven: Yale University Press.

———. 1995. *The Voice of the People*. New Haven: Yale University Press.

Fontana, Benedetto, Cary J. Nederman, and Gary Remer, eds. 2004. *Talking Democracy: Historical Perspectives on Rhetoric and Democracy*. University Park: Pennsylvania State University Press.

Frazer, Michael L. 2007. "John Rawls: Between Two Enlightenments." *Political Theory* 35 (6): 756–80.

Freeman, Samuel. 2000. "Deliberative Democracy: A Sympathetic Comment." *Philosophy and Public Affairs* 29 (4): 371–418.

Freud, Sigmund. [1905] 1938. "Wit and Its Relations to the Unconscious." In *The Basic Writings of Sigmund Freud*, ed. and trans. A. A. Brill. New York: Random House.

———. [1921] 1924. *Group Psychology and the Analysis of the Ego*. Trans. James Strachey. New York: Boni and Liveright.

Galinsky, Adam D., and Gillian Ku. 2004. "The Effects of Perspective-Taking on Prejudice: The Moderating Role of Self-Evaluation." *Personality and Social Psychology Bulletin* 30:594–604.

Galinsky, Adam D., and Gordon B. Moskowitz. 2000. "Perspective-Taking: Decreasing Stereotype Expression, Stereotype Accessibility, and In-Group Favoritism." *Journal of Personality and Social Psychology* 78:708–24.

Galper, Ruth Ellen. 1976. "Turning Observers into Actors: Differential Causal Attributions as a Function of 'Empathy.'" *Journal of Research in Personality* 10: 328–35.

Galston, William A. 1999. "Diversity, Toleration, and Deliberative Democracy: Religious Minorities and Public Schooling." In *Deliberative Politics: Essays on Democracy and Disagreement*, ed. Stephen Macedo, 39–48. New York: Oxford University.

Gangl, Amy. 2003. "Procedural Justice Theory and Evaluations of the Lawmaking Process." *Political Behavior* 25 (2): 119–49.

Gara, Philip. 2005. "McNamara Argues for Empathy in Fighting Nuke Proliferation." *Brown Daily Herald*, April 28. http://media.www.browndailyherald.com/media/storage/paper472/news/2005/04/28/CampusNews/Mcnamara.Argues.For.Empathy.In.Fighting.Nuke.Proliferation-942983.shtml.

Garsten, Bryan. 2006. *Saving Persuasion: A Defense of Rhetoric and Judgment*. Cambridge: Harvard University Press.

Gastil, John, and Laura W. Black. 2008. "Public Deliberation as the Organizing Principle of Political Communication Research." *Journal of Public Deliberation* 4 (1). http://services.bepress.com/jpd/vol4/iss1/art3.

Gastil, John, Laura W. Black, E. Pierre Deess, and Jay Leighter. 2008. "From Group Member to Democratic Citizen: How Deliberating with Fellow Jurors Reshapes Civic Attitudes." *Human Communication Research* 34 (1): 137–69.

Gastil, John, Laura Black, and Kara Moscovitz. 2008. "Ideology, Attitude Change, and Deliberation in Small Face-to-Face Groups." *Political Communication* 25 (1): 23–46.

Gastil, John, Stephanie Burkhalter, and Laura W. Black. 2007. "Do Juries Deliberate?" *Small Group Research* 38 (3): 337–59.

Gauss, Charles Edward. 1973. "Empathy." In *The Dictionary of the History of Ideas*, ed. Philip P. Wiener, 2:85–89. New York: Charles Scribner's Sons.

George, Robert P. 1999. "Democracy and Moral Disagreement: Reciprocity, Slavery, and Abortion." In *Deliberative Politics: Essays on Democracy and Disagreement*, ed. Stephen Macedo, 184–97. New York: Oxford University Press.

Glaser, Jack, and Peter Salovey. 1998. "Affect in Electoral Politics." *Personality and Social Psychology Review* 2 (3): 156–72.

Goi, Simona. 2005. "Agonism, Deliberation, and the Politics of Abortion." *Polity* 37 (1): 54–81.

Goldstein, Arnold P., and Gerald Y. Michaels. 1985. *Empathy: Development, Training, and Consequences*. Hillsdale, N.J.: Lawrence Erlbaum Associates.

Goodin, Robert E. 2003. *Reflective Democracy*. Oxford: Oxford University Press.

Gould, Robert, and Harold Sigall. 1977. "The Effects of Empathy and Outcome on Attribution: An Examination of the Divergent-Perspective Hypothesis." *Journal of Experimental Social Psychology* 13:480–91.

Gutmann, Amy, and Dennis Thompson. 1996. *Democracy and Disagreement*. Cambridge: Belknap Press of Harvard University Press.

———. 2004. *Why Deliberative Democracy?* Princeton: Princeton University Press.

Habermas, Jürgen. [1962] 1989. *The Structural Transformation of the Public Sphere: An Inquiry into a Category of Bourgeois Society*. Cambridge: MIT Press.

———. [1973] 1975. *Legitimation Crisis*. Boston: Beacon Press.

———. 1984. *The Theory of Communicative Action I: Reason and Rationalization of Society*. Boston: Beacon Press.

———. 1990. *Moral Consciousness and Communicative Action*. Trans. Christian Lenhardt and Shierry Weber Nicholsen. Cambridge: MIT Press.

———. 1993. *Justification and Application*. Trans. Ciaran P. Cronin. Cambridge: MIT Press.

———. 1995. "Reconciliation Through the Public Use of Reason: Remarks on John Rawls's Political Liberalism." *Journal of Philosophy* 92:109–31.

———. 1996a. *Between Facts and Norms: Contributions to a Discourse Theory of Law and Democracy*. Trans. William Rehg. Cambridge: Polity Press.

———. 1996b. "Three Normative Models of Democracy." In *Democracy and Difference: Contesting the Boundaries of the Political*, ed. Seyla Benhabib, 21–30. Princeton: Princeton University Press.

———. 1998. *The Inclusion of the Other: Studies in Political Theory*. Ed. Ciaran Cronin and Pablo De Greiff. Cambridge: MIT Press.

Hall, Cheryl. 2002. "'Passions and Constraint': The Marginalization of Passion in Liberal Political Theory." *Philosophy and Social Criticism* 28 (6): 727–48.

————. 2005. *The Trouble with Passion: Political Theory Beyond the Reign of Reason.* New York: Routledge.

————. 2007. "Recognizing the Passion in Deliberation: Toward a More Democratic Theory of Deliberative Democracy." *Hypatia* 22 (4): 81–95.

Hamilton, Alexander, James Madison, and John Jay. [1788] 1961. *The Federalist Papers.* New York: New American Library.

Hatcher, Sherry L., Missi S. Nadeau, Lisa K. Walsh, Meredith Reynolds, Jerry Galea, and Kaye Marz. 1994. "The Teaching of Empathy for High School and College Students: Testing Rogerian Methods with the Interpersonal Reactivity Index." *Adolescence* 29 (116): 961–74.

Held, David. 2006. *Models of Democracy.* 3rd edition. Stanford: Stanford University Press.

Hibbing, John R., and Elizabeth Theiss-Morse. 1996. "Civics Is Not Enough: Teaching Barbarics in K-12." *PS: Political Science and Politics* 29 (1): 57–62.

————. 2002. *Stealth Democracy.* New York: Cambridge University Press.

Hoffman, Martin L. 2000. *Empathy and Moral Development: Implications for Caring and Justice.* New York: Cambridge University Press.

Hogan, Robert. 1975. "Empathy: A Conceptual and Psychometric Analysis." *Counseling Psychologist* 5 (2): 14–18.

Honig, Bonnie. 1993. *Political Theory and the Displacement of Politics.* Ithaca: Cornell University Press.

Hume, David. [1739–40] 2003. *An Enquiry Concerning the Principles of Morals.* Mineola, N.Y.: Dover.

Ivie, Robert L. 1998. "Democratic Deliberation in a Rhetorical Republic." *Quarterly Journal of Speech* 84:491–530.

Jahoda, Gustav. 2005. "Theodor Lipps and the Shift from 'Sympathy' to 'Empathy.'" *Journal of the History of the Behavioral Sciences* 41 (2): 151–63.

James, Michael Rabinder. 2004. *Deliberative Democracy and the Plural Polity.* Lawrence: University Press of Kansas.

Johnson, James. 1998. "Arguing for Deliberation: Some Skeptical Considerations." In *Deliberative Democracy,* ed. Jon Elster, 161–84. Cambridge: Cambridge University Press.

Karpowitz, Christopher F., and Jane Mansbridge. 2005. "Disagreement and Consensus: The Need for Dynamic Updating in Public Deliberation." *Journal of Public Deliberation* 1 (1). http://services.bepress.com/jpd/vol1/iss1/art2.

Kessel, Alisa. 2003. "Teaching Listening for Democratic Education." Paper presented at the annual meeting of the American Political Science Association, Philadelphia.

Kingston, Rebecca, and Leonard Ferry, eds. 2008. *Bringing the Passion Back In.* Vancouver: UBC Press.

Kohut, Heinz. 1971. *The Analysis of the Self.* New York: International Universities Press.

Koziak, Barbara. 2000. *Retrieving Political Emotion.* University Park: Pennsylvania State University Press.

Krause, Sharon R. 2005. "Desiring Justice: Motivation and Justification in Rawls and Habermas." *Contemporary Political Theory* 4 (4): 363–85.

————. 2006. "Public Deliberation and the Feeling of Impartiality." Paper presented at the annual meeting of the American Political Science Association, Philadelphia.

————. 2008. *Civil Passions.* Princeton: Princeton University Press.

Krebs, Dennis L., and Philip G. Laird. 1998. "Judging Yourself as You Judge Others: Moral Development and Exculpation." *Journal of Adult Development* 5:1–12.

Lamm, Claus, C. Daniel Batson, and Jean Decety. 2007. "The Neural Substrate of Human Empathy: Effects of Perspective-Taking and Cognitive Appraisal." *Journal of Cognitive Neuroscience* 19 (1): 42–58.

Lee, Vernon, and C. Anstruther-Thomson. 1912. *Beauty and Ugliness*. London: John Lane, the Bodley Head.

Levy, Jonathan. 1997. "A Note on Empathy." *New Ideas in Psychology* 15:179–84.

Levy, Sheri R., Antonio L. Freitas, and Peter Salovey. 2002. "Construing Action Abstractly and Blurring Social Distinctions: Implications for Perceiving Homogeneity Among, but Also Empathizing With and Helping, Others." *Journal of Personality and Social Psychology* 83:1224–38.

Leib, Ethan J. 2004. *Deliberative Democracy in America*. University Park: Pennsylvania State University Press.

Lipps, Theodor. [1905] 1965. "Empathy and Aesthetic Pleasure." Trans. Karl Aschenbrenner. In *Aesthetic Theories: Studies in the Philosophy of Art*, ed. Karl Aschenbrenner and Arnold Isenberg, 403–12. Englewood Cliffs, N.J.: Prentice Hall.

———. 1907. "Das Wissen von fremden Ichen." In *Psychologische Studien*, ed. Theodor Lipps, 694–772. Leipzig: Engelmann.

Locke, John. [1764] 1967. *Locke's Two Treatises of Government*. 2nd edition. Ed. Peter Laslett. London: Cambridge University Press.

Lodge, Milton, and Charles S. Taber. 2000. "Three Steps Toward a Theory of Motivated Political Reasoning." In *Elements of Reason: Understanding and Expanding the Limits of Political Rationality*, ed. Arthur Lupia, Mathew D. McCubbins, and Samuel L. Popkin. London: Cambridge University Press.

———. 2005. "The Automaticity of Affect for Political Candidates, Groups, and Issues: An Experimental Test of the Hot Cognition Hypothesis." *Political Psychology* 26 (3): 455–82.

Lodge, Milton, Charles Taber, and Christopher Weber. 2006. "First Steps Toward a Dual-Process Accessibility Model of Political Beliefs, Attitudes, and Behavior." In *Feeling Politics*, ed. David P. Redlawsk, 11–30. New York: Palgrave Macmillan.

Macpherson, C. B. 1977. *The Life and Times of Liberal Democracy*. New York: Oxford University Press.

Maner, Jon K., Carol L. Luce, Steven L. Neuberg, Robert B. Cialdini, Stephanie Brown, and Brad J. Sagarin. 2002. "The Effects of Perspective Taking on Motivations for Helping: Still No Evidence for Altruism." *Personality and Social Psychology Bulletin* 28:1601–10.

Manin, Bernard. 1987. "On Legitimacy and Political Deliberation." *Political Theory* 15 (3): 338–68.

Mansbridge, Jane. 1983. *Beyond Adversary Democracy*. Chicago: University of Chicago Press.

———. 1999. "Everyday Talk in the Deliberative System." In *Deliberative Politics: Essays on Democracy and Disagreement*, ed. Stephen Macedo. New York: Oxford University Press.

Mansbridge, Jane, Janette Hartz-Karp, Matthew Amengual, and John Gastil. 2006. "Norms of Deliberation: An Inductive Study." *Journal of Public Deliberation* 2 (1). http://services.bepress.com/jpd/vol2/iss1/art7.

Marcus, George E. 2000. "Emotions in Politics." *Annual Review of Political Science* 3 (1): 221–50.

———. 2002. *The Sentimental Citizen.* University Park: Pennsylvania State University Press.

———. 2003. "The Psychology of Emotions and Politics." In *Oxford Handbook of Political Psychology,* ed. David O. Sears, Leonie Huddy, and Robert Jervis, 182–221. New York: Oxford University Press.

Marcus, George E., W. Russell Neuman, and Michael MacKuen. 2000. *Affective Intelligence and Political Judgment.* Chicago: University of Chicago Press.

Marsilius of Padua. [1324] 1956. *The Defender of Peace.* Trans. Alan Gewirth. New York: Columbia University Press.

Martin, Robert W.T. 2005. "Between Consensus and Conflict: Habermas, Post-Modern Agonism, and the Early American Public Sphere." *Polity* 37 (3): 365–88.

McCarthy, Thomas. 1990. "Introduction." In Jürgen Habermas, *Moral Consciousness and Communicative Action,* trans. Christian Lenhardt and Shierry Weber Nicholsen. Cambridge: MIT Press.

McDermott, Rose. 2004. "The Feeling of Rationality: The Meaning of Neuroscientific Advances for Political Science." *Perspectives on Politics* 2 (4): 691–706.

McGregor, Catherine. 2004. "Care(full) Deliberation: A Pedagogy for Citizenship." *Journal of Transformative Education* 2 (2): 90–106.

Mead, George H. 1913. "The Social Self." *The Journal of Philosophy, Psychology, and Scientific Methods* 10 (14): 374–80.

———. 1925. "The Genesis of the Self and Social Control." *International Journal of Ethics* 35 (3): 251–77.

———. 1934. *Mind, Self, and Society.* Ed. Charles M. Morris. Chicago: University of Chicago Press.

Mehrabian, Albert, and Norman Epstein. 1972. "A Measure of Emotional Empathy." *Journal of Personality* 40 (4): 525–43.

Mendelberg, Tali. 2002. "The Deliberative Citizen: Theory and Evidence." In *Research in Micropolitics: Political Decisionmaking, Deliberation, and Participation,* ed. Michael X. Delli Carpini, Leoni Huddy, and Robert Shapiro, 6:151–93. Greenwich, Conn.: JAI Press.

Mendelberg, Tali, and John Oleske. 2000. "Race and Public Deliberation." *Political Communication* 17 (2): 169–91.

Melburg, Valerie, Paul Rosenfeld, Marc Riess, and James T. Tedeschi. 1984. "A Reexamination of the Empathic Observers Paradigm for the Study of Divergent Attributions." *Journal of Social Psychology* 124 (2): 201–8.

Meyers, Diana Tietjens. 1993. "Moral Reflection: Beyond Impartial Reason." *Hypatia* 8 (3): 21–47.

Michels, Robert. [1911] 1962. *Political Parties: A Sociological Study of the Oligarchical Tendencies of Modern Democracy.* Trans. Eden Paul and Cedar Paul. New York: Crowell-Collier.

Mill, John Stuart. [1861] 1991. "Considerations on Representative Government." In *On Liberty and Other Essays,* ed. John Gray. New York: Oxford University Press.

Morrell, Michael E. 1999. "Citizens' Evaluations of Participatory Democratic Procedures: Normative Theory Meets Empirical Science." *Political Research Quarterly* 52 (2): 293–322.

———. 2003. "Survey and Experimental Evidence for a Reliable and Valid Measure of Internal Political Efficacy." *Public Opinion Quarterly* 67 (4): 589–602.

———. 2007. "Empathy and Democratic Education." *Public Affairs Quarterly* 21 (4): 381–403.

Mosca, Gaetano. 1939. *The Ruling Class*. Trans. Hannah D. Kahn, ed. Arthur Livingston. New York: McGraw-Hill.

Mouffe, Chantal. 1999. "Deliberative Democracy or Agonistic Pluralism?" *Social Research* 66 (3): 745–58.

———. 2000. *The Democratic Paradox*. New York: Verso.

———. 2005. *The Political*. New York: Routledge.

Moy, Patricia, and John Gastil. 2006. "Predicting Deliberative Conversation: The Impact of Discussion Networks, Media Use, and Political Cognitions." *Political Communication* 23 (4): 443–60.

Murphy, Gardner. 1947. *Personality*. New York: Harper and Brothers.

Mutz, Diana C. 2002. "Cross-cutting Social Networks: Testing Democratic Theory in Practice." *American Political Science Review* 96:111–26.

———. 2006. *Hearing the Other Side*. New York: Cambridge University Press.

"National Parliamentary Debate Association." 2008. http://cas.bethel.edu/dept/comm/npda/ (accessed March 17, 2008).

Neuberg, Steven L., Robert B. Cialdini, Stephanie L. Brown, Carol Luce, Brad J. Sagarin, and Brian P. Lewis. 1997. "Does Empathy Lead to Anything More Than Superficial Helping? Comment on Batson et al. (1997)." *Journal of Personality and Social Psychology* 73:510–16.

Neuman, W. Russell, George E. Marcus, Ann N. Crigler, and Michael Mackuen, eds. 2007. *The Affect Effect*. Chicago: University of Chicago Press.

"The 1992 Campaign: Verbatim; Heckler Stirs Clinton Anger: Excerpts from the Exchange." 1992. *New York Times*, March 28.

Nisbett, Richard E., Craig Caputo, Patricia Legant, and Jeanne Marecek. 1973. "Behavior as Seen by the Actor and as Seen by the Observer." *Journal of Personality and Social Psychology* 27:154–64.

Nussbaum, Martha C. 2001. *Upheavals of Thought: The Intelligence of Emotions*. Cambridge: Cambridge University Press.

Okin, Susan Moller. 1989. "Reason and Feeling in Thinking About Justice." *Ethics* 99:229–49.

Omdahl, Becky Lynn. 1995. *Cognitive Appraisal, Emotion, and Empathy*. Mahwah, N.J.: Lawrence Erlbaum.

O'Neill, John. 2002 "The Rhetoric of Deliberation: Some Problems in Kantian Theories of Deliberative Democracy." *Res Publica* 8 (3): 249–68.

Orbell, John M., Alphons J. C. van de Kragt, and Robyn M. Dawes. 1988. "Explaining Discussion-Induced Cooperation." *Journal of Personality and Social Psychology* 54:811–19.

Pareto, Vilfredo. [1916] 1935. *The Mind and Society: A Treatise on General Sociology*. 4 vols. Ed. Arthur Livingstone, trans. Andrew Bongiorno and Arthur Livingstone. New York: Harcourt Brace.

Parkinson, John. 2006. *Deliberating in the Real World*. New York: Oxford University Press.

Pateman, Carol. 1970. *Participation and Democratic Theory*. New York: Cambridge University Press.

Pigman, George W. 1995. "Freud and the History of Empathy." *International Journal of Psycho-Analysis* 76 (2): 237–56.

Polletta, Francesca. 2008. "Just Talk: Public Deliberation After 9/11." *Journal of Public Deliberation* 4 (1). http://services.bepress.com/jpd/vol4/iss1/art2.

Rawls, John. 1971. *A Theory of Justice*. Cambridge: Harvard University Press.

———. 1995. "Reply to Habermas." *Journal of Philosophy* 92:132–80.

————. 1996. *Political Liberalism*. New York: Columbia University Press.

————. 1997. "The Idea of Public Reason Revisited." *University of Chicago Law Review* 64 (3): 765–807.

————. 1999. *A Theory of Justice*. Revised edition. Cambridge: Harvard University Press.

————. 2001. *Justice as Fairness: A Restatement*. Cambridge: Harvard University Press.

Raz, Aviad E., and Judith Fadlon. 2006. "'We Came to Talk with the People Behind the Disease': Communication and Control in Medical Education." *Culture, Medicine and Psychiatry* 30:55–75.

Redlawsk, David P. 2002. "Hot Cognition or Cool Consideration? Testing the Effects of Motivated Reasoning on Political Decision-making." *Journal of Politics* 64 (4): 1021–44.

————, ed. 2006a. *Feeling Politics: Emotion in Political Information Processing*. New York: Palgrave Macmillan.

————, ed. 2006b. "Feeling Politics: New Research into Emotion and Politics." In *Feeling Politics: Emotion in Political Information Processing*, ed. David P. Redlawsk, 1–10. New York: Palgrave Macmillan.

Reeder, Glenn, John B. Pryor, Michael J. A. Wohl, and Michael L. Griswell. 2005. "On Attributing Negative Emotions to Others Who Disagree with Our Opinions." *Personality and Social Psychology Bulletin* 31 (11): 1498–1510.

Regan, Dennis T., and Judith Totten. 1975. "Empathy and Attribution: Turning Observers into Actors." *Journal of Personality and Social Psychology* 32 (5): 850–56.

Rehg, William. 1994. *Insight and Solidarity*. Berkeley and Los Angeles: University of California Press.

Remer, Gary. 1999. "Political Oratory and Conversation: Cicero Versus Deliberative Democracy." *Political Theory* 27 (1): 39–64.

————. 2000. "Two Models of Deliberation: Oratory and Conversation in Ratifying the Constitution." *Journal of Political Philosophy* 8 (1): 68–90.

Reykowski, Janusz. 2006. "Deliberative Democracy and 'Human Nature': An Empirical Approach." *Political Psychology* 2006 (3): 323–46.

Rogers, Carl R. 1967. "The Interpersonal Relationship: The Core of Guidance." In *Person to Person*, ed. Carl R. Rogers and Barry Stevens. Lafayette, Calif.: Real People.

————. 1975. "Empathic: An Unappreciated Way of Being." *Counseling Psychologist* 5 (2): 2–10.

Rosenberg, Shawn W., ed. 2007a. *Deliberation, Participation, and Democracy*. New York: Palgrave Macmillan.

————. 2007b. "Rethinking Democratic Deliberation: The Limits and Potential of Citizen Participation." *Polity* 39 (3): 335–60.

Rousseau, Jean Jacques. [1762] 1988. "On Social Contract or Principles of Political Right." In *Rousseau's Political Writings*, ed. Alan Ritter and Julia Conaway Bondanella, trans. Julia Conaway Bondanella, 84–173. New York: W. W. Norton.

Rowland, Robert C. 1990. "Purpose, Argument Evaluation, and the Crisis in the Public Sphere." In *Argumentation Theory and the Rhetoric of Assent*, ed. David Cratis Williams and Michael David Hazen. Tuscaloosa: University of Alabama Press.

Ruby, Perrine, and Jean Decety. 2004. "How Would *You* Feel Versus How Do You Think *She* Would Feel? A Neuroimaging Study of Perspective-Taking with Social Emotions." *Journal of Cognitive Neuroscience* 16 (6): 988–99.

Ryfe, David M. 2005. "Does Deliberative Democracy Work?" *Annual Review of Political Science* 8 (1): 49–71.

Sande, Gerald N., George R. Goethals, and Christine E. Radloff. 1988. "Perceiving One's Own Traits and Others': The Multifaceted Self." *Journal of Personality and Social Psychology* 54:13–20.

Sandel, Michael J. 1984. "The Procedural Republic and the Unencumbered Self." *Political Theory* 12 (1): 81–96.

———. 1999. "Liberalism and Republicanism: Friends or Foes? A Reply to Richard Dagger." *Review of Politics* 61 (2): 209–14.

Sanders, Lynn. 1997. "Against Deliberation." *Political Theory* 25 (3): 347–76.

Schaap, Andrew. 2006. "Agonism in Divided Societies." *Philosophy and Social Criticism* 32 (2): 255–77.

Schertz, Matthew Victo. 2007. "Empathy as Intersubjectivity: Resolving Hume and Smith's Divide." *Studies in Philosophy and Education* 26 (2): 165–78.

Schkade, David, Cass R. Sunstein, and Reid Hastie. 2007. "What Happened on Deliberation Day?" *California Law Review* 95 (3): 915–40.

Schumpeter, Joseph A. [1942] 1976. *Capitalism, Socialism and Democracy*. 3rd edition. New York: Harper Torchbooks.

Schweiger, David M., William R. Sandberg, and James W. Ragan. 1986. "Group Approaches for Improving Strategic Decision-making: A Comparative Analysis of Dialectical Inquiry, Devil's Advocacy, and Consensus." *Academy of Management Journal* 29:51–71.

Schweiger, David M., William R. Sandberg, and Paula L. Rechner. 1989. "Experiential Effects of Dialectical Inquiry, Devil's Advocacy, and Consensus Approaches to Strategic Decision-making." *Academy of Management Journal* 32:745–72.

Schwenk, Charles R., and Richard A. Cosier. 1993. "Effects of Consensus and Devil's Advocacy on Strategic Decision-Making." *Journal of Applied Social Psychology* 23:126–39.

Smith, Adam. [1790] 2005. *A Theory of Moral Sentiments*. São Paulo: MetaLibri.

Stephan, Walter G., and Krystina Finlay. 1999. "The Role of Empathy in Improving Intergroup Relations." *Journal of Social Issues* 55:729–43.

Storms, Michael D. 1973. "Videotape and the Attribution Process: Reversing Actors' and Observers' Points of View." *Journal of Personality and Social Psychology* 27:165–75.

Stotland, Ezra. 1969. "Exploratory Investigations of Empathy." In *Advances in Experimental Social Psychology, Vol. 4*, ed. Leonard Berkowitz, 271–314. New York: Academic Press.

Strayer, Janet. 1987. "Affective and Cognitive Perspectives on Empathy." In *Empathy and Its Development*, ed. Nancy Eisenberg and Janet Strayer. Cambridge: Cambridge University Press.

Sunstein, Cass R. 2002. "The Law of Group Polarization." *Journal of Political Philosophy* 10 (2): 175–95.

———. 2005. "Group Judgments: Statistical Means, Deliberation, and Information Markets." *New York University Law Review* 80 (3): 962–1049.

Tarrant, Mark, and Adrian C. North. 2004. "Explanations for Positive and Negative Behavior: The Intergroup Attribution Bias in Achieved Groups." *Current Psychology* 23 (2): 161–72.

Thapar, Romila. 1966. *A History of India*. Vol. 1. Baltimore: Penguin Books.

Thompson, Simon, and Paul Hoggett. "The Emotional Dynamics of Deliberative Democracy." *Policy and Politics* 29 (3): 351–64.

Titchener, Edward B. 1909. *Experimental Psychology of the Thought Process*. New York: Macmillan.

———. 1915. *A Beginner's Psychology*. New York: Macmillan.

———. 1924. *A Textbook of Psychology*. New York: Macmillan.

Vescio, Theresa K., Gretchen B. Sechrist, and Matthew P. Paolucci. 2003. "Perspective Taking and Prejudice Reduction: The Mediational Role of Empathy Arousal and Situational Attributions." *European Journal of Social Psychology* 33:455–72.

Villa, Dana. 1992. "Postmodernism and the Public Sphere." *American Political Science Review* 86 (3): 712–21.

Vischer, Robert. [1873] 1994. "On the Optical Sense of Form: A Contribution to Aesthetics." In *Empathy, Form, and Space,* ed. and trans. Harry Francis Mallgrave and Eleftherios Ikonomou, 89–123. Santa Monica, Calif.: Getty Center for the History of Art and the Humanities.

Walzer, Michael. 1999. "Deliberation and What Else?" In *Deliberative Politics: Essays on Democracy and Disagreement,* ed. Stephen Macedo, 58–69. New York: Oxford University Press.

———. 2002. "Passion and Politics." *Philosophy and Social Criticism* 28 (6): 617–33.

Wegner, Daniel M., and Kenn Finstuen. 1977. "Observers' Focus of Attention in the Simulation of Self-Perception." *Journal of Personality and Social Psychology* 35 (1): 56–62.

Wellmer, Albrecht. 1991. *The Persistence of Modernity,* trans. David Midgley. Cambridge: MIT Press.

Wispé, Lauren. 1987. "History of the Concept of Empathy." In *Empathy and Its Development,* ed. Nancy Eisenberg and Janet Strayer. Cambridge: Cambridge University Press.

Wolak, Jennifer, and George E. Marcus. 2007. "Personality and Emotional Response: Strategic and Tactical Responses to Changing Political Circumstances." *Annals of the American Academy of Political and Social Sciences* 614 (1): 172–95.

Wolin, Sheldon S. 1996. "Fugitive Democracy." In *Democracy and Difference,* ed. Seyla Benhabib, 31–45. Princeton: Princeton University Press.

"World Schools Debating Championship." 2008. http://www.schoolsdebate.com/ (accessed March 17, 2008).

Yack, Bernard. 2006. "Rhetoric and Public Reasoning: An Aristotelian Understanding of Political Deliberation." *Political Theory* 34 (4): 417–38.

Young, Iris Marion. 1996. "Communication and the Other: Beyond Deliberative Democracy." In *Democracy and Difference,* ed. Seyla Benhabib, 120–35. Princeton: Princeton University Press.

———. 2000. *Inclusion Democracy*. New York: Oxford University Press.

———. 2001. "Asymmetrical Reciprocity: On Moral Respect, Wonder, and Enlarged Thought." In *Judgment, Imagination, and Politics,* ed. Ronald Beiner and Jennifer Nedelsky, 205–28. Lanham, Md.: Rowman and Littlefield.

Zajonc, Robert B. 1980. "Feeling and Thinking: Preferences Need No Inferences." *American Psychologist* 35 (2): 151–75.

———. Robert B. 1984. "On the Primacy of Affect." *American Psychologist* 39 (2): 117–23.

Made in the USA
Lexington, KY
16 June 2016